Virtual Production

This book, written by industry experts, provides a comprehensive understanding of virtual production processes, concepts, and technology – helping readers get to grips with this nascent technology.

Topics covered are the history of virtual production, underlying technologies, creative potential, and production workflows. In addition, it delivers a detailed overview of the virtual production pipeline, from pre-production planning to post-production finishing. Each chapter explains specific aspects of virtual production, such as real-time rendering, motion capture, virtual cameras, LED screens, game engines, and collaborative workflows. Additionally, the book examines virtual production's ethical and cultural implications, including the impact on actors, the representation of diverse voices, and the democratization of filmmaking.

Whether you're a student, teacher, or industry professional, *Virtual Production* will provide you with a solid foundation for comprehending the fundamental concepts behind a constantly evolving and intricate process.

Mark Sawicki is a seasoned expert in the visual effects and production fields, having worked his way up as an effects cameraman, animator, and compositor to the lead matte cameraman for Illusion Arts. He then progressed to a co-supervisor working on *From the Earth to the Moon* (1998), after which he became a visual effects supervisor and lead cameraman for Custom Film Effects, working on such films as Christopher Nolan's *The Dark Knight Rises* (2012). Mark subsequently began to write books, create video programs for the Stan Winston School of Character Arts, and teach at various film schools. He has now re-entered the field as a virtual production artist and instructor.

Juniko Moody, EdD graduated from the University of Southern California (USC) to enter the industry as a motion control camera and compositing technician, working for New World Studios, Ultimatte Corporation, and Industrial Light and Magic (ILM). She later began working for Eastman Kodak's Cineon project and went on to work for Wamer Digital and Sony Imageworks as a digital artist before working on projects with Walt Disney Feature Animation. She also provided corporate training at Disney and DreamWorks Animation, since then she has been teaching, researching (virtual production and AI) and writing – most notably on the *Filming the Fantastic* books with Mark Sawicki.

Authors

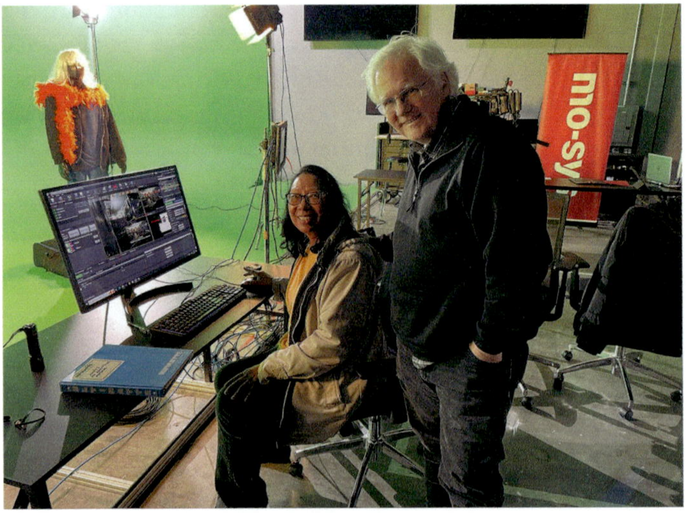

Juniko Moody, EdD and Mark Sawicki

Virtual Production

Essential Elements on a Budget

Mark Sawicki and Juniko Moody

Routledge
Taylor & Francis Group
LONDON AND NEW YORK

First published 2026
by Routledge
4 Park Square, Milton Park, Abingdon, Oxon OX14 4RN

and by Routledge
605 Third Avenue, New York, NY 10158

Routledge is an imprint of the Taylor & Francis Group, an informa business

British Library Cataloguing-in-Publication Data
A catalogue record for this book is available from the British Library

ISBN: 978-1-032-75275-4 (hbk)
ISBN: 978-1-032-73728-7 (pbk)
ISBN: 978-1-003-47316-9 (ebk)

DOI: 10.4324/9781003473169

Typeset in Bembo
by Apex CoVantage, LLC

Access the Support Material: www.routledge.com/9781032737287

Dedication

Bill Taylor ASC
The master magician, my mentor, my boss, my friend
who was the best of the best.

Glenn Campbell
A fan like me who turned pro. We worked together, taught
together, and always had fun. A kind, talented, and generous VFX pro.

We miss them deeply and remember them tenderly.

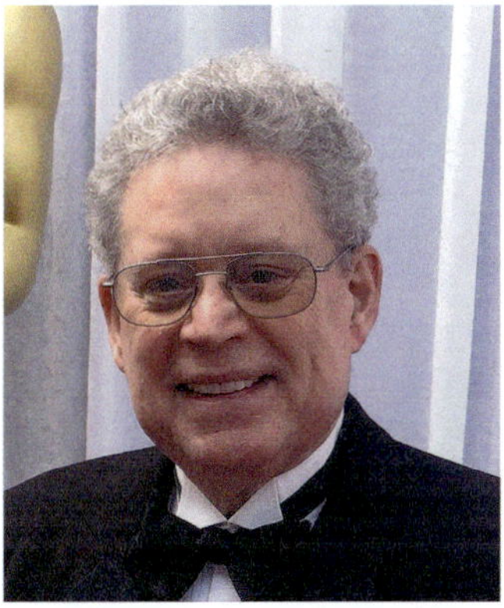

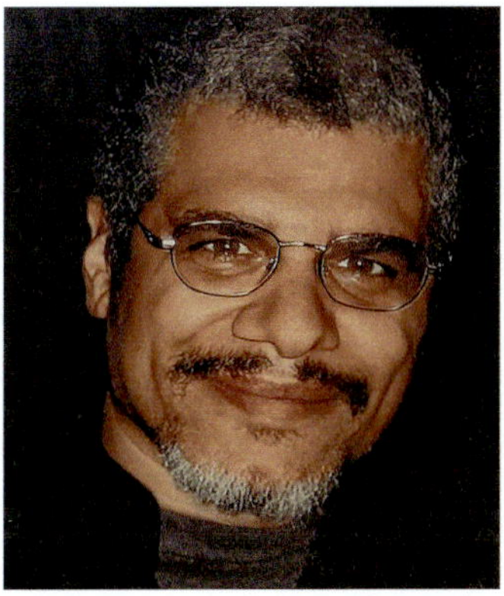

Contents

Acknowledgments

This book would not have been possible without the generosity and help of many talented people. We would like to thank Dr. Geoffrey A. Moore for his insight into the future and the use of his hype cycle diagram. The amazing Victor Perez for his illustrations and tutorials on color. Michael Geissler for the use of his demo stage and his fabulous team at Mo-Sys for sharing their knowledge and enabling our illustrations. Eliot Mack and Bill Warner for their many great office hours that helped us learn Jetset. Lisa Auslen and Brandon Fayette of Fuzzy Door Tech for reviewing our chapter on their ViewScreen product. Birim Yamanlar and the team at Zero Density for sharing their input and illustrations. Edward Dawson-Taylor and Jacqueline Cooper and their excellent team of teachers at https://www.becomecgpro.com/ who taught us the basics of Unreal. Our fabulous expert professionals Erik Wolford, Professor James Brust of Columbia College, production VFX supervisor Lindy DeQuattro, and Eliot Mack for their insightful interviews. Brian Wright, my former TA, now turned pro who shared his astounding student film. My student models from NYFA and Dodge College, Joe Knable, Anika Kumar, Annabella Bandol, Nova Flagerman, and Alana Muchemi, who gave their precious off-time to be in our illustrations. Thanks to the team at Hyper RPG for letting us tour their facility: Zac Lim Eubank, Malika Lim Eubank, Matt Acevedo, and Jo Paloma.

Introduction

The definition of *hype* is an extravagant promotion of something. I've gone to many tech conventions, such as the National Association of Broadcasters (NAB), SIGGRAPH, Cine Gear, and others. At these conventions, I have seen much hype of products to the point when salespeople try to make me believe their product can turn lead into gold. I'm always skeptical of the latest and greatest and was happy to discover that the American research, advisory, and information technology firm Gartner came up with a graph of the life cycle of a new technology called the hype cycle. It is shaped like a spikey bell curve followed by a smaller plateau half as high as the first peak. This unique curve has several sections named from the start as the Technology Trigger, the Peak of Inflated Expectations, the Trough of Disillusionment, the Slope of Enlightenment, and finally, the Plateau of Productivity, where things settle down to the tech that works and delivers. Looking back in history, there have been many hype cycles, such as steam power and the Industrial Revolution. In my career, I've seen the motion control hype cycle and the digital hype cycle, which has blossomed into many branches, such as 2D compositing, computer graphics, game engines, and the internet. Virtual production, too, is following this curve journey amid some unprecedented challenges, such as the COVID-19 epidemic and the slowdown of the entertainment industry. I'm not a futurist by any means, but I did come across an interesting white paper called "The State of Virtual Production 2024" written by Tim Moore, a three-time Emmy award–winning director and co-founder of VU technologies, that provides tools for the virtual production industry. Here are some notable excerpts.

> "The 2030 virtual production industry market forecast has grown to over \$8 Billion, a 32% increase on the initial 10 year industry projections from 2020."
>
> "In the wake of back to back labor strikes last year, the media and entertainment industry experienced a decline of historic proportions in 2023, with a 52% decrease in production spending compared to the previous year and so much collateral damage that the effects have yet to be fully tallied. However in 2024, virtual production earnings have bounced back, with 35% growth in the corporate and education sector, while seeing a 7% decrease in production spending in the entertainment sector.

Over the same period last year. The market is forecasted to be a tale of two cities. As the volatile Media and Entertainment market continues to stifle investment in the industry, a rising number of corporate and higher education virtual studios is set to the highest growth sector this year. With compounding disruption and volatile labor markets, radical transformation is quickly approaching."

"Today's virtual studios aren't getting larger, they're getting smaller, with thousands of micro format virtual studios expected to hit the market in 2025."

" +48% increase in total number of virtual studios around the world in the past two years. -29% size decrease in LED Walls for virtual studios from 2021 to 2023 with a median wall size in 2024 of 6 meters wide x 3 meters tall."

Mr. Moore believes that virtual production is at the start of mainstream adoption by smaller studios. I am pleased that small independent studios will have a place in this rising industry as that is the audience I wish to reach. Our book aims to share our thoughts and actual experiences creating virtual content using various methods that offer the most cost-effective and flexible methodology for combining live actors with virtual cinema content on a budget. We trust our insights will serve you well as you board the rocket ship called Virtual Studio.

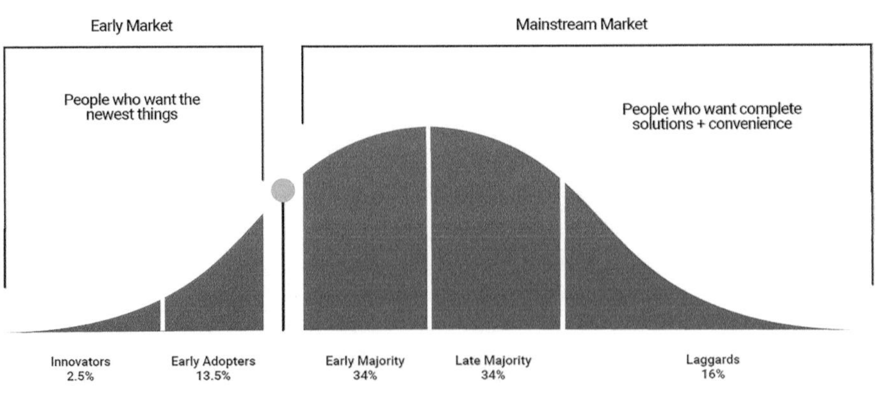

Figure 0.1 *The virtual production hype cycle.*
Source: Courtesy of Geoffrey A. Moore, Author, Speaker, Advisor, Philosopher

Chapter 1

Visual Effects Influences on Virtual Production

Early In-Camera Effects

> **Paintings and miniatures** with multiple film exposures inside the camera created the first virtual sets. Masking film from exposure while it is still inside the camera is the first form of composting.

When one examines the history of film visual effects, one sees that we have been doing virtual production and in-camera VFX since the beginning of cinema. One of the earliest techniques for set extension was the glass shot invented by Norman Dawn. This simple yet elegant method placed a sheet of glass in front of the camera, on which the set extension was a painting, such as the upper level of a castle entrance.

The painting was a virtual simulation of a real castle.

The glass shot was called in camera, as the final result could be seen through the viewfinder. Even in the silent era, camera moves could be made with a glass shot as long as the camera was panned or tilted at the lens's nodal point. The nodal point was a location in the center of the lens where all the light

DOI: 10.4324/9781003473169-1

rays converged. If the camera were panned or tilted on this point, there would be no perspective change between near and far objects, and synthetic additions such as the painted castle would remain locked to the background instead of pulling away from the live-action element as would happen if you panned the camera from the standard mount of the camera body. While the nodal point allows pans and tilts, it cannot compensate for dolly in and out moves as those will reveal the perspective. As long as the depth of field was significant enough to allow both the painting and the live background to be in focus, the illusion could be very successful, depending on the quality of the rendered painting.

The drawback to the glass shot was the need for a great deal of light to obtain depth of field, which relegated many shots to being done outdoors in the sunlight. Because the sun moves across the sky throughout the day, one was locked into shooting the glass shot at a specific time so the static-painted shadows would match the natural shadows. The setup required the glass shot frame and camera support to stay on location until the artist finished the painting to begin photography. You would also hope that the weather would remain the same. To address these issues, Dawn invented the latent image matte painting process, in which a matte consisting of a black card would block out the area on the frame where the painting was to be so photography could commence rapidly. The technique capitalized on the ability of film to be exposed multiple times to create double exposures or selective area exposures. The camera person would shoot several takes with this matte that prevented the film from being exposed in the area to be replaced by a painting. After the takes were photographed, a few hundred feet of film were shot with the matte for test footage. After the shoot, only a few feet of film were sent to the laboratory for processing and development. The remaining partially exposed film was held in refrigeration as a latent image. When the processed film returned, it was placed in a special matte camera in the artist's studio that could be both a projector and a camera. The negative was projected through the camera lens so the artist could trace out where the live-action component was and begin to paint in a sky and a castle. The bottom of the painting was painted black to prevent re-exposure of the live action in that area. The test footage was used to shoot short exposure tests exposing the painting on top of the latent footage. The final composites could be executed when the exposure, blend, and painting were refined. Each take was placed into the matte camera to combine the painting with the live action for the final composite. The tracing process is called rotoscoping, and the idea of separating the photography of the live-action element and the photography of the painting on top of the live-action latent was one of the first examples of post-production. This method saved a tremendous amount of time on set and allowed the artist the proper time to execute good-quality artwork. Since neither of the elements, live action or painting, was duplicated in this compositing process, the quality of both painting and live action was first generation, meaning the same as that of original photography.

The latent image technique was only possible as the motion picture medium became standardized and refined. In the pioneering days of cinema, visual effects that made use of a second pass or exposure, like the latent image process, would suffer from one image erratically bouncing against the other as there did not exist a method to keep the film in exactly the same place in the camera during subsequent exposures. Fortunately, a method of standardized perforation holes (Bell and Howell perforations) and registration pins in cameras that were designed to fit perfectly inside these holes on either side of the film frame would hold the film in place during each and every exposure, making sure that elements would not drift but lock together without jitter. In practice, there was a big full-fitting pin on one side and a small pin on the other side to allow for film shrinkage so perforations wouldn't tear.

While the registration pin system made the latent image process possible, it took away the ability to make moves in the original photography. A move could be created in post by copying the latent composite in an optical printer with a camera pointed at a projector. The camera would copy a portion of the composite film directly and execute a pan or tilt by moving the printer lens. The quality of this method was reduced as there would be a significant increase in contrast and grain. Because of this, latent image shots were rarely duplicated and were just cut into the film like regular shots. The drawback to this was that for decades, matte painting shots were "lock-offs" by necessity and could have the jarring effect of seeing a static shot surrounded by moving camera shots.

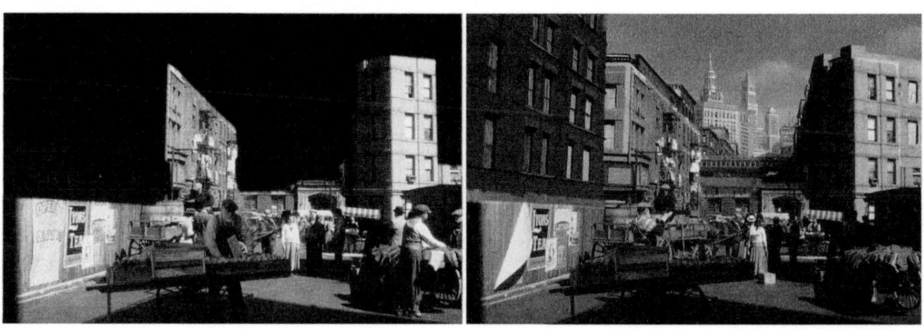

Figure 1.1 *The latent image matte shot. A black matte prevented exposure in the area of the painting. Later, the painting would be exposed in this area while the bottom half was black, preventing additional exposure to live action. Since both exposures were on the same piece of film, no duplication was required, and the quality was as good as a glass shot with the advantage of adding the painting in post-production.*

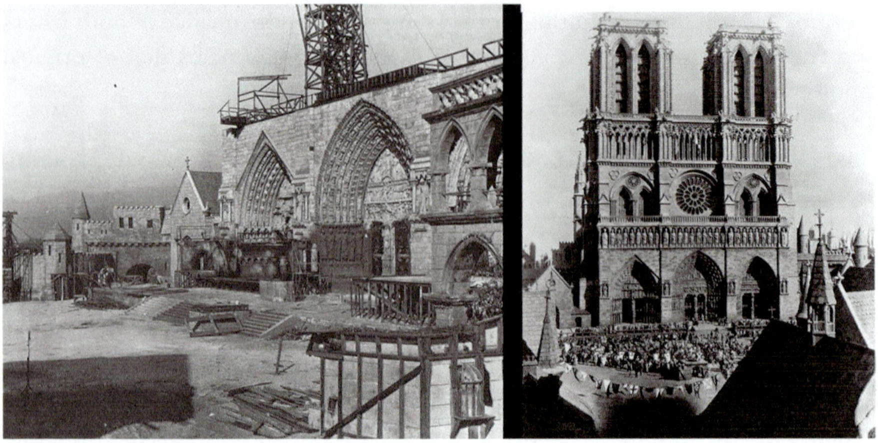

Figure 1.2 *From the 1923 version of The Hunchback of Notre Dame. The magnificent set was only built to the top of the entrance arch. A foreground miniature completed the illusion of the magnificent structure. The advantage of the miniature was that the lighting would match as the sun changed position, allowing a longer window of time for the composite to be shot.*

Another early solution to the in-camera set extension would be the hanging miniature. This method had an advantage over the glass shot in that the shadows would track with the live-action shadows as the sun moved. A dimensional miniature could look very convincing when shot in natural light. Some purists complain about miniature shadows with this technique. What miniature shadows mean can be explained by examining a tall telephone pole and its shadow on the ground. An actual pole will have a sharp-edged shadow near the base, but as you look at the end of the shadow, it will get softer and less sharp. The distance between the top of the pole and the ground could be 40 feet or more to display this effect. A miniature pole may only be four inches tall, and its shadow would be sharp the entire distance. This slight difference is a minor defect in a very successful traditional technique. The drawback of the hanging miniature was once again the time used on set for setup, let alone the construction of a miniature.

Optical Printing

> **A special camera and projector assembly** called the optical printer was one of the first post-production compositing tools.

Linwood Dunn is credited with inventing the optical printer mentioned earlier for the film *King Kong* in 1933. One can think of the printer as the After Effects compositor of the film era. The Bell and Howell registration system allowed the printer to do any number of effects using multiple exposures such as split screens, blue screens, blow-ups, post moves, etc. The Eastman Kodak company began to make unique films meant for duplication that enabled post effects to become more practical. The technological progress of film duplication was a work in progress for decades. Black and white films were much easier to copy in the early days than color. To understand the quality mismatch in early color film duplication, you can examine the dissolves used in the classic film *Forbidden Planet*, made in 1956. To address the quality hit in film duplication, they only copied the film during the dissolve and then cut back to the original photography. If you watch the picture, you will see a high-quality shot suddenly become contrasty and soft right when the dissolve starts, and then it becomes high quality again at the end of the dissolve. Eventually, the film duplication process became good enough that the entire beginning and end of both A and B shots could be duplicated with the dissolve, with no discernable difference from the original. Another printing method used fine-grain black-and-white separation film to copy the color negative onto three rolls of black-and-white film. One roll copied the negative through a red filter, the next through a green filter, and the last roll through a blue filter to obtain fine-grain positive records of each primary color. These were then recombined in three separate exposures onto color film to achieve high fidelity. Generating three rolls of film to copy one was expensive, but it was a while before Kodak developed a full-color intermediate film to simplify color duplication.

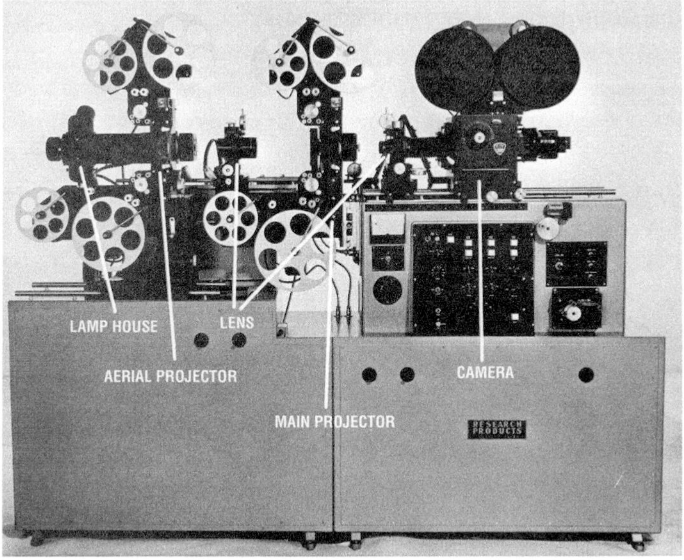

Figure 1.3 *The two-headed optical printer was the photochemical version of After Effects in the days before digital.*

Rear Projection

> **Rear projection screens** displaying movie clips were the first live background imaging method used before LED screens were utilized for live on-set compositing.

Willis O'Brien was a pioneering stop-motion animator who created the effects for *King Kong*. He utilized the rear projection technique to combine live action and animated puppets to make a significant impact, and his method was one of the first examples of the later-coined term WYSIWYG at the dawn of digital in the 1990s. WYSIWYG stands for "What you see is what you get." This term was adopted as visual effects artists struggled with early digital files and compositing. Cineon files, for example, were not only hard to image on a screen, but also, when they were finally viewable, they looked strange and of low contrast. An additional viewer app had to be added to see the image with normal contrast. This confusion came from the difficulty in grasping what we were looking at, which was the same contrast as negative film except that it was positive. We still see this today in RAW files from digital cameras, and now we have viewing systems that allow us to work with images with normal contrast. In the case of O'Brien, rear projection introduced WYSIWYG in a different context. The live-action performers could see what was projected on the screen behind them and react to the action. Conversely, when the rear projection technique was used one frame at a time in a stop-motion miniature, the animators could see what the live actors were doing in the projection and animate the stop-motion puppets appropriately.

Film duplication using projection had similar issues with optical printing with added ones. The grain of the film (the tiny bit of silver embedded in the emulsion that creates a film image) would increase and become more pronounced. The contrast would increase enormously, particularly in black-and-white film due to the Callier effect, in which the silver granules would block more light disproportionately than the transparent portions of the film. The image projected from behind through a translucent screen would be soft. When shooting a rear projector screen, you are also shooting directly towards a projector light source; you would often get a "hot spot" in the middle of the image, meaning the image would be bright in the center and become darker on the edges. Lens focal lengths had to match, or puppets or people moving along the Z axis (forward and back) would not grow and shrink properly. Rear projected images are very dim. Here are the brilliant solutions to address these issues.

- To decrease the grain, one could shoot the background image in a larger film format, such as 65mm film, project the print, and shoot the rear projection composite onto 35mm film to reduce the grain size.

- To decrease the contrast, the negative film used to shoot the background image or "plate" was flashed at the lab to slightly fog the film in dark regions. When the print was made, the lab slightly fogged the print film, generating density in the clear areas or white regions of the film. This created a low-contrast projection plate with no absolute blacks or whites. When copied, the contrast would still increase but to a normal level.
- Hot spots were handled using long focal length lenses on the projector, such as 100mm, which required a long throw. Another technique involved placing a sheet of glass with a coin glued to it in front of the projector lens to dodge and dim the light in the center of the image. (The coin would be so out of focus that you would still see the image it was blocking, but now the center of the image would be dimmer.)
- Multiple projectors projecting and overlapping the same image could handle a dim projection for live action. For miniature rear projection, you could shoot at one-second exposure times.
- Softness remained an issue until the front projection process was developed. In this process, the image is projected onto a retro-reflective screen using a two-way mirror to hide the actor's shadow.
- The new Scotchlite™ screen is made of millions of tiny parabolic mirrors that direct light back towards its source. We see it used on the many road signs that reflect our car headlights so we can clearly see them. Even though the image is projected on top of the performer, it is never seen as it is far dimmer than the image off the screen, whose mirrors reflect light 1,000 times brighter than a white card. The front projection system allowed for sharp projected images and larger screens.

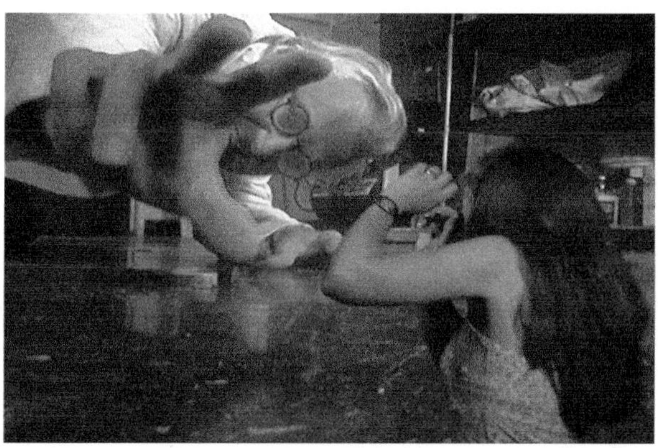

Figure 1.4 *Rear projection was the crude precursor to today's LED volumes. Both methods have a number of challenges. For projects with modest budgets, the green screen technique is more cost effective.*

Lens Angles And Perspective

Shoot the background movie clip to match or enhance the desired illusion of the foreground scale and perspective.

This is the most critical component of any traditional or virtual production technique. With rear projection, it can get confusing, especially if you have a moving image. An excellent way to think about conventional rear projection is to imagine it as a projected still or, even better, a photo blow-up. Once you shoot a locked-off background, the camera position and focal length will be locked for a given distance. Now, let's say you blow up that background to a 16 x 9 foot backdrop. If you shoot the background with a 35mm lens and then rephotograph it with a 35mm lens so it fills the frame, a figure standing in front will fit right in. If you dolly in on your performer, they will get larger, and the background will get larger, but the background will have no dimensional change or perspective. As you dolly in, the performer will change in perspective, but the backdrop will get larger as if it were a zoom. You can get away with this with subtle moves, but it is still a cheat. If you rephotograph the 35mm background with an 18mm lens, you can fill the frame and have the background look normal, but the figure in front will appear oddly large. If the performer moves closer to the camera, they will grow abnormally fast and further give away the illusion.

The Datasheet

Take copious notes to ensure accurate duplication of scale, perspective, and lighting for the background and the foreground elements.

Due to errors in matching elements in most VFX shots that involve compositing two or more elements, data sheets were used to ensure everything matched. Here is an example from a typical student project. Let's say you're making a romantic comedy but need a house. Your grandmother has a house that you can use for free. Hooray! The only problem is that Grandma's house is in the mountains, and your story takes place on the beach. Your VFX supervisor says no problem, just shoot the house, and we'll find a beach on the internet, and it'll be fine. So you do that and get the composite back. It looks okay for the first second, but it soon starts looking peculiar. The house looks like it's leaning, shadows are going in the wrong direction, and the trash can seems too big. This is because the compositor did their best with a found element.

The proper method would be to use the data sheet that listed the focal length, frame rate, shadow direction, tilt angle, film stock (sensor size today), etc., when shooting the house, and then resetting the camera to those exact same settings when shooting the ocean will result in an excellent shot. The proper perspective can be verified by projecting lines from the top and bottom of a window frame from the house to the vanishing point that lies perfectly on the horizon atop the ocean. Matching the tilt prevents the house from looking like it is leaning forward.

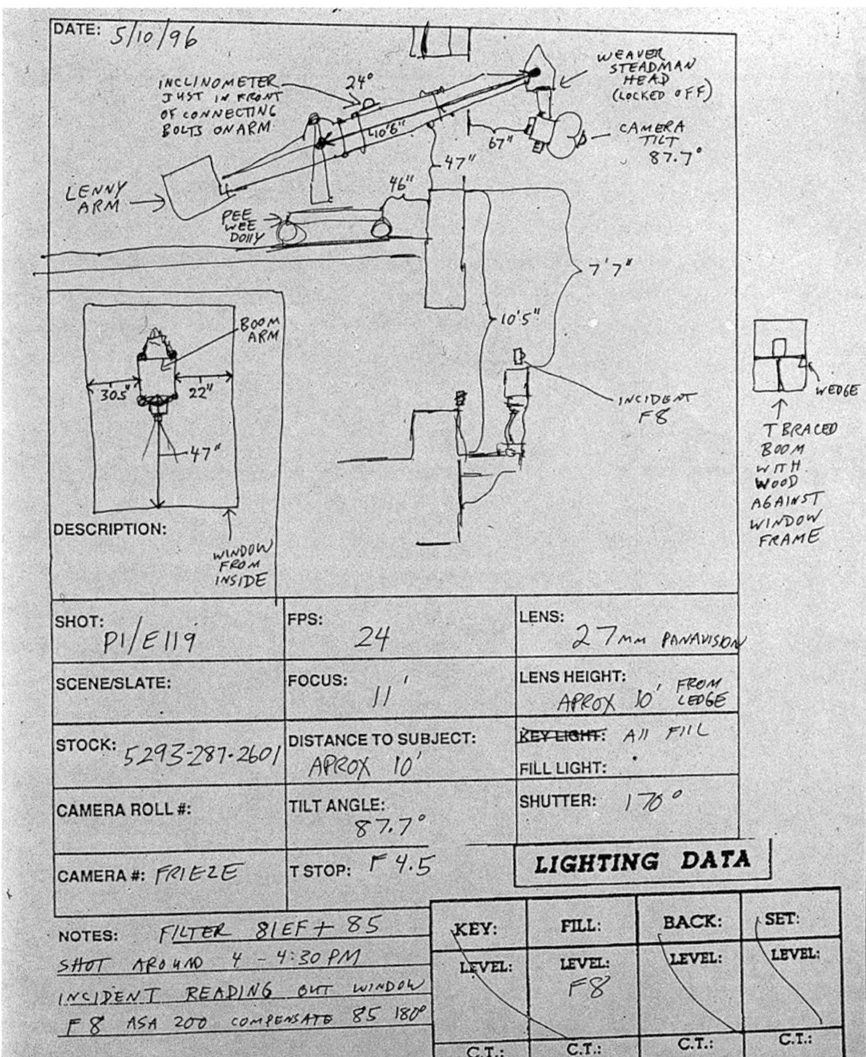

Figure 1.5 *A traditional data sheet.*

The data sheet process is beneficial when executing color backing composites like blue or green screens. For example, a shot of a figure hanging off the ledge of a building uses a typical data sheet from the film *The Glimmer Man* and a partial set that the actor can hang from above a green screen.

Color Backing Technique (Blue and Green Screen)

> **The blue screen technique** resulted in a higher-quality composite than rear projection as all elements were usually of the same generation when duplicated. The method also allowed for broader freedom of camera placement and wider compositions.

The advent of the optical printer enabled post–traveling matte composites. The term *traveling matte* means that the matte, instead of being static as used in the latent image system, usually consists of a moving human figure silhouette where each frame is different, conforming to the performance. The first method of making a traveling matte was using rotoscoping to trace around each frame of the performer's image to make a frame-by-frame animated traveling matte. This method is still used today for various situations in digital compositing. While this process worked, the edges were inconsistent and jittery due to unavoidable human error in tracing. Frank Williams invented one of the first photographic traveling matte processes in 1918. It involved shooting performers in front of a black background and extracting a matte using the contrast difference between the performer and the black. An excellent example of Williams's process is the scene from *The Invisible Man* 1933 in which the invisible man disrobes except for his white shirt and battles with the local townspeople. The drawback to the Williams process is that the inclusion of anything close to the black tone will make it impossible to create a matte, and roto enhancement will need to be used.

Oddly, one of the first uses of color backing was invented in 1927 by C. Dodge Dunning, and refined by Roy Pomeroy it was called the Dunning Pomeroy process. This process made use of the color-canceling properties of color filters. In this case, if you hold an orange filter in front of your eye and look at a blue screen, it will be dark, but if you look at an orange wall, it will be seen clearly. In practice, a background image was printed on a large glass plate as a transparent orange image. This was placed before the camera lens while an actor beyond was lit with orange lights. Beyond the actor was a blue screen. When viewed through the camera, the actor's image passed right through the orange background transparency, and the areas of the transparency that had orange dye were made dark and visible by the blue screen. When the black-and-white film was processed, a perfect seamless composite, including perfect blurs, was created. Instead of a large transparency, the process was usually done by bi-packing the background in the camera with the raw stock. This placed the orange positive of the background in contact with the raw stock during exposure, thereby printing the background while simultaneously recording the actor. The process created composites suitable only for black-and-white movies.

One of the first color films to use the blue screen technique invented by Lawrence Butler was *The Thief of Baghdad* in 1940. This blue screen technique used the color separation process mentioned before with a slight twist to create a matte. The blue separation appears like a positive image of an actor on a transparent background. If this black-and-white film is laid atop the original negative image, then the positive and negative images of the actor cancel out, creating a silhouette while the background remains transparent. When this combination is copied onto high-contrast film, you obtain a traveling matte of a transparent actor on a black background. When this matte is printed back, you obtain a black silhouette of the actor on a clear field that can be used as a traveling matte or "hold out" that will hold out the exposure of the actor's area when copying the background. After this exposure, all three separations are printed to obtain the actor's image in the background.

This was a big step forward over the rear projection technique as it provided that both foreground and background were the same generation, so you never had the drawback of a direct comparison between the projected image's quality and the performer's first-generation quality in front. In other words, in rear projection, the actor was first generation, and the background was always a copy photographed through a screen. In optical printing, all elements had the same quality of reproduction, which was better than projection as it was a direct film-to-film copy with no screen in between. The big drawback of the blue screen technique during this period was the blue halo or flare around the actor. This was caused by imperfectly fitting mattes that revealed part of the blue screen around the actor.

Petro Vlahos

> **Narrow wavelengths of light** can act as filters to create mattes. With video signals, mathematical algorithms can be used as filters to create even more complex functions and matte logic.

Vlahos was one of the leading engineering geniuses of the motion picture medium in visual effects. The blue halo problem was a long-standing issue in the blue screen technique for over a decade, and the performer could not wear blue. The first brilliant process he helped perfect, which won an Academy Award in 1965, was the sodium vapor process, which used the Technicolor three-strip camera. This camera, used for such films as *The Wizard of Oz* and *Gone with the Wind*, ran three black-and-white films through the camera simultaneously, which were, in turn, exposed to separate red, green, and blue exposures through the use of a prism that split the image coming from the lens. In the case of the sodium vapor process, the Technicolor camera was modified to allow two films to run through the camera; one was a color film, and the other was black and white. The original camera prism, whose purpose was to assist in separating the red, green, and blue light for photography, was replaced with one that transmitted all wavelengths of light except for the slim sodium wavelength to be exposed to color film. The prism reflected the sodium wavelength, exposing a black-and-white film to create a traveling matte.

The yellow screen was only lit with sodium vapor light while the actors in front were lit with traditional tungsten movie lights. As a result, with the color film, the actors could wear any color against a black screen (because only the sodium vapor wavelength was filtered out), and the black-and-white film showed a silhouette of the actors against a white or clear screen. This brilliant development eliminated any halo (as the area behind the actors was black), and any color could be used. The technique was most famously used for Disney's *Mary Poppins*. While this method yielded excellent results, the focal length of lenses was limited to accommodate the prism. Disney Studios was the primary user of this technology due to the exotic nature of the equipment. It was last used in 1990 for the film *Dick Tracy*. I can only imagine that this process inspired Vlahos to come up with his spectacular color difference process to remove the blue halo for the blue screen technique and bring back some foreground color for the 1959 film *Ben Hur*. In the Vlahos patent, the primary matte is extracted similarly, but he discovered that the only difference between the blue and green records was for the colors blue and yellow. That being the case, he invented a method of creating a synthetic blue record from the green record, enabling some blue information to remain in the performer while the screen behind stayed black. The blue halo was gone, and yellow colors could be reproduced. (As you will see in the color management chapter, yellow is made from the combination of red and green. If you merely used the green separation for both green and blue, yellow objects would turn white. Using a red, green, and synthetic blue, you bring back a true yellow.) This invention led to Petro's company Ultimatte for both video and digital. The use of video and digital brought about the use of green screens as they had much more information in the green channel of electronic media. His contributions built the foundation of all the digital keyers used today.

Petro Vlahos Color Difference System

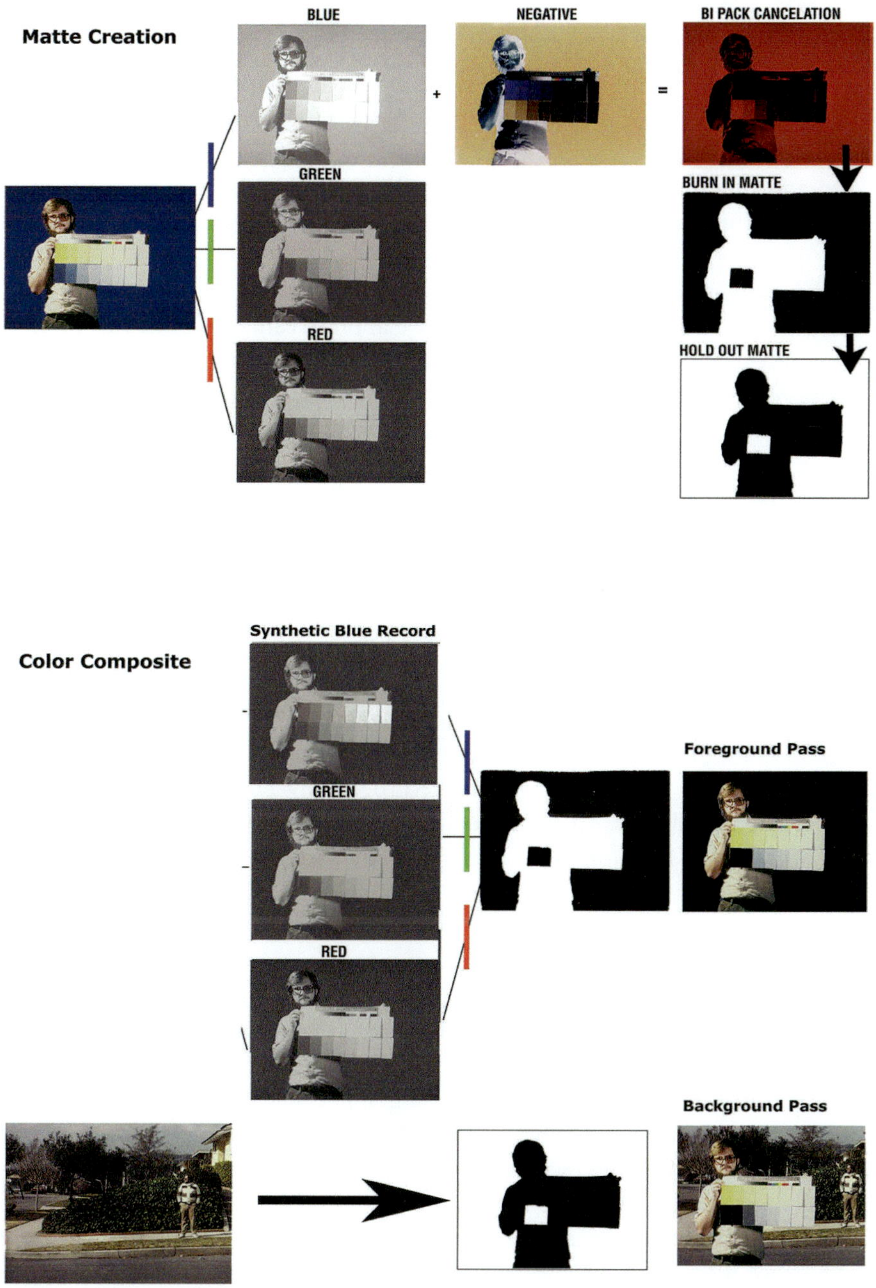

Figure 1.6 *The brilliant Vlahos method created a matte by overlaying the positive blue separation atop the negative to cancel out the figure and make the screen area clear to create the traveling matte. To obtain a synthetic blue separation, Vlahos combined the green and blue records to keep the screen area dark while also darkening the yellow tones in the synthetic blue record to keep them yellow. Having yellow areas clear for all three records would turn yellow to white. This system preserved more colors and eliminated the blue fringe that plagued earlier methods.*

Motion Control

Camera moves in composite shots have to match. Even with static camera shots, there may be moving objects or scenery that have to be composited in. A camera move may have to be repeated multiple times to add different related elements. So there needed to be a mechanical way to duplicate camera moves.

The earliest rigs had gears and markings with wheels turned manually. Animation stands were the most elaborate camera rigs at this time because, unlike tripod heads, they did not need to be mobile so stayed in one room and could be built very large. Electric motors were added to the gears, and hand-turning was replaced with remote controls. Eventually, computer controls and software allowed movement to be recorded and played back.

Programmable and repeatable animation stand development influenced repeatable mobile tripod camera heads, camera rail systems, stage motion control rigs, and today's camera crane rigs.

Visual effects practitioners have long aimed to accommodate a live camera. As early as 1949, Olin L. Dupy patented the Dupy Duplicator, which could record pan and tilt data on sound media to be repeated later. This system was used in the 1948 film *Easter Parade* for a matte painting composite. However, it was not widely used.

Zoran Perisic shot the fabulous orbiting spaceship shots for Kubrick's *2001: A Space Odyssey*" in 1968, which was more of a direct precursor to the motion control of the digital age. Using a precision Oxberry animation stand, Zoran could log exact camera positions using cranks and read out numbers for zoom, pan, and tilt. A model spacecraft was photographed as a still picture, cut out, and glued to an animation cel. This cel was placed on a black background, and an animated frame-by-frame camera movement was made to show the ship slowly getting bigger in the frame and moving left to right. This was photographed with a hole punch and frame marking on color film to indicate a zero start point. After Zoran shot the animation, the color film was removed and held as a latent. At this point, the spaceship photo was painted over with white paint and once again placed atop a black background to result in a white silhouette against black. The camera was loaded with black-and-white film with a hole punch for zero and run forward up to the same frame the animation started on the latent color film. The frame-by-frame move was repeated by moving the hand cranks and zooming to each number recorded to repeat the move manually. Once this animation was done, the film was processed to create a black silhouette on clear film. Now, both the black traveling matte and the latent image were bi-packed (two strips of film running together) in the camera so the matte would protect the spaceship exposure on the latent. The final pass was to shoot a matte painting of the Earth for the background, which could have a different move. Once again, this painstaking technique enabled first-generation quality in the elements of a classic film.

In 1977, electronics came to the rescue when camera movements could be recorded in real time and played back later without being done a frame at a time. This method enabled that year's breakthrough VFX in *Star Wars* and *Close Encounters*. In the case of *Star Wars*, identical moving elements could be made that would be blended later on in the optical printer. A beauty pass would be the dramatically lit model against a blue screen; the engine pass would be two tiny light bulbs with a fog filter shooting the identical move but at two seconds per frame to overexpose and blow out the tiny lights to make them appear to be engine exhaust.

Motion control is alive and well today as a viable technique for various effects. The film *Darby O'Gill and the Little People* (Disney 1959) served as the template for scale effects for *The Lord of the Rings* (2001). While the remarkable work in Disney's film could only pan and tilt the camera on nodal, the VFX artists for *Lord of the Rings* used motion control to accomplish tracking and dolly shots by having computer-controlled set movers keep all the characters aligned to avoid the elements misaligning when the camera moved along the Z axis.

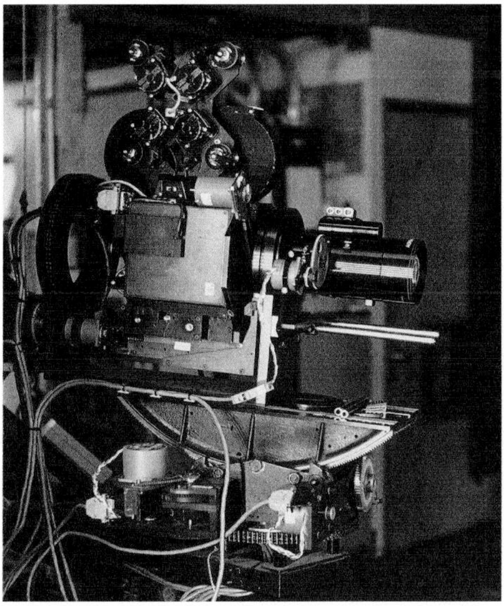

Figure 1.7 *Motion control was a huge step forward, allowing for freedom of camera movement. In the days before tracking, all elements were shot using repeatable camera controllers such as this Illusion Arts camera, which was controlled by stepper motors actuated by a computer.*

Virtual Production Fundamentals

There is much overlap and new terminology. Virtual production is an evolving field and concept.

To begin, we'll clarify some terminology with definitions.

- **Virtual Reality**: Computer-generated simulations of a 3D image or environment that can seemingly be interacted with using special electronic devices such as gloves with sensors and goggles with screens inside.
- **Augmented Reality**: A technology that superimposes a CGI image on a user's view of the natural world to create a composite. An example would be a game character composited atop a cell phone's camera view of a live environment.
- **Virtual Production**: Uses real-time game engines, motion capture, and other software to combine live action into a synthetic environment to aid with or complete final production shots for film and television.

Under the heading of virtual production, we have other terms.

- **LED Volume**: LED or light-emitting diodes make up a wall composed of many tiny lights that can display an image, such as an actor's background. A single wall can provide the background but not light the foreground. Several of these walls are stitched together to provide a left and right wall, background, and ceiling to create a volume. This volume can provide interactive light from the image on the screens, as seen on a shiny chrome helmet worn in the show *Mandalorian*.
- **Virtual Camera**: The camera inside a game engine that mimics the lens characteristics and motion of the live-action camera on set.
- **Pre-Viz/Previz**: A rough version of a production done in CGI, live action, or a hybrid combination. It is used as a video template for the production, like a living storyboard.
- **Post-Viz**: Live-action production shoot combined with previz elements to provide a rough composite as a check before finishing.
- **Tech-Viz**: Technical previz to assess how to shoot certain scenes.
- **Production-Viz**: Capturing final imagery in camera during production, such as shooting close-ups of actors in front of an LED volume.

Why Virtual Production?

The virtual production processes described in this book may seem nothing more than technological extravagances. Why would people spend so much effort, innovation, money, and continual learning to complicate an already overly complicated process? Ironically, the answer is control. There is a meaning to the madness. This continual evolution has always had the singular goal of absolute artistic control over executing a creative vision.

Up to now, we have covered the history of camera control and compositing. This was the beginning of an epiphany that filmmaking's most essential controlling aspects needed to serve a creative vision without compromise. Think of the evolution of animation production epitomized by the Walt Disney Studio, and you have a process in which every stage of the production is controlled without that control being threatened by the variables of live action production. From design to execution to post-production, every element visible on the screen has been meticulously planned and executed. Unlike motion picture films, animation movies were not hindered by the physical limitations that loom large in movie making.

These limitations are obstacles to a creative vision. Limitations like location, terrain, weather, lighting, equipment (compatibility, matching, and mobility), people, animals, props, sets, distances, physics, and even time cost the production an absurdly unpredictable amount of logistical planning, financing, and problem-solving. Movie producers always wanted the same control afforded to animation studios, where the creative control was basically under one metaphorical or physical roof because the most essential aspects of animation creation are drawing and painting. The two-dimensional artwork could be designed and directed by a few people with the same creative vision without fighting relentless natural obstacles in the real world or at least limiting real-world influences.

Even television production was capable of ultimate control because it relied on permanent sets, which allowed time to be spent on dialogue, camera blocking, acting, and storytelling instead of battling the environment. Designed more like theater than filmmaking, television production was limited to sets used every week. Television could be produced at a faster and more reliable rate than movies, resulting in long-running episodic shows similar to radio.

Separating photographic processes from real-world time and place is more than an extravagance in movie making. It is a necessity that leads to complete control of the movie-making and storytelling processes.

A comprehensive history of computer graphics appears in *Filming the Fantastic with Virtual Technology*, Chapter 2, "Filming on the Digital Backlot." https://www.researchgate.net/publication/340241451_A_brief_history_of_computer_graphics

With its involvement in motion control and 2D/3D graphics, the computer merged with television and movie making – the result was virtual production.

Over time, computer software and processes allowed movie makers to operate like animation studios. Control over location, environment, weather, time of day, lighting, compositing, stunts, physics, physical effects, characters, actor performance, props, camera movement and repeatability, costuming, surrealism, photorealism, and psychological time has made producing today's blockbuster movies like the production of an animated movie combined with a virtual video game. Even the separate pre-production, production, and post-production stages are now fused into parallel iterative workflows and pipelines not limited to one metaphorical or physical roof but produced simultaneously worldwide in different time zones, churning 24/7 with near-instant editorial results.

(Incidentally, introducing AI text-to-picture or text-to-video is a step towards camera-less storytelling in which the production uses only 2D imagery without original camera photography. However, AI imagery still uses a reference library of images created with cameras or drawings/paintings. It can be argued that AI can generate imagery only through derivative use.)

Workflow From Linear to Iterative

In the past, the production model was pre-production, production, and post-production. Today, there are efforts to condense all these processes. In traditional pre-production, you had the script that, once approved, was sacrosanct. Today, not so much. As things are shot, finished, and off to editorial, we can change our minds today and reshoot with a different line or environment. Once the shooting starts, the footage can instantly go to the editorial, post, and back again for on-the-spot refinement. If a prop needs to be added, the virtual art department is informed, and the prop is added to the master scene (within the Unreal Game Engine), and the pickup shot is made. This type of instant iteration is not cheap and only applies to large-budget pictures shot in LED volumes. The same miracle of camera tracking and virtual cameras can be used with the green screen compositing technique. Both methods have pros and cons.

LED Pros

- Uses director sessions for rapid iterative workflow.
- The final image is possible on set in real time.
- You can make changes on the fly, such as set, lighting, or even animation tweaks, and ingest them immediately.
- The cinematographer can obtain interactive lighting in a volume.
- You can also shoot green for the background and use the wall for lighting and reflection. (In this case, the green only surrounds the performer while the outside of the green patch has the background image.)

LED Cons

- There is a lot of expense, purchase, setup, operation, and maintenance.
- The LED method relies on very powerful machines on set.
- The LED process requires a lot of preparation before production.
- LED walls have issues. Moiré, color quality, sync, flicker, etc. can limit the types of shots you can achieve.

Green Screen Pros

- Green screen composites can be easier to change after shooting.
- The green screen technique is less expensive.
- The quality of the foreground and background will be the same.
- There is no mismatch of set extensions outside the screen. (Set extensions beyond an LED wall can show the join unless corrected by even more technology.)

Green Screen Cons

- Performers can't see the environment.
- Interactive lighting will have to be simulated.
- While getting a final composite on set is possible, finishing is usually done in post.

Basic Hardware Components for Virtual Production

Shoot the background movie clip to match or enhance the desired illusion of the foreground scale and perspective.

To begin, the camera used to photograph the live action is usually a high-end camera such as an RED or Sony Venice for shooting motion picture–quality images. These cameras differ from consumer cameras in many ways but mostly resolution, and, more importantly, they have a synchronization signal output that consumer cameras do not. As we will see in the next chapter, this sync signal is very important to provide the amount of data needed for the virtual camera to be a twin to the live camera. The lenses for these cameras need to be calibrated to send information about lens aberrations to the virtual camera as well. Subtle distortions are always found in any lens, such as barrel distortion, in which straight up-and-down objects like telephone poles tend to bend as they get farther from the center and closer to the edge of the frame. Pincushion distortion has the opposite effect. There are often color offsets as well. When this information is missing from a tracking system, the live action can appear to slide across the floor during a pan. These cameras are also designed to allow encoders to be attached to the zoom and focus of the lens so the virtual camera can mimic these adjustments.

Regarding the camera's location in space, two methods are primarily utilized: inside out and outside in. The inside-out method, such as the Mo-Sys system, uses a secondary tracking camera mounted to the live-action camera. The tracking camera has a ring of infrared emitters surrounding the taking lens. This camera points to the ceiling, on which hundreds of little retro-reflective materials are positioned as small and large dots attached to the ceiling. The infrared emitters illuminate the dots for the tracking camera that can image infrared. They can now see a constellation of targets that can be used to detect the motion of the camera along every axis dolly in and out, up, down, etc. This is used as positional data to manipulate the virtual camera inside the engine.

Inside out – A tracking camera is attached to the cinema camera, and markers are placed on the stage.

The outside-in method uses a system such as Qualisys, which is popular for obtaining motion capture data from performers in suits. In this case, markers are placed on the camera, and an assortment of the same type of infrared-emitting tracking cameras are positioned above the stage to observe the camera from many angles. These observational cameras detect and inform the virtual camera where the live-action camera is in space, much like a performer's limbs are detected to manipulate a computer-generated character. Of the two systems, the inside-out method is the most cost effective.

Outside in – Tracking cameras are placed above the stage and follow the cinema camera.

Central Computer on Stage

We'll discuss this in more detail in the hardware chapter. For now, the main computer controls the LED wall or volume by broadcasting the image from the virtual camera inside the Unreal Game Engine. The camera can shoot both the performer and background together as a finished in-camera shot, or, if using a green screen instead of an LED wall, the engine can composite the signal from the live-action camera on top of the image generated by the virtual camera, or a hardware compositor such as an Ultimatte can be used to do the live composites.

On-Set Recorders

Signals from the live-action camera, the virtual camera, and the composited image are recorded separately onto high-end recorders such as Blackmagic HyperDeck.

Lights and Other Gear

As mentioned, a high-end LED wall or several walls can create a volume, or you can buy a can of green paint. The rest of the equipment remains traditional, with the usual collection of movie lights, dollies, tracks, C stands, sound gear, etc. We'll focus on these in more detail in the next chapter.

Summary

To summarize, the two main options for virtual production are time and money. If you want everything done in real time and in camera using LED walls, a brain bar of talented engineers to run Unreal, tracking, assets, and the wall, you will be spending a great deal of money, usually reserved for high-budget studio pictures. If you have a limited budget and more time, you can achieve good virtual production results by shooting green screens with live previz composites, tracking them, and finishing them in post. This book will focus on the latter technique.

According to *The Virtual Production Glossary*, a brain bar is "The team of artists and engineers operating the equipment that drives a smart stage or any space used for virtual production. Areas of responsibility include content distribution, image manipulation, camera tracking, recording, and creative visualization of data. Also known as volume control or mission control."

(2024, September 19). https://vpglossary.com/vpglossary/brain-bar/

Chapter 2

Technical Fundamentals of Virtual Production

Hardware, Synchronization, and the First Virtual Studio Backlot

Camera Evolution

Frame rates, frame separation, and frame labeling are essential elements to synchronizing cameras, synchronizing recording and playback instruments and for editing the movie.

In movie cameras, frame rates are expressed as frames per second (fps), frame separation is the black lines between frames (a result of the camera mechanism), and frame labeling is edge/key numbers printed on the film in a film manufacturing process.

It is of utmost importance to clearly understand the live-action camera in relation to the tools that manipulate a virtual camera. Much had changed since those halcyon days of yore when we hand-cranked ribbons of film through a camera housed in wood to make movies. The principles behind that early technology remain with us and have been enhanced and modified over the years. Let's begin with the history of frame rates.

DOI: 10.4324/9781003473169-2

Early Silent Film and the Flicker Problem

The way a movie camera captures images is simple. A mechanism pulls the film forward using a claw that engages the sprocket holes in the film. Once positioned in the camera gate, the film is held static while a shutter in front of it allows light to come through to expose an image. After the exposure, the shutter closes, preventing light from hitting the film, and then the film is pulled forward again and held static for the next frame to be exposed when the shutter comes around again. The exact same process is used when the film is projected. We see the static frames projected, and then the shutter closes to introduce a black cycle while the film is pulled down to the next frame, and the shutter opens again. There is one problem, though. We perceive a flickering image if this cycle doesn't happen fast enough. This is why early movies were sometimes referred to as the flickers. This was particularly troublesome as the camera and projector were hand-cranked, and there needed to be a way to regulate or standardize the speed.

Thomas Edison determined that the flickering effects would disappear if the images flashed by at around 46 frames per second, creating the persistence of vision phenomenon that made it look like a moving picture instead of a series of pictures. This high speed was difficult and costly to achieve with the cameras of the time since most movies were hand cranked at around 16 frames per second. The solution was to utilize a three-bladed shutter on the projector so each held frame was flashed on the screen three times. Three flashes multiplied by 16 frames per second gave us 48 flashes, creating a flickerless movie.

Edge Numbers

In the early days of editing, shots were chosen and assembled by merely looking at the images, deciding what take was what, and cutting the movie together with a bit of trouble and often guesswork. As the industry became more sophisticated, a better way had to be found to organize and identify all the footage. A system was developed in which edge or key numbers were printed on the raw stock along the edge outside the sprocket holes. These letters and

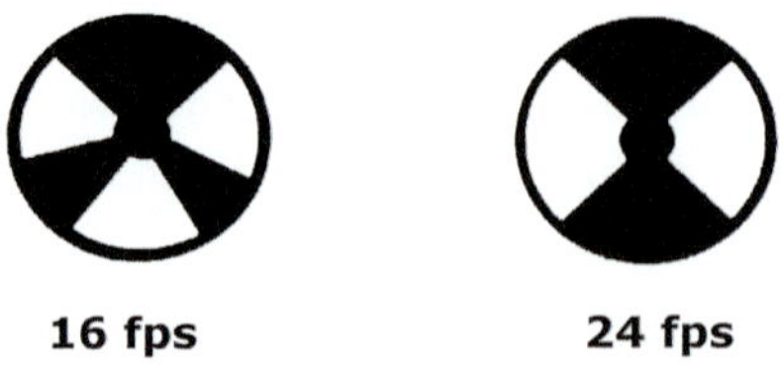

Figure 2.1 *Rotating shutters used to remove flicker. 16 fps x 3 flashes per frame = 48 images per second. 24 fps x 2 flashes per frame = 48 images per second, fast enough to eliminate flicker.*

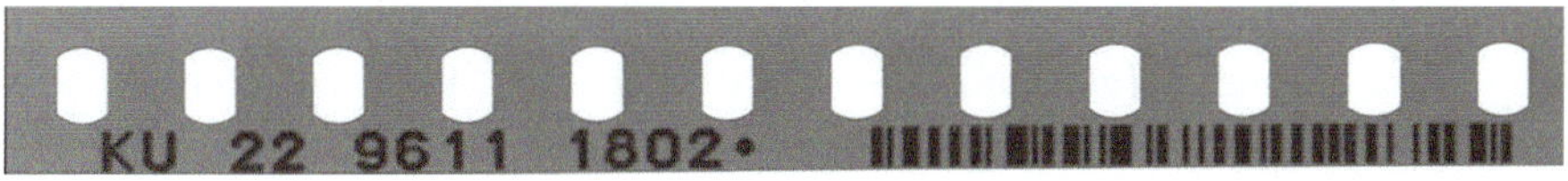

Figure 2.2 *Key numbers printed on the edge of the film along with a machine-readable bar code.*

numbers would identify the stock and advance at even intervals. This proved invaluable in matching the print with the negative for the entire filmmaking process. This good idea will be repeated later for video in a different way.

Here Comes Sound

When sound films arrived, it was determined that to get good fidelity from the sound, the film would have to run at 24 frames per second. Thankfully, by this time, motors were beginning to be used on cameras, which enabled them to run faster at a steady speed along with projectors, and the switch to a two-bladed shutter kept the movies going: 24 frames per second flashed two times equals 48 flashes per second.

Here Comes Video

In video electronics, frame rates are controlled by frequency, frame separation uses fields, and frame labeling uses timecode.

The flickering issue applies not only to movies but also to our electric lighting. During the early days of power generation, Edison and Westinghouse competed, using two different forms of electrical transmission. Edison used direct current, a constant stream of positive and negative energy that moved in one direction supplied through two wires. Westinghouse developed an alternating current that generated power that switched from positive to negative and back again. Westinghouse won the day as AC (alternating current) could be generated more inexpensively, travel long distances, and increase or decrease voltage through transformers. These advantages outweighed the fact that DC (direct current) would energize a light without flicker. AC, by its very nature, introduces a light that pulses.

Street lamps and electric home lighting could not be allowed to flicker, so a frequency had to be decided to prevent it, and that is where 60 hertz or 60 cycles a second going from plus to minus voltage coming out of our outlets was arrived at. In Britain, 50 cycles were chosen. These two power frequencies are important because they became the basis of the video frame rate. In the US, it was initially 30 frames per second, half of the 60 Hz, and in Britain, the video was 25 frames per second. Transferring video frame rates to film was quite a challenge, and it was often done with a device called a Kinescope, which had a movie camera that photographed images off a television monitor. The quality was not the best. However, it enabled us to preserve classic comedies like the famous Jackie Gleason show *The Honeymooners*. Around that time, Lucille Ball decided to shoot her episodes on film in front of a live audience, allowing us to see pristine images of her comedy *The Lucy Show* for generations.

Interlace

Unlike film, which captures an image all at once when the shutter opens, television had to break up the image into small components called scan lines that enabled the image to be broadcast vast distances in small chunks that were reassembled on the receiving end: the television set. Early television had images that were made up of 525 lines. You can think of a line as a narrow slit of image information, like looking outside through the tiny gap of a Venetian blind. These lines were created using a scanning electron beam along the sensor's surface, receiving the image projected on it by the lens. Odd lines were scanned to speed up the scanning process, then immediately followed by even lines. Each collection of lines was called a field. Each odd and even field was shown at 1/60th of a second. To the eye, the two fields interlaced and merged as one image, creating a 30 frames-per-second video with no flicker. This can provide an appearance of more immediacy or the sense that something is happening now. This is why interlace is a preferred format for sports or live broadcasts.

On the other hand, film gives the impression of something grand or historical. It is the result of the lower frame rate as well. Having more dark intervals

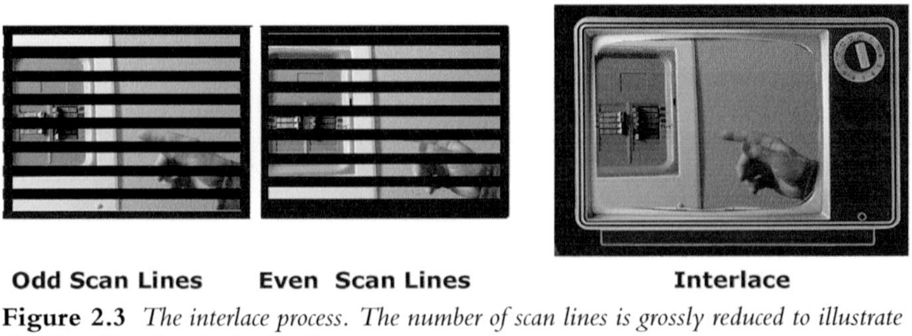

Figure 2.3 *The interlace process. The number of scan lines is grossly reduced to illustrate the idea of interlace in the broadcast.*

excites the imagination. I've always sensed that movie stars become diminished when I see them on television. They're a star on the big screen, but on TV, they're just a regular Joe. The lowercase letter i following a video format resolution (e.g., 1080*i*) indicates it is an interlaced media. If the video is captured like a film with the image captured all at once, it is indicated with the lowercase p for progressive capture.

Here Comes Color Television

Now, it gets awkward. When black-and-white television came to the US, the market exploded. Some reports say that in 1949, 100,000 TV sets were sold each week. A decade of black-and-white broadcasting was set in place, and now, with color introduced in 1953, the engineers had to figure out how to add color to the existing black-and-white signal as this tremendous legacy had been created. To get under the hood, I'll let my friend cinematographer Dave Stump, ASC, explain what changed from his book *Digital Cinematography* (2014).

> **In 1941, the US monochrome television standard** had a frame rate of 30 fps at 525 lines. The audio signal was combined with the video signal by modulating an audio subcarrier at a frequency of 4.5 MHz. In 1953, the US National Television System Committee (NTSC) added a color television standard that it hoped would be backward compatible with existing black-and-white television sets. Two new chrominance components were combined with the original black-and-white luminance signal by adding two subcarrier frequencies. Engineers discovered an interference between the line frequency and subcarrier frequencies, so they changed the frame rate by 0.1% or 29.97 fps.
>
> Stump, D. (2014). *Digital Cinematography: Fundamentals, Tools, Techniques, and Workflows* (1st ed.). Routledge.

Putting 24 fps Movies Into 29.97 fps Television

As I mentioned, interlace plays a big part in converting movie frame rates into video frame rates. If we slow down the movie film from 24 fps to 23.97, it will fit into the 29.97 frame rate. We can fit four frames of a movie into five frames of video. We can do this with the 3/2 pull-down system where three frames of film equal three full video frames (both odd and even lines), but the other two frames are made up of odd lines from one frame and even lines from another to create an extra synthetic frame. A strange combination of fields from two frames executed every two frames had an odd look but was a mild

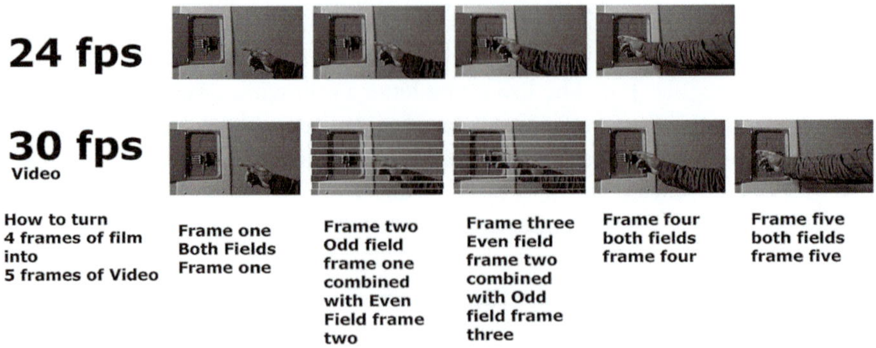

Figure 2.4 *The clever method of combining fields from separate frames created additional synthetic frames to allow for conversion. The synthetic frames looked odd but allowed the public to see movies on television.*

enough compromise to get past most audiences. This is the origin of the 23.97 fps rate on digital cameras. Film shot at 24 fps was slowed to 23.97 in the video transfer machines.

Timecode

As I mentioned, having a labeling system to identify every image on a medium is an absolute necessity for editing. We use timecode instead of key numbers for video. The numbers are divided into hours, minutes, seconds, and frames. The last two numbers will be recycled accordingly, depending on your frame rate. If you shoot at 24 fps, the last digits of the time code will go from 0 to 23, then back to 0. At 30 fps, the code goes from 0 to 29, then back to 0. The timecode does not synchronize cameras. It is beneficial for editing as several cameras can use the same timecode at the start of a take to assist in lining up pictures and sounds. Timecode does not prevent drift over time between cameras and does not synchronize all the events required to create a digital image. Once again, this is an elegant explanation from David Stump.

Timecode is used to synchronize video, film, audio content, and music and provides a time reference for videotape editing. It eventually led to the invention of nonlinear edit systems such as Avid and Final Cut Pro.

The timing data in SMPTE timecode is an eight-digit, 24-hour clock. The count consists of 0–59 seconds, 0–59 minutes, and 0–23 hours. The second number is subdivided into several frames, which vary depending on regional acquisition frame rates. In the United States and the

Americas, it is 24 fps for films; in Europe, Uruguay, Argentina, and Australia, 25 fps for NTSC broadcast in the United States, Canada, Mexico, Colombia, and so on.

Stump, D. (2014). *Digital Cinematography: Fundamentals, Tools, Techniques, and Workflows* (1st ed.). Routledge.

Drop-Frame and Non-Drop-Frame Timecode

Another clarification from Dave Stump.

Black-and-white broadcasting was based on a non-drop-frame timecode that assumed a frame rate of 30 fps, so programming broadcast at 29.97 fps created a problem; a 1-hour program was now 3.59 seconds longer than an hour according to clock time, leading to an error of almost 1.5 minutes over a day. To correct this error, a drop frame timecode was invented. No picture frames are deleted using drop frame timecode; instead, some of the numerical timecode labels are dropped. To make an hour of timecode match an hour on the clock, drop frame timecode drops frame numbers 0 and 1 of the first second of every minute, except when the number of minutes is divisible by 10. This creates a drop frame rate of 18 frames each 10 minutes and very closely compensates for the difference in frame rate, leaving a residual timing error of roughly 86.4 milliseconds per day.

If you are shooting digital, the correct camera timecode frame rate is either 23.976 fps or 29.97 fps. Both non-drop frames for syncing audio recorded at 29.97 fps. The correct frame rate for a recording studio that will be synced to true 24 fps shooting is 30 fps, regardless of whether the camera is running at 24 fps or 30 fps. This is because the audio does not have to correspond to the film speed. Still, rather to the video speed, the editing is done in video.

Stump, D. (2014). *Digital Cinematography: Fundamentals, Tools, Techniques, and Workflows* (1st ed.). Routledge.

The Camera Shutter

Sensel (sensor element) is a short-form word like pixel (picture element). A sensel is a light-detecting element of an image sensor.

The original film cameras had a simple shutter that could go from 180 degrees to zero to adjust exposure or create fades and dissolves. The angle of the shutter has a lot to do with the appearance of movement. In the film *Saving Private Ryan*, for example, the battle scenes were shot with a much smaller shutter angle that decreased the exposure time and, therefore, the length of the blur, creating dynamic stroboscopic imagery. Conversely, using a much wider shutter, such as 270 degrees, will significantly increase the size of motion blur and yield an unusual dream-like effect. A 355-degree shutter would have the moving headlights of a passing car create a long streak of light. For most movies, we have a legacy experience of seeing images recorded with a 180-degree shutter, so that would be the default.

Attempts were made to reproduce the rolling shutter effect with an electronic shutter that would activate a line of sensels (a single element of an image sensor that detects light) and send data line by line down the sensor. This proved problematic with moving imagery, which would displace the image during the image scan, creating stretching effects. The current method is to have a global shutter that exposes all the sensels at once to create a "progressive" (like film) frame-by-frame capture.

Resolution

Output image resolution for film is measured in millimeters (mm). Video and digital output resolution is measured in pixels.

Higher resolution with motion picture film just meant using bigger film. The 65mm movie film will have more detail than the consumer Super-8 film. One gets to use a much bigger area of light-sensitive crystals. The light-sensitive emulsion will be the same; it will just spread out on a larger piece of plastic backing. With digital cameras, it's all about the sensor. You could have a large 4K sensor (indicating the number of pixels it can generate) that could deliver less resolution by just cropping in the sensor. Here is a list of some common resolutions.

- HD 1280X720
- FULL HD 1920X1080 (indicated as 1080i or 1080p)
- 2K 2048X1080
- 4K 3840X2160

The 2K and 4K are considered film resolutions. As mentioned previously, the letter designation at the end of a resolution figure indicates the type of capture: 1080i means an interlaced video while 1080p means a progressive capture. Newer resolutions, such as 6K and 8K, have entered the professional market; 8K digital is similar to the VistaVision film format, in which 35mm film was shot on its side over a larger area of film, equaling the combination of two normal frames. The caveat of using larger resolutions with virtual production is the sheer magnitude of the data. The difference between 2K and 4K is not twice the amount of data but four times. You must have tremendously expensive computing power to handle an 8K live shoot. One strategy to address this issue is to do live tracking and compositing in real time at 1080p while recording a 4K image. One can see a live composite as a low-rez version of the shot while the 4K data is sent up to the cloud to be combined with slowly rendered 4K Unreal backgrounds and eventually be brought back to the set in the afternoon to see the final 4K. For independent films I would strongly consider shooting in high def and rendering the final composite from high def to 2K. With our amazing capability to capture ultra–high resolution imagery for motion pictures, it seems a shame that so many pictures eventually appear on mobile phones. It reminds me of the famous line from the film *Sunset Boulevard* (made in 1950, at the advent of television) uttered by the silent film star Norma Desmond character: "I am big; it's the pictures that got small."

Genlock

Genlock stands for generator locking. Using frequency-locked reference video signals (blackburst or tri-level), frame starts and ends for every shot are synchronized for multiple devices. Genlocking requires a sync generator that all other audio, video, or digital devices are connected to. Genlock is preferred because it avoids delays or latency. Low-latency livestreaming is especially important during live broadcasting. It is important to ensure that all devices can accept the sync signal that is generated. Devices include cameras, recorders, computers, trackers, etc.

Multi-camera productions such as sitcoms need to have all the cameras synced so their shutters all open simultaneously at the same frame rate to allow for seamless live or post editing. An example can be doing live switching between cameras that are not genlocked when you switch from one camera to another. Camera one could have its shutter open, but camera two would have its shutter closed when switched, leading to a black frame at the edit. Modern-day switchers do not use genlock, as they have an internal buffer that stores video images that are released at the appropriate time to keep all signals in sync. The downside of this is that buffering takes time and does not allow for the real-time synchronization needs of virtual production.

Synchronization is accomplished by using genlock, the drumbeat that keeps all the technology in line. Hi-definition genlock uses a tri-level signal that tells all cameras to start outputting pixel number one at exactly the same time. Scan lines will all start drawing from left to right at the exact same time and speed. This synchronization signal is so precise that care also needs to be taken with the length of cables used. If all cameras have the same length of cable, there will be no issues with the genlock. If one cable is a hundred feet longer, that physical distance and extra wire will slow the signal down in relation to other shorter cables, which require a delay mechanism to slow the signal in the other cables. While this is a consideration, it is rarely an issue.

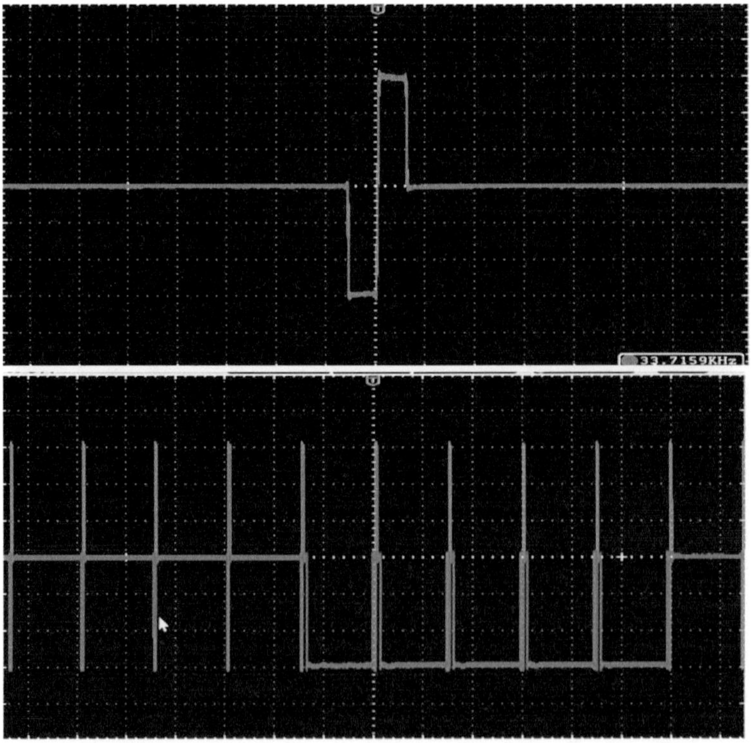

Figure 2.5 *The top image shows the tri-level genlock sync pulse with a negative pulse below, a ground pulse in the middle, and a positive pulse at the top to signal the start of a scan line. The bottom image displays the first four lines as having only a negative pulse, yielding dark lines.*

Genlock is critical for virtual production as you have so many systems that have to be synchronized to work primarily with the real live-action camera, tracking data, and their virtual counterparts. If you would like to learn more in-depth information on video systems, I find Doug Johnson's site most valuable: https://www.youtube.com/@djp_video.

Tracker Camera and Encoders

This data-gathering camera is attached to the primary live-action camera as used with the Mo-Sys system. The camera has a ring of infrared LED emitters surrounding a taking lens. The emitters illuminate a number of retro-reflective targets on a ceiling. (It could be a wall, floor, or screen as well.) The camera, in turn, takes an image of this constellation of targets to let the computer know where in space the live-action camera is. This data is sent to the Unreal Game Engine to inform the virtual camera where it needs to be to match the live-action camera.

This system needs to be genlocked. This tracking method is known as inside out and has been a mainstay for virtual production. Other systems that are outside in use a multitude of cameras to watch the live-action camera and derive its position in space. Other systems use radio sensor technology. The encoders refer to sensors that send out signals regarding the location of the zoom and focus controls.

Yikes! Too Much Info – Just Tell Me What to Do

Believe me, I feel your pain. Here is my take on virtual production for schools. Bare bones for a school is to get a proper camera such as a RED or a Blackmagic design or some model that is professional and can take a genlock. Next, you need to get a tracking system such as Mo-Sys that also comes with a virtual production plug-in. Next, you need ample hardware to run the Unreal Game Engine with video connectors. If you have that, all you need is a good fabric green screen (digitalgreenscreen.com) and enough lights to light it and your subject, along with a boom microphone and sound recorder. We'll cover these items later in this chapter.

The LED wall can wait unless you happen to have one lying about; then just plug it into the other equipment.

The important takeaway from our camera history lesson is setting up your live-action camera.

I have used this for students' projects and my personal films. This sample is from a RED Epic.

- Camera set to 23.97 progressive capture.
- 180-degree shutter.

- ISO native 800.
- Resolution 1080p.
- Genlocked.
- Non–drop frame timecode.
- Color temperature daylight, i.e. 5500K. (There is a trend of moving away from 3200K, but that's okay too. We'll cover this in the color chapter.)
- For a RED camera record Wide Gamut view at Rec. 709; more on this in the color chapter.

Hardware

Hardware Pricing

There are many ways to achieve virtual production shots. Mainstream LED volume methods are costly, while post-tracking and conventional cameras are not. To provide some longevity for this book, actual figures will only be provided for ranges illustrated by the number of dollar symbols, much like those used for restaurants.

- $ = 0–500 dollars
- $$ = 500–1,500 dollars
- $$$ = 1,500–5,000 dollars
- $$$$ = 5,000–10,000 dollars
- $$$$$ = 10,000–100,000+ dollars

Computer for Real-Time Rendering

The following is the recommended hardware for Unreal Engine 5.0 for Windows. For further documentation for other systems, such as Macintosh, consult the Unreal Engine site (https://docs.unrealengine.com/5.3/en-US/hardware-and-software-specifications-for-unreal-engine/).

Example: Lenovo laptop CPU Intel i7-975OH 2.6Ghz $$$
RAM 8 G.B.
Storage 1 TB HDD+256 GB SSD
GPU GTX 1650
Display 15.6″
O.S. Windows 10

While a laptop works well when dealing solely with the Unreal software, it is better to obtain a tower that can quickly add video input cards. Laptops, for example, don't have the customary SDI inputs used for professional camera systems. A workaround for this would be the purchase of a Blackmagic Design

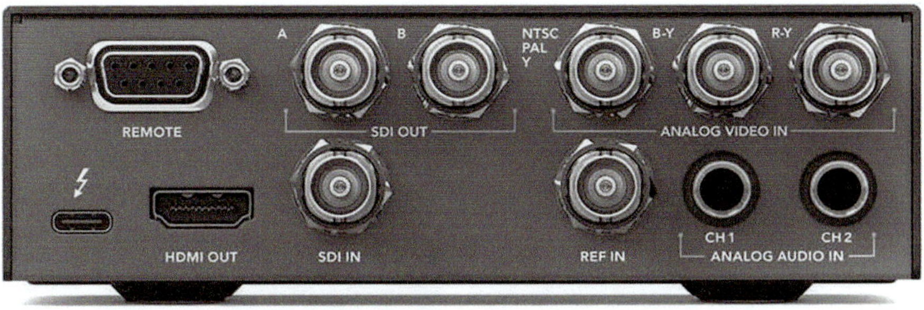

Figure 2.6 *Blackmagic Ultra Studio $$.*

Ultra studio that can take several video inputs and output the signals via a Thunderbolt 3 port if your laptop is so equipped.

A Proper Render Engine

A virtual studio often handcrafts its own custom hardware to handle the demands of virtual production running both the Unreal Engine and a connected LED volume. I'm happy to announce that the Zero Density company has taken on this cumbersome task and provides the hardware to work with their spectacular software called the EVO II. Here is a description from their site:

> **Where high-end servers lack the specialized specifications** of gaming hardware, gaming systems don't come equipped with essential professional 24/7 operational features such as redundant power supplies and rackmount capabilities. Until now, no engine on the market could deliver everything in one package.
>
> So we made our own, re-engineered the concept of rendering Hardware that supports game engine-based virtual productions, and unleashed the full potential of our Reality5 virtual production platform.
>
> From PCBs to power cabling and cooling, we meticulously reviewed every component and developed better alternatives in-house when industry-standard components fell short.
>
> The resultant EVO II is the most advanced real-time virtual production render hardware platform today.
>
> (2024, September 19). https://www.zerodensity.io/platforms/evo-ii/

Software and hardware are priced separately.

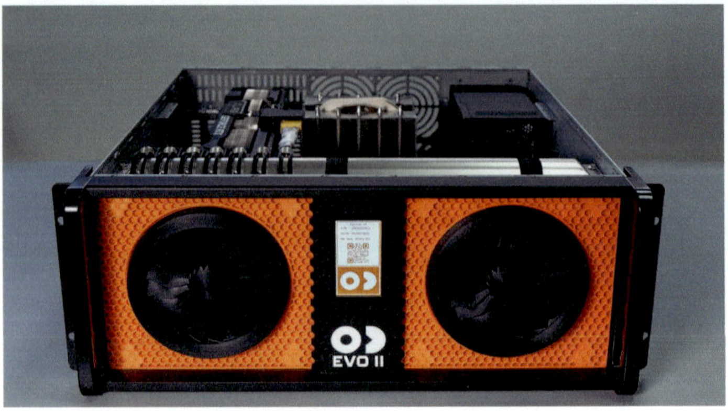

Figure 2.7 *Zero Density computer $$$$$.*
Source: Image courtesy of Zero Density.

Affordable Cameras

Live-action cameras have a wide range of choices. For post-tracking techniques where footage is shot wild, there is no need for a sync generator signal. Once the live-action frames are rendered, they become the basis for tracking the movement by using software such as Nuke or After Effects. You won't have data for focus, so that would be handled by eye.

Examples of low-end cameras that can be used in this manner are as follows:

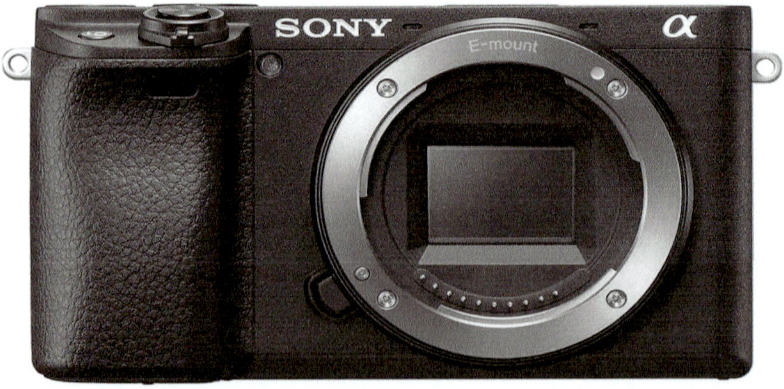

Figure 2.8 *Sony A7 $$ can record a good color signal in 4:2:2 color space that is good for green screen composites if you are using a recording chip that is fast enough. The numbers represent sampling rates: 4 samples the luminance value at 4 million times a second while the other numbers represent the color sampled at 2 million times a second. All three colors of RGB are derived from Luminance and the two color signals. The best composites would be done with a 4:4:4 signal, but in most cases, 4:2:2 is fine.*

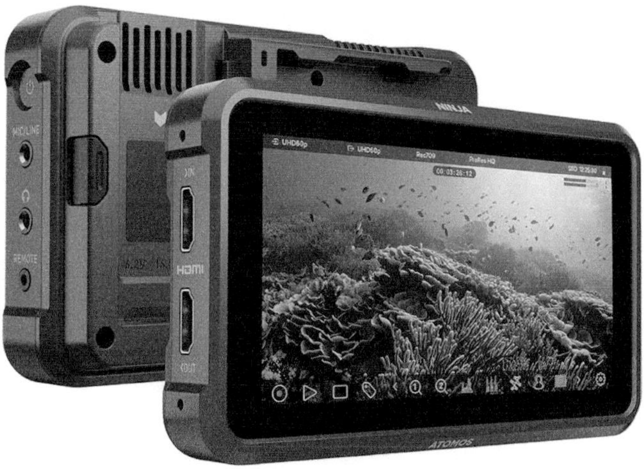

Figure 2.9 *The Atomos Ninja is a 5.2″ 4K HDMI recording monitor. It can also record ProRes RAW up to 6K with compatible cameras. The idea is that while small camera cards can't record high-resolution images, camera sensors are still capable of sending that information to higher-end recorders like the Atomos. $$.*

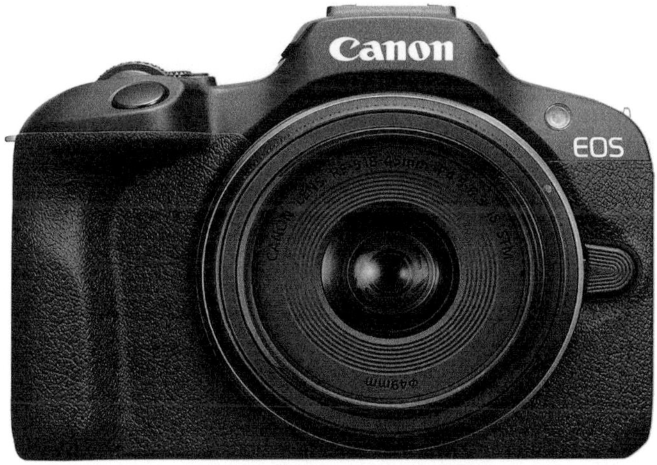

Figure 2.10 *I suggest this Canon R100 camera, which works with the Dragonframe stop-motion software through its USB port with live view capability. Dragonframe has a previz keyer capability to import still frames from an Unreal render to use as a background and align and light your subjects against green to match the still. After that alignment, you switch to video mode and record the live action. It is a less expensive alternative to a full video switcher. I have used this system for simple class projects concentrating on perspective and lighting match of live action to still backgrounds. Canon $$ Dragonframe software $.*

Professional Cameras for Live Tracking

These cameras have genlock capability to allow for live tracking.

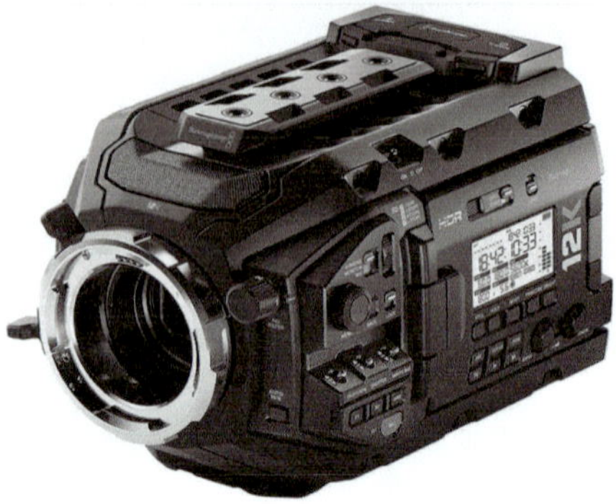

Figure 2.11 *Blackmagic Ursa $$$$.*

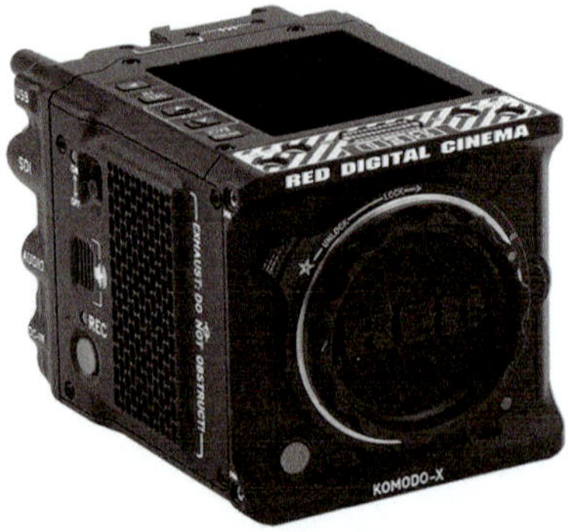

Figure 2.12 *RED Komodo $$$$$.*

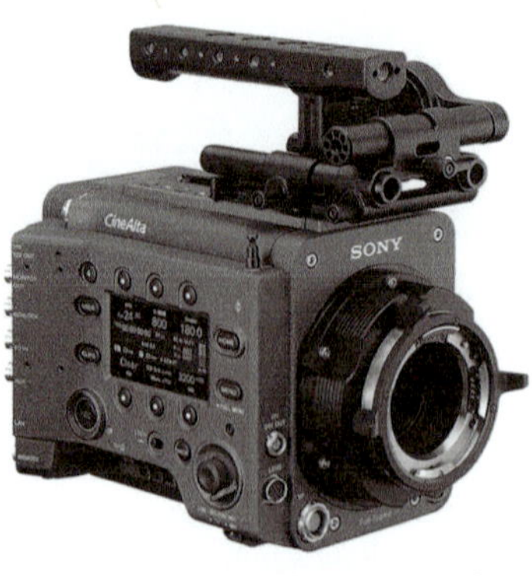

Figure 2.13 *Sony Venice $$$$$. I suspect that, due to the release of the Sony virtual production tools that work with this camera to detect moiré distortion and balance color on LED walls, this will be the go-to camera for high-end VP work.*

LED Walls

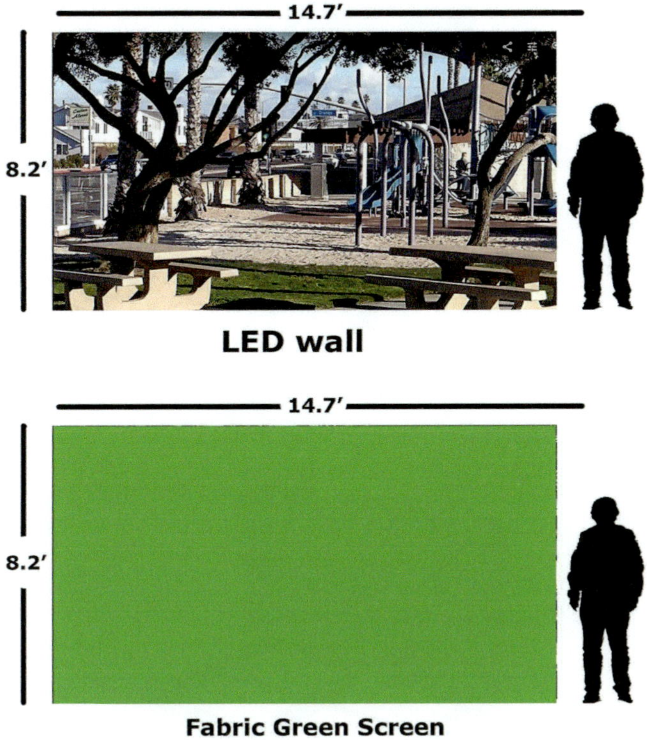

Figure 2.14 *LED wall rental $$$$ (per day): rentforevent.com (https://www.vu.network/). Paint and fabric screens from digitalgreenscreen.com $ (purchase). Also Planar.com to rent stage.*

Lighting and Grip

Nothing has changed with the standard grip package of C stands, flags, nets, apple boxes, and the like, but the new LED lighting instruments are fabulous. The Aputure line in particular has the LS 600 D Pro unit that puts out 8500+ Lux at 9.8′ with far less power than an HMI without the ultraviolet risk and heat. Furthermore, its color rendering index (CRI) is rated at 96, over and above the 90 recommended for contiguous spectrum sources. The LEDs in these lights pay far more attention to obtaining the full spectrum of light than some Spikey LED walls. The other advantage is instantly switching the color from 6500K to 3200K or anything in between. They are beautiful lights, but that being said, if you are on a budget, you can save money by renting the quickly becoming outdated tungsten filament movie lamps. They rent for far less than the latest LED fixtures because they are out of fashion. Yes, they will be hot and not as efficient with electricity. Still, the light they emit is excellent for good reproduction, as it has been for years. As for sound, the standard boom pole microphone and mixer still hold true.

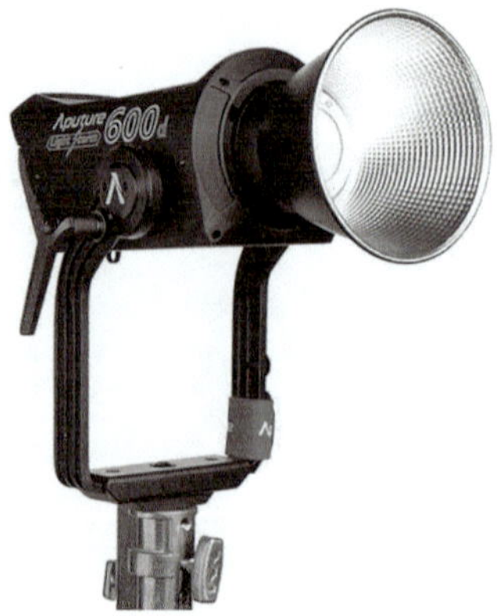

Figure 2.15 *The Aputure 600 D Pro $$.*

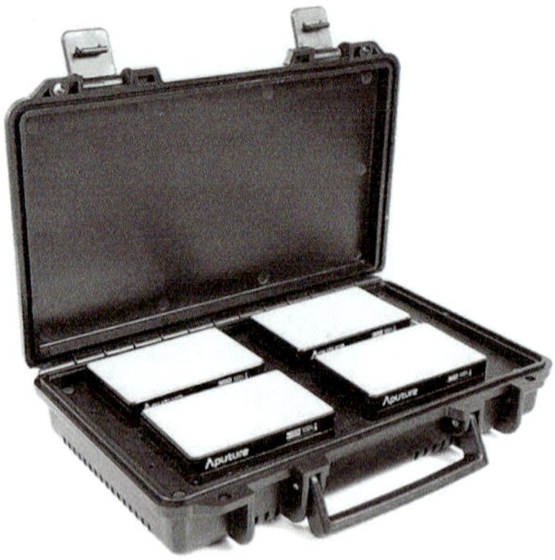

Figure 2.16 *The Aputure MC four-light panel kit $$.*

The Turn-Key Studio

Filmmakers on a budget have traditionally cobbled together a borrowed this and that to put up a short-term stage to shoot their movie. As you can see from the variety of choices and the complexity of the technology, kludging things together can be perilous, and you only need one point of failure to stop a shoot cold. Should you have the resources, the ultimate alternative is to rent a turn-key stage with turn-key technicians to make the magic happen. Studios such as Vū Studio (https://www.vu.network/virtual-studio) have several fully equipped and functional stages ready to go.

Planar manufactures camera-ready LED walls with good color space. Their pixel pitch distance is much closer than others, at 1.5 and 1.9mm.

As far as the cost to rent these fabulous facilities, the saying I think of is "If you have to ask . . . you can't afford it." Pulling a figure out of the air would be $$$$$$ per day. When one gets to that level one has complete control and can work fast and iteratively.

Sound

Using the boom microphone has traditionally been the best way to capture a performance. During emotional scenes, the boom operator can anticipate and react quickly to sudden changes in volume, such as a scream, which will be recorded far better with the microphone at a distance than with the reduction of sensitivity on a volume control. Lavalier microphones are prone to pick up the ruffling of clothing but also are always "present," meaning the microphone is always close to the actor, creating an unusual homogenous intimacy between all the characters, much like a dubbed movie for which all the replacement voices have been recorded close to a microphone. The other issue with sound and the LED volumes that has been noticed is the potential for echo off the LED walls. While that can occur on a hard-painted green screen stage, one can put up curtains or sound-absorbing materials outside the green screen area to cancel the effect. In a volume, all the screens need to be seen so that solution is unavailable. Using a green fabric screen is the best solution as it serves to improve the recording environment and is a compositing tool.

Zoom H4 Audio Recorder $
https://zoomcorp.com/en/us/
Audio Technica 2020 microphone $
https://www.audio-technica.com/en-us/at2020

Summary

Many moving parts and variables go along with the virtual production processes. To avoid the confusion that arises from a data dump, our plan is to share our experience and the choices we made creating our case study films to demonstrate how to integrate all this information into action. Keep in mind that the most complicated things are made up of a lot of simple things. Like old-time filmmaking, the journey will bring surprises, missteps, frustration, confusion, laughter, and joy. Stick with it, and you, too, will make virtual production movies.

Chapter 3

Color Management

Photography has always been a product of light. Images displayed on a screen involve the science of light and color, which is an interplay between light and our human vision system. For production, there must be a means of maintaining light and color consistency throughout the production in order to control and match design intention to final public display output.

Light

Light takes up a tiny bit of what is called the electromagnetic spectrum. This spectrum is composed of radiant energy that travels with wave motions. A wavelength is the distance from the top of one wave to the top of the next, while frequency is the number of waves passing a given point in one second. Light travels at about 186,000 miles per second in air and about two-thirds that speed as it goes through ordinary glass. Lenses work on this slowing principle by bending light as it travels from one medium to another.

In the case of a lens, light travels through the air and then through the various thicknesses of glass in a convex lens, where the lens is thicker in the middle than on the edges. Different glass thicknesses bend or refract the light rays so a

DOI: 10.4324/9781003473169-3

magnifying glass can focus a hot spot of light from the sun's parallel rays to burn through paper at a specific distance from the lens. The distance from the center of the lens to the focal point where the light rays converge is the focal length.

Wavelength

We describe different parts of the electromagnetic spectrum by broad divisions and precise wavelengths. This spectrum of radiant energy goes from the extremely short wavelengths found in gamma rays and X-rays to the extremely long wavelengths found in radio, which can be miles long. What we call light is right in the middle. Everything before and after light is called radiation. If we can see the radiant energy, it's called light; if it is invisible to the eye, it is called radiation. The terms *infrared* and *ultraviolet light* are misnomers as both wavelengths are radiation. The wavelengths of light span from 400 millimicrons (millionths of a millimeter) to 700 millimicrons: 400mm represents a deep blue, and 700mm represents a deep red. Ultraviolet radiation wavelengths begin below 400mm, and infrared radiation starts above 700mm.

White Light

Suppose a prism refracts a beam of light into its component wavelengths. In that case, we will perceive a rainbow of colors going from blue to cyan to green to yellow and finally to red. The narrow cyan and yellow bands result from blending blue and green, creating cyan, and red and green combined to create yellow. When the primary colors red, green, and blue are presented to the eye together in roughly equal amounts, they blend into what we perceive as white light. However, white light is in the eye of the beholder due to how our brain interprets what it sees. If we are in a room lit by traditional light bulbs with a tungsten filament, our eyes will perceive that the pages of the book we're reading are white. Suppose we were to turn off all but one of the light bulbs and open the drapes to let the sunlight stream in to light the book. In that case, the page would still appear white because our brain adjusts for the now much bluer light coming in to the room. By comparison, the one tungsten light bulb will glow with warm yellow light because our eyes have adjusted to daylight. This remarkable flexibility of our brains presents a problem with media, as film, video, and digital media don't have this capability; they can only be designed to expect and record a certain kind of white light. To make that work, we need to define "white" light.

Color Temperature

Scientists used heat and a black body radiator to define different combinations of the primary colors that create the perception of "white" light. A black body is a substance that emits no radiation. The best example would be a black hole out in space where no light escapes. Since we don't have one of those on Earth (thankfully), we can create a black body by making a black box of graphite with a viewing hole in it that we can take measurements through. As this black body is heated, it will glow like a piece of metal heated by a torch. As the temperature rises, the black body will go from red to yellow to several shades of white (blends of red, green, and blue). At specific points, we assign a temperature to the white glow. This temperature is called Kelvin. Kelvin is used in science and is based on the Celsius scale, where a change of one degree Celsius equals one degree in Kelvin. The main difference is in the units of measurement, 273.15K + 0 Celsius, which is the approximate melting point of ice. The absolute zero in Kelvin is much lower than that. Using this method, two standard white blends were found for media: tungsten at 3200K and daylight at 5500K. Daylight is tricky as the sun never stays put. At noon, the sun is quite blue, while at sunset, it is much warmer. Today's consumer cameras often use graphic icons to represent these color temperatures, such as a light bulb icon for 3200K, a sun icon for 5500K, and a sun in shade icon for cooler daylight.

5500K Or 6500K? Which Is It?

> **Throughout history, painters and photographers recognized sunlight** at midday to be a trusted and repeatable light source. Before artificial light, sunlight was a standard source. Today, different devices measure sunlight differently, but it continues to be a reference source.

For years, film has been manufactured in two sensitivities. Tungsten film would reproduce colors accurately under 3200K tungsten light. Daylight film would reproduce colors accurately at 5500K daylight. Filters were used to convert one color temperature to another to accommodate situations where the appropriate film was unavailable. The 85 filter was orange and used to warm the daylight 5500K to 3200K. The 80B converted 3200K into 5500K. I noticed recently that 6500K is being used for standard daylight or D65 viewing standards. My research has discovered that the difference lies in the sun being a perfect black-body radiator.

Still, the graphite black body is a close simulation, and the Kelvin temperature described for that is the temperature of the heater that makes it glow. The sun being read directly through the atmosphere is 5500K. In other words, the 6500K is correlated with the 5500K and is essentially the same thing. I have never found a default 6500K setting in a camera, but I have seen them as defaults on LED walls. The difference between the two temperatures is relatively minor, anyway. Still, annoying little variables like this can drive one to distraction. In practice, I keep the camera at 5500K, and the LED wall can be set to the default as it will inevitably need color correction, as seen in the LED chapter (https://en.wikipedia.org/wiki/Color_temperature).

Printing Film

After processing, the negative was copied to print film that created an image using three layers of images. One layer had an image made with cyan dye, the next with magenta dye, and the third with yellow dye. These secondary color dyes are combined by overlapping to create a full-color image through a subtractive color mixture. For example, when magenta and yellow overlap, we see red on the projection screen as white light passes through. Yellow and cyan overlap to create green, and cyan and magenta over each other make blue. One gets a dark neutral tone or black if all three dyes overlap. A wide array of variations in the saturation or intensity of the dyes against one another gives a beautifully wide color palette to reproduce the colors we see in nature. There have been times when art students who were painters took my color class and pointed out that when painting with watercolors, their primary colors are red, blue, and yellow. While this mixture can produce many colors on the canvas, to get a full range, the red would be magenta, and the blue would be cyan.

To obtain superior contrast in movie film prints, some processes would leave the processed silver in the film to make the dark regions even darker, as the silver particles were very effective at blocking the projector light. A similar method is used for printing books and magazines. When images are prepared for book illustration, the file color space should be in CMYK. The CMY, of course, stands for the cyan, magenta, and yellow dyes used to print the picture. The K represents a black ink pass to increase the contrast in the picture, much as was done keeping silver in motion picture prints.

The Density and Exposure Curve

Now that we had defined the various wavelengths of light and color temperature standards, we had to come up with a way to describe accurately how the film captured light and turned it into an image. Light on Earth has a tremendous brightness range. If we start with a black card that only reflects 1% of the light that hits it and compare it to the sun itself, the sun is 20,000 times brighter. This enormous dynamic range is far larger than we can perceive all at once with our eyes. For humans, the eye and the brain compensate so that when outdoors, our irises shrink to limit the amount of light allowed in, and our brains favor the range of light between the black card and, let's say, a bright shirt that reflects 90% of the light falling on it. Anything brighter than that is listed as a super white, such as glints, candle flames, light bulbs, and the sun.

As so happens, film responds to light in a similar manner. Film's response to light was discovered and plotted on a curve called a D (density) Log E (exposure) curve, sometimes called the H and D curve, named after Hurter and Driffield, the two scientists who invented the curve in the late 1800s. It is still very much used today, plotting the sensitivity ranges for analog and digital media. The process used for film involved a particular instrument called a sensitometer to expose a strip of film through a wide range of neutral density filters that varied in density from completely opaque to clear glass in evenly stepped variations in opacity like a series of gradually darkening sunglasses that went from clear to a little darker, then darker, then darker in even steps until no light came through at all. Once a strip of film was exposed in this way, it was processed to reveal a gradation of tones. This film, in turn, was analyzed in a densitometer, which amounted to a small light meter that measured the density of the film over the range of steps. This data was then plotted out as a density over exposure curve.

It was discovered that the silver halide crystals in film slowly began to sense the light with increasing density in small increments, called the toe, until there came a series of exposures that responded equally to the changes of the filters used in the sensitometer, called the straight line portion, until the exposure

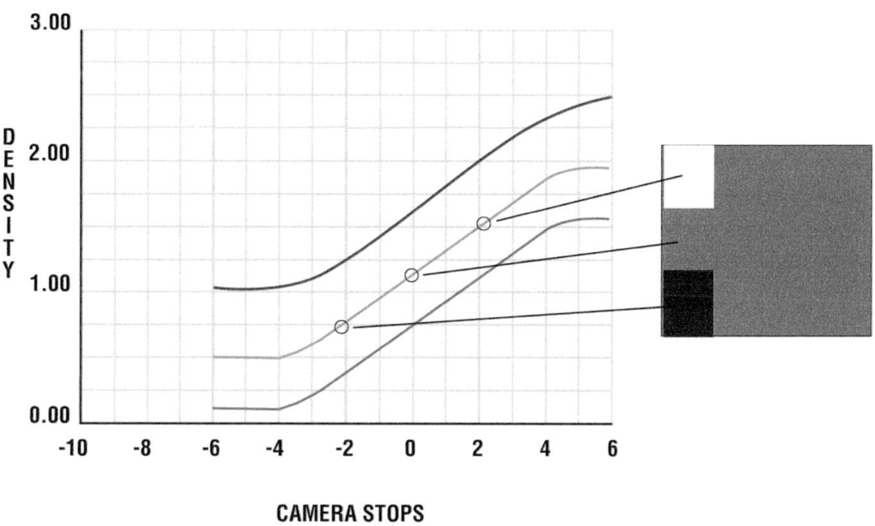

Figure 3.1 *The D log E curve shows the sensitivity range of film and, when well exposed, places the white, gray, and black standards on these points of the curve with plenty of room to change the exposure and color.*
Source: Filming the Fantastic, First Edition

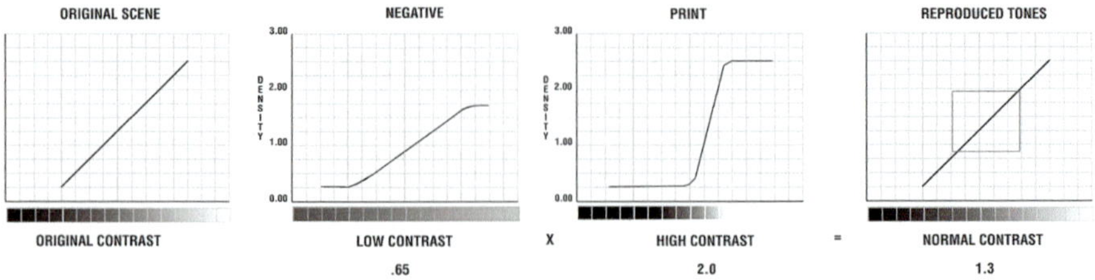

Figure 3.2 *The simple pipeline of film image reproduction. Low-contrast negative captures the high dynamic range of light while the high-contrast print normalizes sections of the negative to create a pleasing color-corrected and readable image of the original subject.*
Source: Filming the Fantastic, First Edition

came to a point where the increase in density began to have smaller differences than before, called the shoulder, until it reached a point where the film could go no darker. This curve interpreted the range of exposures with a certain contrast given the term gamma. Essentially, gamma was the angle of the curve. The steeper the angle or more straight up and down the curve, the higher the contrast would be as the small, even changes in the exposure would respond with large changes in the film.

Conversely, when the angle of the curve became lower, the contrast would lower as the even changes of exposure reflected as smaller changes in the film. The control of gamma or contrast became a good tool for capturing as much of the brightness range as possible during photography. These curves become separate red, green, and blue curves when shooting color.

The Film Duplication Process

Shooting on negative film where the exposed silver halide crystals turn to opaque silver after developing had very low contrast. A low-contrast film can capture and condense big brightness ranges. For example, if the light in a scene doubles from 50 to 100 on low-contrast film, the density, if starting with the same number, might go from 50 to 75. The brilliance of this method of capture is that when the film is printed on high-contrast film (a steep curve), it takes the smaller increments of the negative densities and increases them again to reproduce an image similar to what the eye would see. The typical film reproduction pipeline is to go from a negative with a gamma of .65 and copy it onto print film with a gamma of 2.0 to obtain a normal contrast of 1.3 for projection.

One might ask why the final contrast isn't 1.0. It is slightly higher to compensate for the dim ambient light in theaters coming from exit signs and walkway lighting.

Gamma 1.0 was used for duplicating onto intermediate film stock to create visual effects or big print runs. An example would be a simple dissolve, where the negatives of shots A and B were copied onto the intermediate to become low-contrast positive images. These were then rephotographed in an optical printer to create a new internegative that would closely match the original negative in contrast and quality before going to the final print stage.

In the early days of digital, a great deal of confusion occurred when looking at digital scans of negative film, as the image was a very flat, low-contrast positive image. Artists were expecting normal-contrast imagery. The flat image had the characteristics of a low-contrast negative, except that it was positive, which enabled a large amount of density and color correction. This is why RAW images, DPX files, and the like look flat.

Laboratory Aim Density System (LAD)

There are different types of color reference charts. One of the simplest is the gray card. In the final film print, as in a digital image, red, green, and blue are in equal amounts. This reference is an indication that lighting and exposure are correct, so everything else should be lit and exposed correctly also.

The gray card is actually 18% gray. Why not 50%? Because this standard is driven by the human vision system, which perceives 18% gray to be the middle value between white and black on a logarithmic or exponential scale.

When a motion picture laboratory made thousands of prints to be distributed worldwide, a system was devised to ensure that each print would have consistent, identical colors. Eastman Kodak invented the laboratory aim density (LAD) system based on a gray density that appeared to the eye to be halfway between white and black (90% reflective and 1% reflective). This gray tone was read on a densitometer to reach aim densities for all the primaries: red, green, and blue. Kodak would supply a color negative control film called a "Girl Head" that consisted of a photograph of a woman next to a patch of white, gray, and black, along with three primary colors and a gradation of gray tones. The most important was the gray patch, which had densities of red at .80, green at 1.20, and blue at 1.60.

The numbers are not the same across all the primaries due to surrounding compensating dyes that equalize the color absorption characteristics of the dyes that are not perfect. This is why the color negative has an overall orange appearance. At the end of the pipeline, the print of the gray patch will be the exact measurement in all three colors. Another way of checking the result is to lay the print of the control strip on top of a standard viewing light box and compare the gray to a .90 neutral density filter. If the gray matches, all the other tones and colors will fall in line and be consistent.

Standard Illuminant

Evaluating film prints over a standard lightbox balanced to 5500K and with a color rendering index (CRI) color rendering index above 90 was important. A CRI of 100 is the continuous daylight spectrum that approximates pure daylight. Traditional matte painting artists worked on their paintings under a skylight and viewed film strips in magnifiers against it. This ensured that the same daylight source illuminated both painting and film, enabling the artist to paint according to what the film reproduced.

Color Space

The previous sections compressed into a nutshell the fundamental elements used for film to capture and reproduce color. One question that needs to be answered is how much color the film is reproducing. A series of experiments were done in the 1920s to determine how many colors a human can see. These findings were compiled by the Commission Internationale de L'eclairage (CIE) in 1931 to document this color space and created the CIE chromaticity diagram. Instead of a 2D slice of a rainbow, this diagram depicts a slice of a 3D cone that looks like a horseshoe with an arc showing all the wavelengths of light from 400mm to 700mm. All the colors blend towards the center to create white. There is a point called the Planckian nexus that depicts where all three colors are blended equally, which happens to be 6500K or the correlated daylight color temperature of 5500K. The bottom of this arched horseshoe is oddly flat without wavelength markings. This is because, within the human eye, we have color sensors called cones that are sensitive to red, green, and blue light. Some colors, like magenta, don't have a wavelength because they blend two wavelengths and the sensation of two cones sensing them together. After creating this diagram, we could plot how many colors the film could reproduce. The film process captures a large portion of the human perception gamut but not all of it. Video and digital cameras captured even less when they were first introduced, and today, they are quickly overtaking film as the motion picture media of choice.

The Digital Dilemma

The fundamental principles of wavelength, color temperature, sensitometry curves, viewing standards, aims, and the CIE diagram served the film world well for the better part of a century. Kodak, the leading film manufacturer, was extremely helpful in setting standards and laying the groundwork for what was to come. Fuji Film and Agfa began making film with their subtle differences in manufacturing. Once digital came about in the mid-80s, we found ourselves in a cornucopia of different curves, sensors, file formats, etc. The challenge is in sorting it all out, and fortunately, there is a new book that does just that.

The Color Management Handbook for Visual Effects Artists by Victor Perez

The best source for understanding and sorting out all our new color issues is the book *The Color Management Handbook for Visual Effects Artists*, published by Focal Press in 2024. Mr. Perez has succinctly defined the issues and prescribed solutions to our festering problems with consistent imaging. In brief, the industry has suffered from the fathers' sins by using technological Band-Aids on top of ever-changing technology. One such band-aid was using a gamma curve to change the contrast of a video signal so it displayed properly on a cathode ray tube.

The CRT has a coating of phosphors that glow when it is hit by an electron beam. Unfortunately, the response didn't match the input. In other words, if you doubled the voltage, the phosphor didn't glow with twice the brightness, so you had to add a curve to the signal to correct the deficiencies in the CRT to display the picture correctly. Technology moved on, and we have liquid crystal displays (LCD) that don't have this issue, but they sit alongside millions of CRTs that do, so the curve became a universal Band-Aid grandfathered into many displays.

The list goes on, of course, but I can think of no better explanation of this cobweb of fixes than one from Victor himself.

Display-Referred Workflows

In the beginning, there were film cameras, and they shot in film negative stocks. All you needed to do was to develop the film negative and convert it into positive, apply a light to it, and voila: cinema projection. The whole process was analog – a physical support and a chemical process – and everybody was happy.

However, if we wanted to put a film on TV, we needed to convert the physical support into an electronic signal, so we used a telecine (practically a video camera that taped the negative recording against a light). So, we had a magnetic support that was still analog – not perfect for a few reasons, but still, everybody was quite happy with it.

But then people started getting personal computers, accompanied, of course, by CRT monitors – roughly the same technology as the TVs of the time – so the image capabilities of both TVs and PCs were more or less the same. This meant that any image document required a correction by the software attempting to visualize it, more or less correctly, on the CRT monitor, and I mean "more or less" because every CRT monitor was built without standard criteria for color. And every type of software was doing its own thing to represent color.

Then computers and monitors evolved, and finally everything complied with the newly established sRGB Color Space (yay!), so my image is going to be displayed correctly as the monitor and the software are aligned in terms of color, and so are the websites full of images I browse on the super-slow internet. In the meantime – we are still in the 90s – the film scanner has been invented; the digital intermediate is born and used for the first time to digitally restore and remaster Walt Disney's 1937 classic *Snow White and the Seven Dwarfs*. The process is also known as DI; we scan the original negative, converting it into Cineon file sequences in gorgeous 10-bit – a higher bit depth than the 8-bit sRGB we use for watching videos of cats on the internet. Everything was processed in digital after the scan, but at the end – cough cough – for the delivery, we print it back again in a film strip to be projected in analog as before, so the digital part was just in the middle (hence, intermediate) until digital projectors became good enough, affordable, and popular (without mentioning the contribution of the stereoscopic boom created by James Cameron's *Avatar*).

Digital cinema also changed the rules in the chain of distribution, as film rolls did not need to travel anymore. The new digital cinema packages were transmitted over the internet. Cinema was becoming entirely digital but not end-to-end just yet, until digital cameras landed. No longer did we need to scan film negatives – couth cough; images from digital cameras, though, were converted to the same Cineon file sequences we used for film scans to keep a consistent workflow. And then the TV became digital and abandoned the less ecological CRT to become LCD, but during the time of transition to digital, they had to build inside the software of the digital TV the same "defects" of the image reproduction that CRTs had naturally so everybody could see the same corrected signal that could be reproduced by a crap old system – a smart move for consistency but a headache for everything else. And since TVs became digital – meaning they have a computer inside – TV contents started evolving with the same speed as computers.

Very quickly, we stepped from standard definition – remember the old NTSC and PAL systems? – to the new world of unified high definition (with its three versions: 720pm, 1080i, and 1080p). Yet all of them had the same color space, which is a tweaked version of the sRGB used for computers. This color space for the TVs was standardized to a recommendation made by the International Telecommunications Union and become the standard for HDTVs: recommendation number 709 or ITU-R 709. That is a long and complicated name; let's just call it Rec 709. The Rec 709 maintains the same primaries and white point of the sRGB but changes the gamma encoding (its transfer function) slightly to represent the images with a better color quality in these new devices.

But why stop evolution here if we can get greater resolution, bigger color spaces, and higher bit depth? Computers get better and more affordable, technology evolves, the pursuit of image quality never stops, and here we are at 4K HDR UHD TV, but just when the trend was "bigger is better" and while the market was focused on making bigger screens and more powerful projectors . . . people decided to watch content on their phones and tablets. The war of devices was on: portability versus bigger screens.

So the process that was once called digital intermediate became significantly more complex, with elements coming from very different sources, and needed to be visualized for processing on the same sRGB monitors but delivered for displays with the same capabilities of computer monitors and for better screens. So how can you work colors, bit depths, and dynamic ranges you cannot visualize? Of course! Using LUTs to convert from a device to another device, depending on where the image was generated and where we want to transfer it now! Yep . . . that is a lot of LUTs. Furthermore, once the project is finished and the master final delivery is archived, what will happen in a few years when displays get even better? Our precious materials that came at a high cost will become simply obsolete.

This mess relies on one single issue: all corrections to adapt the content to be correctly visualized on the screen implied changing the actual data of the images to be adapted to every display, so as soon as the technology changes, our files must change to adapt to that new technology, to the display. This is known as display-referred workflow.

Perez, V. (2023). *The Color Management Handbook for Visual Effects Artists: Digital Color Principles, Color Management Fundamentals & ACES Workflows* (1st ed.). Focal Press.

Scene-Referred Workflow

Victor's explanation was the best I've ever seen. When he speaks of LUTs, he's referring to look-up tables that convert image data numbers from a camera to

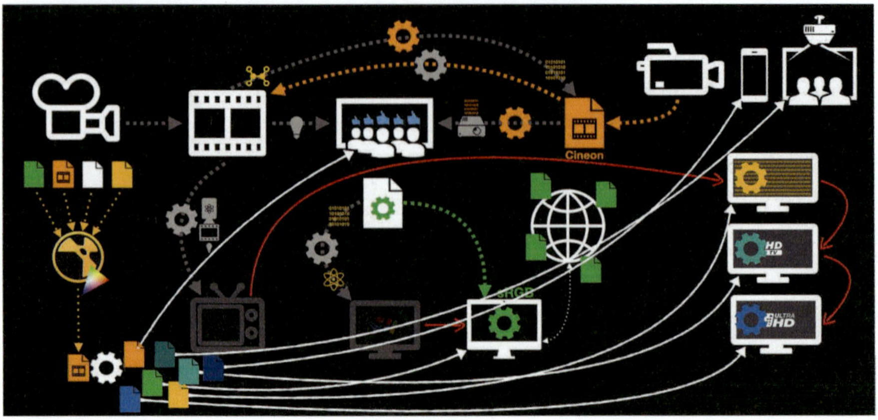

Figure 3.3 *The alarming complexity of dealing with competing technologies using the display-referred pipeline.*

Source: Perez, Victor. *The Color Management Handbook for Visual Effects Artists: Digital Color Principles, Color Management Fundamentals & ACES Workflows*. Focal Press, 2023. Image courtesy of Victor Perez. ©2023 Victor Perez. All rights reserved.

a predetermined set of numbers for a display device. An LUT can convert a flat, raw image into a viewable normal-contrast image. Victor says the ultimate answer to the color babble problem is the Academy Color Encoding System (ACES).

In a nutshell, since we know the range of human vision, let's create placeholders for every color a human can see. This means those recommendations Victor spoke of, such as Rec 709, Rec 2020, and Rec 2065, all have unique color gamuts, but it's okay because they are all within the master ACES color space, and there is no need to convert anything to anything. Furthermore, ACES is future proof along other lines: any format resolution, any frame rate, every visible color, high bit depth (16-bit float), high dynamic range of 30 stops. Regarding the latter two advantages, the 16-bit float was a good choice as it has enough precision to handle the visible spectrum without being too heavy in storage and computation. For the last, the human eye can distinguish up to 24 stops, so unless humans suddenly evolve, we're covered there.

This unified color space becomes the central working hub for visual effects compositing as all the numerous inputs and gamuts get placed into the ACES color space; compositing is executed within the space, and when sent out to the different displays, the content will output to each needed color space for the device.

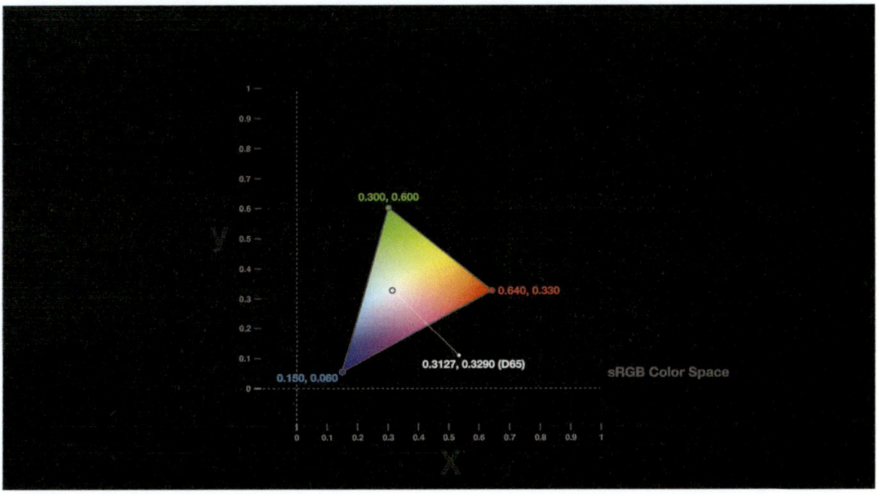

Figure 3.4 *The sRGB color gamut cut out from the chromaticity diagram was a boon for keeping all colors aligned with computers and the internet. The circle in the middle shows the white point of the D65 color temperature.*

Source: Perez, Victor. *The Color Management Handbook for Visual Effects Artists: Digital Color Principles, Color Management Fundamentals & ACES Workflows*. Focal Press, 2023. Image courtesy of Victor Perez.

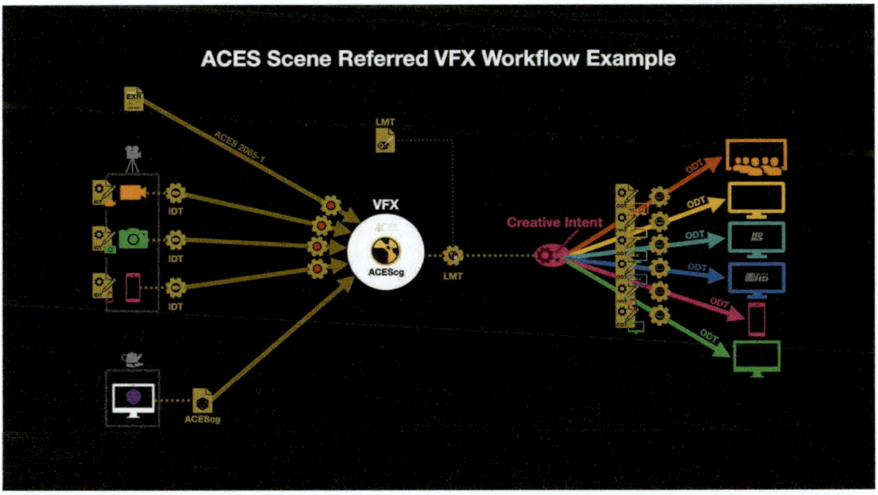

Figure 3.5 *The brilliant scene-referred pipeline using the ACES color space to keep consistent color for today and the future. Mr. Perez has made videos showing how to integrate ACES and the scene-referred pipeline into After Effects and Nuke.*

Source: Perez, Victor. *The Color Management Handbook for Visual Effects Artists: Digital Color Principles, Color Management Fundamentals & ACES Workflows*. Focal Press, 2023. Image courtesy of Victor Perez.

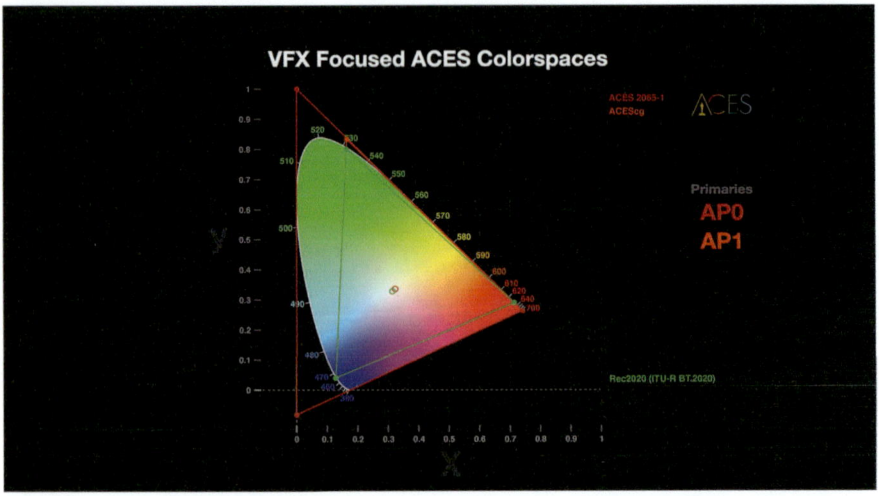

Figure 3.6 *ACES created placeholder numbers for all the colors the human eye can see, as plotted out in the red triangle surrounding the CIE chromaticity diagram. The green triangle shows the improved color space of Rec 2020 compared to sRGB.*
Source: Perez, Victor. *The Color Management Handbook for Visual Effects Artists: Digital Color Principles, Color Management Fundamentals & ACES Workflows.* Focal Press, 2023. Image courtesy of Victor Perez. ©2023 Victor Perez. All rights reserved.

Display-Referred Versus Scene-Referred Workflows

In a professional setting, the hands-down winner is scene referred, and if one has the inclination, resources, and the need to handle multiple inputs and outputs, go the way of the future. The display method may also be a good choice for students and independent filmmakers if they don't need to accommodate many variables, especially if they are creating a demo reel. One case in point is to shoot and render in the same format and color space. For green screenshots, a good practice is to shoot the live action with Rec 709 color space and have the format be Apple ProRes 4:4:4:4 or 4:2:2 at least. This leaves plenty of color data for pulling good composites.

When the Unreal backgrounds are recorded, do a final render as a JPG sequence that uses sRGB (the still version of the video Rec 709) to keep the color consistent. EXR renders would accommodate matching color space as well. Essentially, since you primarily have just the live action and a CG background, make sure they are both in the same space, and the complexity of the process goes away. Do a final delivery render as Apple ProRes 4:2:2 in high definition, and you will have a good sample reel. Once you show it around and get a big contract to do your big-time movie, then, by all means, move over to the studio pipelines of scene-referred workflow.

Chapter 4

The LED Screen

Introduction

The popularity of the *Mandalorian* series gave rise to the use of LED technology as an image "volume" for creating in-camera synthetic environments. While this provides a unique new process for film production, it is not a one-size-fits-all technique. The method provides some solutions but has many challenges that are best addressed with other methods, such as the green screen compositing method.

The LED Wall

Most of the time, the LED wall is displaying a 3D environment such as that created in Unreal. When the Unreal virtual camera and the live camera are linked, any camera dolly movement will result in a matching perspective change in the foreground and background (LED wall). Any zoom camera movement will not result in a perspective change in the foreground and background but will appear as a cropped background change.

DOI: 10.4324/9781003473169-4

The common names for the video screen used for virtual production are the LED wall and the volume. The term *wall* focuses too much on the instrument rather than its purpose. I prefer to think of it as a doorway because that is what it recreates. Instead of looking at the LED screen as a large TV set, think of it like an open garage door with your camera inside the garage looking out. As the camera moves forward, the things closest to it get bigger faster than items farther back to create a dolly effect with a perspective change. This dimensional capability makes this screen different from old-school rear projection. From the camera's viewpoint, it appears to be traveling through space. From the stage and crew viewpoint, we see an image within an image called the frustum that shows a slice of the camera's viewing angle as it intersects the screen. As the camera moves closer to the LED screen, the frustum shrinks as the fixed camera angle passes through a smaller screen section. This can disconcert the performer as it deviates from a conventional display. However, in the camera viewfinder, everything looks correct.

Rear Projection

By comparison, a rear projection setup is as if the camera inside the garage took a picture looking out the door opening and then blew that up to be wallpaper on the closed garage door. From the vantage point of the camera, the original image looking out the door and a picture of that image blown up and attached to the closed door would look the same. The drawback is that the blown-up picture is locked in space and time. If you were to move the camera closer to the blown-up image, there would be no perspective change because you are looking at a flat picture. Moving the camera forward doesn't look like an accurate dolly move but more like a zoom because all objects in the image get

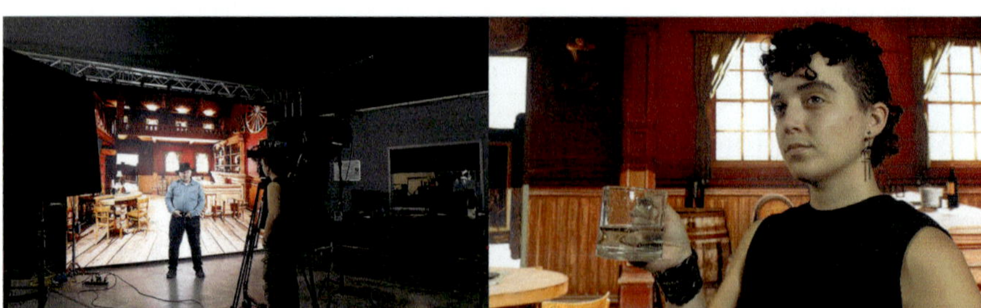

Figure 4.1 *Traditional rear projection captures a specific viewpoint in time. The image (like wallpaper) cannot change in perspective as the camera moves closer. It just sees a smaller portion of the screen. An LED wall allows for a dynamically moving image that shows perspective changes as the camera moves in, just as if you were shooting a real set. The picture on the right shows the advantage of any background image technique as reflective and transparent objects such as glass are recorded realistically, and there is no danger of matte lines around the figure as in an in-camera composite.*

more prominent by the same amount. There is no dimensional change. We merely see less of it as we get closer to the blow-up.

For many schools that purchased LED screens but did not follow through with having them controlled by the Unreal Game Engine and a tracking system like Mo-Sys that ties a real camera to a virtual one in the virtual set to allow for dimensional change, the screen will remain a rear projection tool. This is

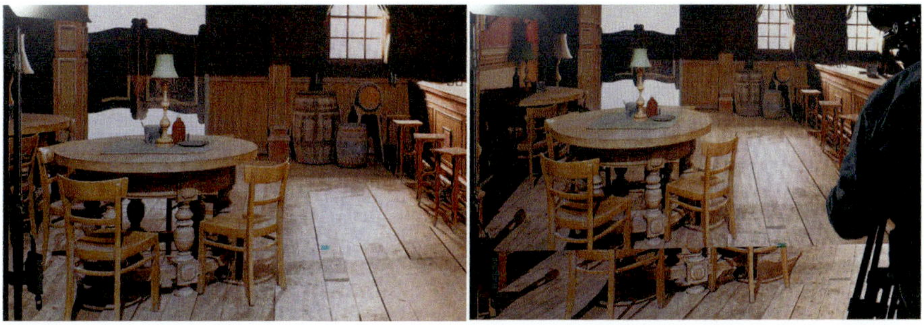

Figure 4.2 *A picture within a picture. On the left is a traditional rear projection view, in which the perspective is locked, and pushing in on the image will only enlarge it. On the right is the Frustum image atop a static image of the scene; within the frustum, we see what the camera is seeing with a perspective change. Note how we see more of the top of the table and the chairs pulling away from the table as they are closer to the camera, just as they would appear in a real dolly move.*

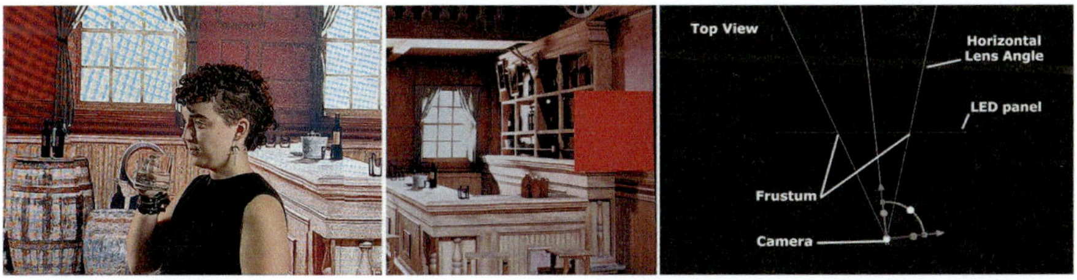

Figure 4.3 *Some issues with LED walls. On the left we see a Moire pattern generated when the camera sensor interferes with the LED display along with poor color reproduction of the background. The middle image shows a panel drop out. The LED wall is made up of a number of square panels, and one panel can inexplicably blank out on occasion. A simple restart usually solves this issue, but it can be nerve wracking. The right view shows how the frustum is generated on the screen as it displays a slice of the camera's viewing angle. As you can see, the camera is shooting the screen from a slight angle. Even though the image changes properly in perspective, it is locked to the plane of the physical wall. This creates issues of wall extensions as the outside image of the environment will be a direct perfect feed, but the image shot off the wall can have a slight distortion. This translates into a mismatch in which buildings and windows don't align perfectly. A traditional solution was to blur the blend between the two. A recent development by the Mo-Sys company has addressed this issue as we will see in a later chapter.*

not bad; it allows for much greater student safety when shooting car shots. No trailer cars, permits, closed streets, etc. are required to make a believable illusion of a vehicle traveling down the road. The automobile can be raised above the floor on wheeled dollies to safely position it on the set without needing to start the engine. The shiny reflective surface of the car will also give some interactive light on the vehicle to further enhance the illusion of movement.

> **The LED screen is not always a lighting tool** for foreground subjects. Be sure to light them appropriately using standing lights and/or interactive light sources.

It should be noted that a single LED screen does not provide interactive light for a human subject. If the actor's lights are turned off, they will appear as a black silhouette on a flat screen in front of the image. The expensive volume configurations of multiple LED screens surrounding the performer provide true interactive light on them.

Types of LED Screens

US engineer Nick Holonyak developed the light-emitting diode (LED) in 1962. They first had a red color, but by the 80s, green and blue diodes were created so that full-color image display could be created by the additive color process of combining the values of each diode to arrive at a single color when seen from a distance. Screens that use this system of three adjacent single-color diodes are called direct in-line packages, or DIP. There is also a surface-mounted diode, or SMD, screen, which contains only one diode that emits multiple colors.

DIP screens are lower in cost, have better heat distribution, have longer life, are brighter, and consume less power, making them ideal for outdoor displays. The SMD screen has a smaller footprint, which places the diodes closer together to help lower the risk of moiré patterns, which are discussed later. SMDs also have higher color uniformity, which makes them better suited for virtual production.

LED Screen Issues

Moiré Patterns

Moiré is a series of wavy circular patterns that appear in the camera when the evenly spaced LEDs conflict with the evenly spaced sensels in the camera sensor. Current remedies are keeping the video screen soft or limiting the camera

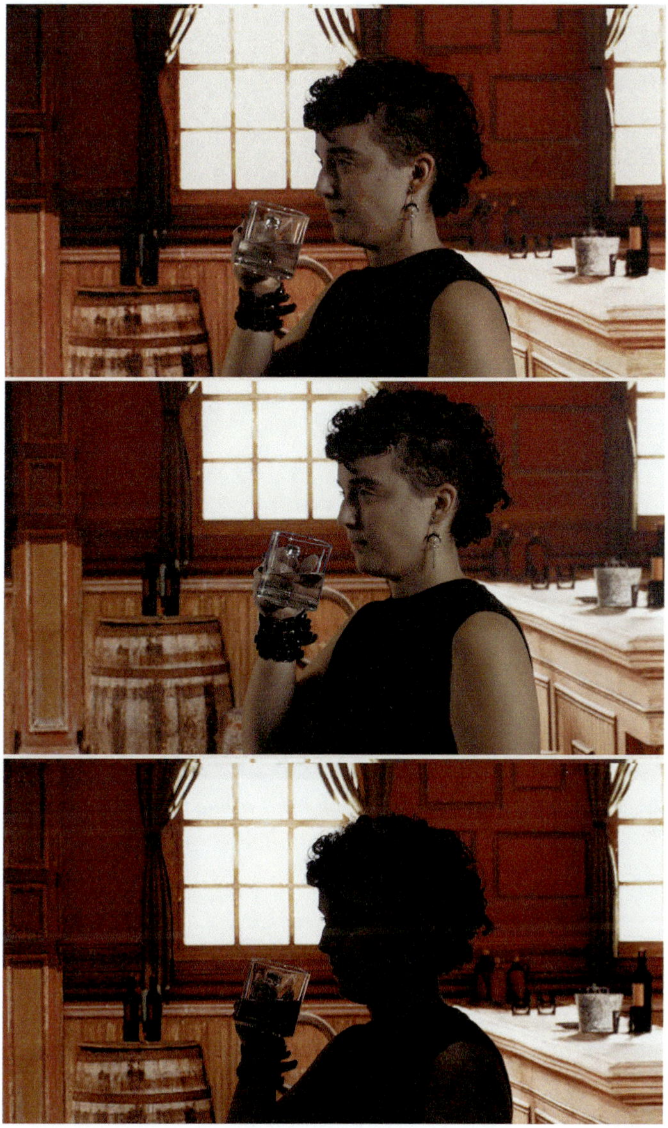

Figure 4.4 *The top image shows how a glass cup distorts the background projected on the LED wall. The middle photo shows the same glass composited after the foreground was shot against a green screen. While the glass does not distort the background, the background quality is superior to the LED image as it is a first-generation image not copied off a screen. The bottom image shows the figure against the LED wall without front lighting to illustrate that the LED panel does not provide lighting in the foreground unless a "volume" of surrounding LED walls is used from the top and sides. A single wall will provide reflections off shiny surfaces in the foreground and image distortions seen through glass.*

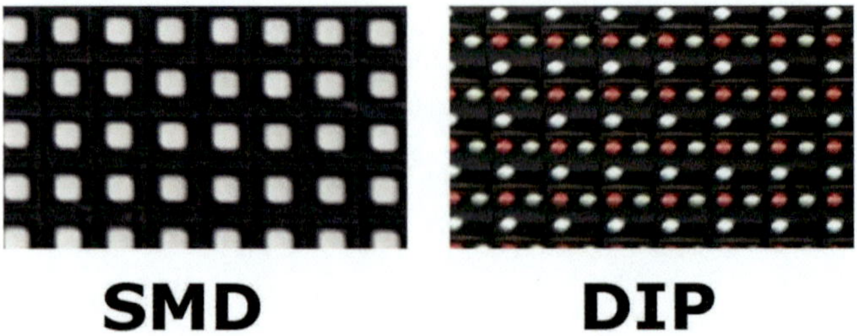

Figure 4.5 *The differences between three separate RGB LEDs (DIP) and an all-in-one LED (SMD) are proximity and color fidelity.*

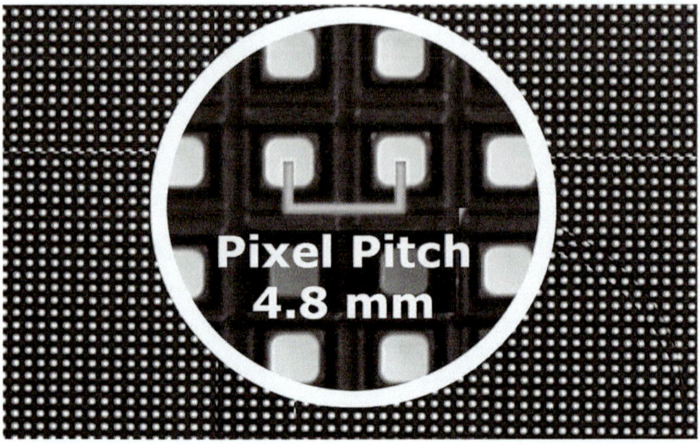

Figure 4.6 *A common pixel pitch of 4.8mm helps reduce the occurrence of moiré patterns.*
Source: Image courtesy of screen-led.com

position to places where it does not happen. Others are getting a much more expensive screen with a tighter pitch dimension, placing the individual LED lights closer together, or putting a much larger screen farther away.

Another brilliant solution is to shoot on film rather than digitally, as the silver halide crystals in the film are organic and randomly placed in the emulsion and cannot cause a moiré like the regimented sensels in the digital camera sensor. Some have tried low pass filters that blur the image before it reaches the sensor to alleviate the problem. When I spoke to a seasoned, award-winning cinematographer about virtual production and LED walls, he said, "No one's gonna tell me where to put my camera." This hit the nail on the head, as this issue is an example of the tail wagging the dog. The aesthetic comes first. If the cinematographer wants the camera at a specific place to get the shot and a moiré issue arises, it is time to bring in the green screen. It is my philosophy for limited budgets to primarily use the screen for close-ups, where it is customary to place the background out of focus (eliminating moiré) and accommodate things like eyeglasses that can have a realistic reflection.

For complete freedom of movement and angle, I would use green or blue screens for high angles, low angles, long pans, dollies, and the rest of the film-making vocabulary. The background color and focus can be adjusted in the post, and a pristine image is obtained instead of the second-generation copy of an image off the screen.

One last thought on moiré patterns is they can also occur in set windows and be seen by the eye! If a foreground set has thick quarter-inch plexiglass windows, they can reflect the LED image so the reflection interferes with itself internally in the plexiglass and cause a moiré pattern right in front of your eyes! The surefire solution to this issue is not having windows in sets and adding the reflections in post-production. Car windows seem less susceptible, but it is something to look out for.

Flicker

The refresh rate of an LED display is measured in Hz. If you are shooting at 24 frames per second and your screen display is set to 48Hz, each image will display twice for each frame of the camera. Many use the rule that the display should be at least four times the frame rate. The manufacturer screen-led.com recommends at least 1000Hz to eliminate flicker. Keeping all components genlocked is essential. Adjusting the shutter angle can also be helpful. Ultimately, test ahead of time and stick to the settings that work.

Color

> **If an LED screen is being used in a VFX shot**, color consistency should be maintained between the foreground subject and the background. Color reference charts and instruments should be used to check color temperature, saturation, hue, contrast, and brightness. Don't trust your eyes. In this situation, the LED screen is less of a light source than a background element display. Just like in the editorial process, when compiling an entire show, color management and correction are accomplished with references, measuring instruments, and software.

We can understand color challenges by examining an earlier transition from tungsten to LED movie lights. Movie lights were traditionally inefficient and power-hungry tungsten filament bulbs. Despite these drawbacks, the light had a beautiful continuous spectrum where every wavelength was represented, and film and digital media could reproduce much of the gorgeous color we see with our eyes. However, during the transition to LED lights, it was discovered that the light emitted from LED was "spikey," meaning that very narrow regions of the spectrum were used to combine into a peculiar "white" light. With the invention of chip on board (COB) arrays, an assortment of LEDs could be placed close together with a broad spectrum of light mimicking tungsten or daylight.

In figure 4.7 the top image is photographed under full-spectrum daylight, while the bottom image is illuminated by white light provided by an LED wall. Even though the gray card has been color-corrected to a neutral gray, the skin tone and the peppers' colors are not reproducing correctly under the spikey illumination. The goal is to match the color and contrast, but there will always be a perceptible loss of quality reproducing an image off the LED screen.

LED walls' primary purpose was to image bright billboard displays, and they did not have to have the full-spectrum light that cameras needed. These panels had arrays of red, green, and blue LEDs arranged close together so the impression of an even white display was perceived much like a television set at a distance. Some schools purchased these types of lower-cost screens, making it

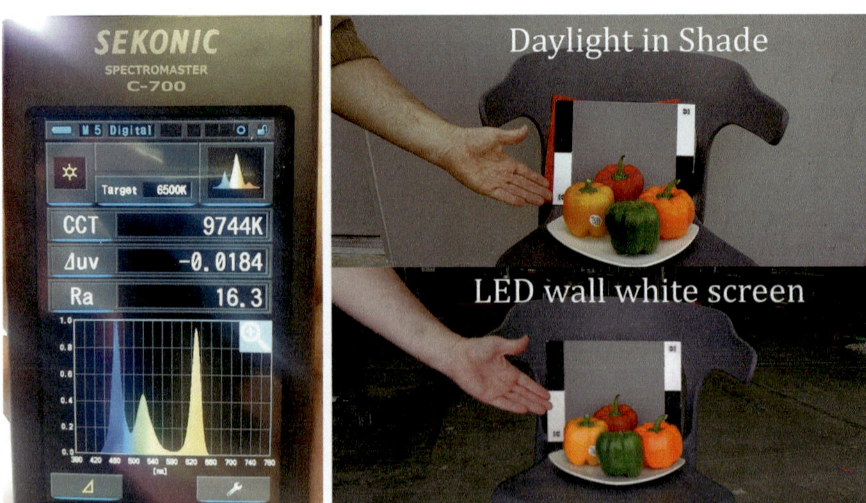

Figure 4.7 *A color temperature meter reading an LED wall on the left shows the harsh spikey transitions between the colors of light emitted from LEDs. A full-spectrum reading would show a smooth, even blend of all the wavelengths. Note the reddish tint of the arm lit by the LED light.*

challenging to obtain good color when a digital camera recorded an image of them.

Here is an example of what can go wrong on a student project. A picture of an Unreal set was displayed on an LED screen composed of RGB LEDs and looked great to the human eye. The subject was lit with daylight-balanced light and looked great as well. The monitor on the camera showed some disparity, but the crew ignored it as it looked great on the stage.

After the shoot, the dailies were viewed, only to find a correctly colored actor against a bright magenta background. A complete disaster! The error was locked into the shots. You could correct for the environment or the actor, but they would never match. The tough solution would be to painstakingly rotoscope (trace around the actor's image to extract them from the background) to enable separate color corrections; in this case, I told the students they should

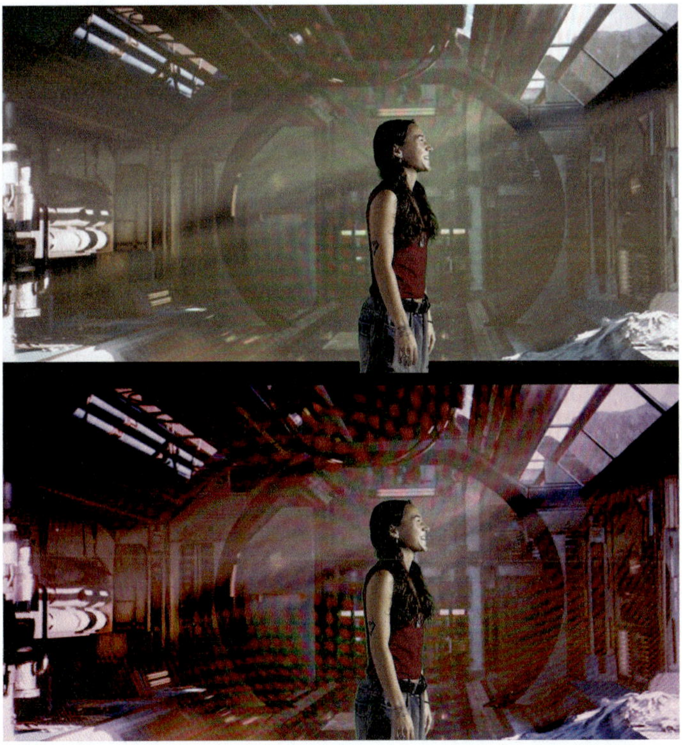

Figure 4.8 *What you see is not what you get. The top image is an approximation of how the subject and LED image appear to the human eye on set. The bottom image shows what the camera records. The color is glaringly off on the screen while the subject is correctly rendered, and an annoying moiré pattern appears (the red dots above her head), which can become worse if color correction is used to fix the screen while using a roto matte to preserve my correctly exposed model.*

turn their film into a black-and-white movie. They were pleased. The rule of thumb here is never to trust your eyes to balance the screen. What matters is what the camera sees.

Sony to the Rescue

The Sony Corporation has acknowledged and addressed the challenges of moiré and color issues with LED walls. At Cine Gear, they demonstrated their virtual production toolset as a plug-in for the Unreal Game Engine. This impressive toolset has an on-set moiré detector that provides a visual overlay on the camera viewfinder, indicating when a moiré pattern occurs. Much like a manual focus helper that creates outlines around focused objects, the detector will let everyone know during a camera shoot if and when this anomaly will happen. While this is a godsend, the problem I see is that, once again, the technology is wagging the dog. I often envision where the DP and director find the perfect angle for the talent and detect the moiré. In this scenario, the director typically says to shoot it anyway and fix it in post. No creative wants their vision dictated, especially by a technical anomaly. When I discussed this potential problem with my cinematographer friend, he agreed and said the solution would be to hold the shot and crack open the stop to reduce the depth of field and make the wall soft to lessen the moiré. The Mo-Sys company devised a focus limiter so the focus on the wall would stay just soft enough to avoid a moiré to deal with the issue before it becomes a fix-it-in-post scenario.

The moiré detector is a handy tool, especially for productions that are open to compromise. The other great tool is the color calibration tool, which balances any number of LED walls to the Sony camera. The tool can calibrate some walls: SONY, ROE, Absen, INFiLED, Unilumin, Alfalite, Samsung, and LG. The way it works is a ready-made chart with an assortment of color boxes displayed on the wall. The live-action camera rephotographs this chart and adjusts the output of the wall so that the specified colors land on the camera sensor's sensitivity curve in the proper spots. It is an automated closed-loop system miming the manual testing process historically used to balance color. The one caveat for these great tools is that you must use a Sony camera, typically the high-end VENICE.

OpenVPCal LED Wall Camera Calibration

There is good news for schools that are using different camera products. Netflix has come to the rescue by creating an open-source calibration tool for in-camera visual effects pipelines, including the LED wall available here: https://github.com/Netflix/OpenVPCal.

Calibrating for the Unreal Game Engine Image

Fortunately, thanks to the Epic engineers' foresight, they have included a computer graphic equivalent of the Macbeth color chart in one of their starter projects. In this case, a real Macbeth chart is placed next to the computer-generated chart as a control to assist in adjusting the screen's color.

Summary

When working with LED walls, make an effort to test the wall ahead of time for color reproduction and flicker. Don't rely on monitors alone to evaluate the image. Shoot something and take it all the way through your pipeline to see the end product. Moiré issues can be particularly tricky as they might not appear in the camera's raw output even after normalization but may show up after color correction enhances the image. While many of the issues listed here are rapidly being solved by manufacturers of walls to accommodate the needs of cinema, there are many schools and companies who have already purchased walls and need a return on that investment. This book hopes to provide workarounds and alternatives for facilities and schools with limited resources.

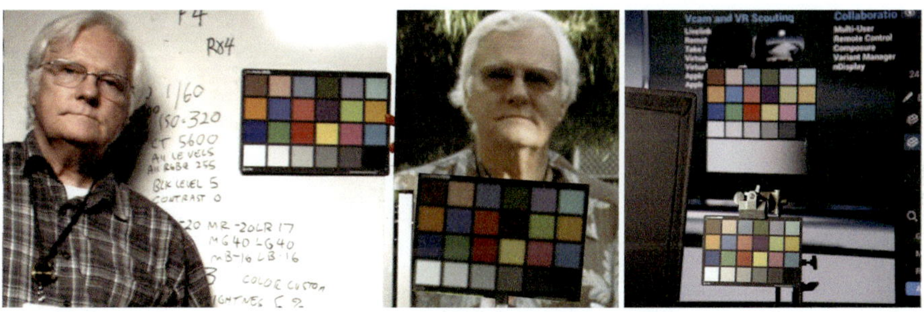

Figure 4.9 *The digital equivalent of the Macbeth chart is available in the virtual production setup in the Unreal Launcher. This is useful to double check the color calibrator you are using or if you are balancing the color manually.*

Chapter 5

The Unreal Game Engine as a Virtual Studio Backlot

Overview

Game engines such as Unity and Unreal can render CGI in real time, allowing for real-time gameplay. This ability also lends itself to virtual production as it is now possible to shoot and combine live action with an animated and interactive CG environment. Currently, the Unreal Game Engine is the leader in virtual production. The parent company, Epic Games, has many excellent tutorials for the software and also provides the Unreal Marketplace (now fab.com), where CGI environments, sets, props, and characters are sold that can be used for film production at amazingly low prices and sometimes for free.

As of this writing, the Unreal software is free, but it may become subscription based like many other products after this book is published. Nonetheless, this part of the process is the most affordable. For example, fab.com has complete and finished CG environments, such as a spacecraft interior. Many settings can be purchased for under $100. This is shockingly affordable if you consider the talent and time it takes to create a set. For example, let's use the animation guild pay scale for 2024 for a CG modeler only for a journey class, $1766 per week. In the author's experience with both traditional models used in the film

DOI: 10.4324/9781003473169-5

Daylight and CG models used for the TV series *From the Earth to the Moon*, both techniques typically took four to six months to complete before photography began. So if you had only one person, such as a modeler, take six months to build a set, the cost for their weekly salary would be $42,384. This does not include the designer, texture artists, painters, animators, etc. How can you buy a finished set for so low a figure?

Much like any mass-produced product, the price point comes from mass marketing. If an entrepreneur spends six months of sweat equity creating a set and sells it for $100, they only need to sell 1000 of them to make $100,000. It becomes a win-win all around. The only drawback is that a mass-marketed set would not be unique and, much like a studio backlot, would be used repeatedly by those 1000 people with slight modifications in coloring and prop placement. The purchaser of these sets will also have to rely on reviews and due diligence to ensure the set is ready for virtual production. Is it photorealistic enough? Does it have a poly count that is low enough to run in real time? All computer graphic objects comprise a multitude of polygons that make up the surface. More polygons, like a million, would be able to reveal all the wrinkles, nooks, and crannies of a surface but would take a lot of time to render.

Game characters are designed to have as few polygons as possible while creating the illusion of detail. One example is the skin texture of the dinosaurs in *Jurassic Park*. They had relatively few polygons, and if you looked at the model's surface, it would appear smooth without scales. A texture map called a bump map was used for the scales, creating the illusion of dimensional scales by drawing a 2D representation of scales. If the light changed direction, the bump map would sense that and redraw the scales with shadows painted in the new appropriate direction.

Here is an example of what can happen in a school setting. A school has purchased virtual production hardware equipment that will run a low-poly ballroom set with no trouble at all, but when a student brings in their jungle set composed of hundreds of trees and foliage blowing in the wind, the school's system may not be powerful enough to handle that much data.

In cases like this, clever production design can come to the rescue by perhaps rendering a large swath of trees slowly and not in real time to prepare a video that can play in real time on a polygon plane positioned just behind a few full CG trees to create the illusion of hundreds of trees appearing on the screen but done in real time as you are using a blending of 2D and 3D to eliminate the heavy lifting of an all-3D set.

Photoreal Assets

While the marketplace is an excellent resource for sets, they often look "gamey," meaning game-like and plastic. Clean, futuristic sets often work well, as those environments tend to look plastic in real life. Other sets, such as the subway, have a bit of both, where the plastic seats and chrome pipes were enhanced by a lot of dirt and scuff added atop all the elements to elicit a better feeling of being real, much like the miniatures used in the past would be scruffed up to take away the too-perfect look.

There are cases, however, where one must have accurate photoreal set pieces. Another resource called Quixel.com Megascans can provide these assets. These objects are derived from photogrammetry, in which a real object such as a boulder is photographed dozens of times from assorted angles to provide a full 360-degree view. When the photos are stitched together, they create a dimensional photoreal object. The photography is usually done in ambient fill light conditions so as not to bake in the light direction on the asset as that will be provided by the virtual key lighting inside Unreal. The drawback is that Megascan models tend to be data heavy, and one must have powerful hardware to enable real-time rendering.

Characters

Virtual production often uses synthetic characters that play alongside the live action. https://www.mixamo.com/#/ has many characters and skeletons, pre-recorded walk cycles, and performances from motion-captured live actors that can be used to animate the characters. The characters can either be hand animated, use pre-recorded motion capture, or use a live performance using motion capture from an off-screen performer animating the character in Unreal.

How Unreal Is Used for Filmmaking

In virtual production, Unreal is mostly:

- A content library organizer.
- A world-building/layout tool.
- An image renderer – interactive or not.
- A timeline for moving objects.
- An interactive programming tool.
- A real-time compositor.

Content for the engine (assets) come from places like the marketplace (fab.com), Megascans, and Mixamo or are created by artists in Maya, Photoshop,

Blender, 3D Max, etc. The content comes from various tools and file formats, and the artists working in a virtual production can be from all over the world. For high-end projects that use large teams, a system has to be put in place to organize all these assets throughout the movie's life cycle.

Perforce – Data Management

In any production, there must be remote means for production management, data management, asset tracking, asset and element check-in/out, and data storage. Without these processes being automated, there is a risk of data loss, which is work lost. Large studios usually have a dedicated production department for such needs. Independents with fewer personnel need to rely on automation and cloud services. Ideally, production tracking and data verification are executed after every shot take.

The Helix Core system built by Perforce handles all the complex versioning and management of data for complex projects. For example, an artist in Amsterdam creates a Photoshop background for a virtual production in Los Angeles. His Photoshop file was converted for use inside Unreal and was used for an LED wall shoot on February 14. This footage has gone over to editorial in New York, which wanted a change in the background by adding a cloud. The Amsterdam artist gets the instruction and makes the change to create a new version that is sent on March 1. On March 5, a pickup shot is done using the new background and then back to editorial. This interactive process goes on and on with any number of assets and versions. It can get horribly complex and confusing if not tracked. The Helix Core handles all that as a go-between for the production and Unreal, ensuring the correct version of an asset is used at the proper point in the process. Costly mistakes of using the wrong version of an asset are avoided with this tool, which has become a mainstay in the industry.

Unreal – File Naming Conventions

Assets such as textures, meshes, etc. are stored under Unreal's headings.

- ENV (environment)
- Vehicle
- Char (character)
- Prop

The main asset types are labeled in the following manner:

Description	Unreal Term	Prefix	File Type
• Non-deforming model	Static Mesh	SM_	FBX or Obj
• Deforming model	Skeletal Mesh	SK_	FBX
• Texture	Texture	T_	Png, Jpg, TGA
• Material	Material	M_	FBX or null
• Animation	Animation	A_	FBX
• Blueprint	Blueprint B.P._	null	

Worlds are made up of levels.

- A level is made up of a collection of actors/assets.
- An asset in the previous list can be static or dynamic mesh with texture maps.
- Unlike a character asset, an actor can be a virtual camera or light that can be manipulated within the scene.

The World Outliner

The outliner window contains all the referenced assets that make up your scene. It is invaluable for quickly finding a specific asset. Once the asset is found, clicking on it reveals its details. A camera asset called a cinematic actor in Unreal jargon will have the details of sensor size, focal length, f-stop, position, rotation, and more. Each of these parameters can then be adjusted to modify the asset.

The Sequencer

The sequencer is where everything comes together to create a shot in Unreal. The sequencer is an editor window for level sequences/containers for timelines. It is used to create and preview cinematic sequences in real time and to animate anything on your level. For example, you can bring your environment into the sequencer with a cinematic camera "actor." In the sequencer, you can animate the camera to make a dolly move within the set and preview the move. Once approved, you can output the virtual camera view into a movie in the sequencer.

Learning Unreal in One Class Session

Unreal is a highly complex software, and it requires constant dedication and learning to be adept at all aspects of this ingenious tool. On the other hand, producers, directors, and filmmakers just need to know the bare-bones basics. The primary purpose of Unreal is to provide a set with lights and a camera. All one needs to know is how to create a camera, bring in a set, light it, and move it or have it linked to a live camera by a third-party asset. This is the basic breakdown of my quick-start tutorial for filmmaking students.

- Create a blank starter scene (no assets). Using the basic objects provided in Unreal, create a plane and place a cylinder atop it.
- Create a sun and position it to light the plane and have the cylinder cast a shadow.
- Create a cinematic camera in the scene.
- Create a sequencer.
- Use the sequencer to animate the camera moving past the cylinder.
- Render a movie from this simple move.
- After this exercise, import an environment from fab.com by adding it to your basic starter scene. In version 5.4, you will have to close out and reopen Unreal for this new map to be included in the content window.
- Use the lights included with the environment or make and manipulate your lights.
- Once again, create a cinematic camera and make a move.

At this point, I have the students import a static mesh character as a stand-in. Using the stand-in and the camera, they scout the set for camera placement and create a previz storyboard in the sequencer or even do screen grabs of the camera view to plan out and make a storyboard for their movie short.

Back to Reality

As one scouts in Unreal, it is essential to use the proper camera settings so they will match the live-action camera settings. The sensor size and the lens focal length will be the most important. Suppose the school uses a Blackmagic camera with a Super 35 size sensor 24 x 14mm. In that case, you should also set the sensor size of the virtual camera to that dimension. Furthermore, the typical complement of lenses for that size sensor is 18mm, 24mm, 35mm, 50mm, 85mm, and 135mm. Make sure you use focal lengths that are available for the camera you're using at the school. Also remember to make use of the cube as a measuring device. The basic cube is one meter in all direction and can be stretched to any size. To find the height of your virtual camera, use the cube as a measuring stick from the set floor to the middle of the sensor on the virtual camera icon. This will provide the height you need for the real camera. The detail window of the virtual camera will show the tilt angle that you will match using an angle finder on your real camera. These measurements are the key to matching Unreal backgrounds with live action green screen elements for static shots.

Chapter 6

Capturing Light Itself

Radiance Fields and Gaussian Splats

The Nature of Light

For 2,000 years, the nature of light has been explored and debated. Is it a ray, a wave, or a particle? While the topic is still theoretical and there is no consensus (like electricity), this theoretical hindrance does not prevent practical use. For today's practical purposes, mathematically and in software applications, it is all of these.

Light Fields – 3D Volumetric Light Data

In 1996, Marc Levoy and Pat Hanrahan introduced the concept of the light field, which is the capture of the amount of light traveling in every direction through every point in space. This is a volumetric process for light data capture. Volumetric processes for lighting have precedent in the development of holographic **imagery.**

DOI: 10.4324/9781003473169-6

The Hologram

The hologram was invented by Dennis Gabor in 1948 but was not practical until the development of the laser in 1960. In 1962, Yuri Denisyuk of the USSR, Emmett Leith, and Juris Upatnieks at the University of Michigan captured a light field practically. It involved reflected laser light off an object and a reference laser beam to create an interference pattern, which captured the light field.

Looking at the photographic plate holographic image in regular light, it looks like a foggy mess. When illuminated by the laser, you can see the object, reproduced perfectly in three dimensions, that changes its appearance as the viewer alters their angle of view. To get an idea of the difference between a regular photograph and a hologram, all you need to do is cut off a corner of the hologram. You can still see the entire object, only with fewer viewpoints. A regular picture reveals a portion of the subject, losing most of the information. The drawback to holograms is that they are challenging to create and view under typical lighting conditions.

The Plenoptic Camera

A plenoptic camera is a light-field camera. By 2005, light-field cameras could photograph the light field in a scene including light intensity and direction points, allowing for changes in focus and depth adjustments after a photo is taken. Today, the plenoptic camera is used extensively in industrial optical inspection.

Another idea for capturing light fields was proposed by Gabriel Lippmann in 1908, which he called integral photography. This consisted of a camera that used thousands of glass beads acting like tiny microlenses laid on top of the film emulsion to capture the object from an extensive array of angles supplied by the displacement of the many lenses. This clever idea came to fruition in 2006 when Stanford researcher Ren Ng launched the Lytro light-field camera. The imagery astounded the world because, for the first time, you could refocus an image after the fact. The multi-lens approach captured light in depth to shift the focus after the image was taken using the original data captured instead of synthetic sharpening tricks. This sharpening effect also took place over space, meaning you could focus on the background and then switch to focusing on the foreground, just like the lens on a camera.

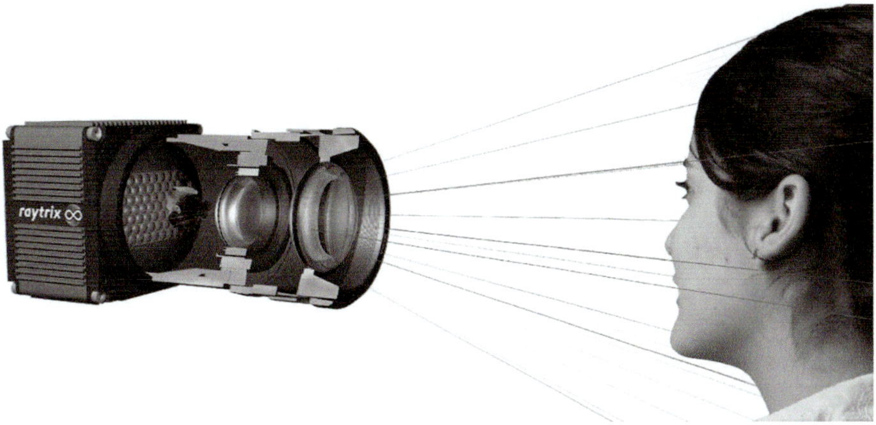

Figure 6.1 *shows the plenoptic camera. Instead of using many images to capture the subject from various viewpoints, a single lens captures the subject as an aerial image within the camera. This image is then refocused by a microarray of tiny lenses to record a variety of viewpoints onto the sensor. This information can then be used to create a 3D model of the subject.*
Source: Courtesy of the Raytrix GmbH Company (www.raytrix.de).

Photogrammetry – 3D Geometry Data

Photogrammetry uses multiple 2D photos taken from multiple perspectives to create a 3D map by calculating the many points into triangular polygons. Previously widely used in surveying, architecture, and archeology, it became a common technique used in 3D mapping without modeling.

Rather than creating a 3D environment by building one piece at a time, a geometric environment or object can be created from multiple photographs.

Photogrammetry is a form of volumetric 3D data capture but is an indirect measurement because it uses image-based measurement from photographs. It does not measure objects directly. This process requires much computational effort to convert 2D information to 3D data.

In our first book on virtual production, we covered the progression of techniques for capturing as much of the real world as possible. A traditional camera can capture only one viewpoint and lens angle to translate our 3D world into a 2D picture. Towards the end of the 19th century, a brilliant scientist, Aimé Laussedat, invented a process of studying parallax differences between images of an object shot from several viewpoints to deduce distance and depth information to create a 3D object. The process was named photogrammetry by Prussian architect Albrecht Meydenbauer in an article written in 1867, which shows how early this remarkable technique appeared.

The process involves shooting a static object with many images from different angles, such as 360 degrees around the subject. This assortment of stills has slight overlaps but can be combined and calculated to create a 3D object from this oversampling. Fortunately, we have software that handles these calculations and can make a 3D model very quickly. Photogrammetry has been used extensively to faithfully recreate models of objects and even people for use in CG environments and saves a great deal of time modeling these props from scratch.

A common practice is to place the object in an evenly lit lightbox for shadowless lighting to obtain the proper number of images. The object is then attached to a rotator to be spun in even increments and photographed at various angles from high to low, central to the subject, with the same lens to provide the proper number of sampled images. Once the 3D object is made, it will be evenly lit from all sides, allowing the CG artist to add a virtual key light to enable creative lighting. In the case of a human subject, dozens of cameras surround the performer, and they all expose their images in synchronization to capture, for example, a jump in mid-air.

The process had some drawbacks, as the model frequently needed cleaning up when too much occlusion of one part of the object obscured another. When this occurs, holes in the model need to be filled in. Reflective and transparent objects are also a challenge.

LiDAR

LiDAR stands for light detection and ranging. LiDAR can generate point cloud data. It was originally developed in the 1960s for atmospheric research and meteorology. By the 1970s–1980s, it was used for topographic mapping and environmental monitoring.

It is more accurate than photogrammetry because it uses laser pulses to measure distances and can create detailed data under vegetation to the ground. It is a direct measurement of surfaces. Therefore, the data can be used to measure and scale objects to match the scanned geometry.

Today it is used for high-resolution 3D mapping and widely used in autonomous vehicles and geospatial applications.

A point cloud consists of data points in three-dimensional space that represent the shape or surface of an object or environment. The data comes from a 3D scanner. Point-cloud data is different from light-field data because one is geometric X, Y, Z coordinates while the other is light intensity and direction U, V. Typically, point-cloud and light-field data complement each other. So, while it may be possible to generate geometric data from light fields or generate light data from point clouds, both would involve more complex processing procedures.

In the 1980s and 1990s, point clouds were commonly used to depict 3D shapes and environments. In the 2000s, improvements like better laser scanners, sensors, and algorithms; faster software; and multiple sensors resulted in scans with increased data, better precision, reduced noise, and the capture of more complex shapes with textures and reflectivity.

Another method that can scan real objects and create a polygonal model is light detection and ranging (LiDAR). This process became possible in the 1960s when light amplification by stimulated emission of radiation (laser) was developed. The LiDAR process uses a laser's coherent beam of light to scan an object by shining the laser at the subject and measuring the time it takes to reflect the laser back to its source. An object 10 feet away would have a far quicker reflection time than an object 20 feet away. By rapidly scanning an object thousands of times and recording all the bounce-back measurements, an incredibly detailed 3D model can be created.

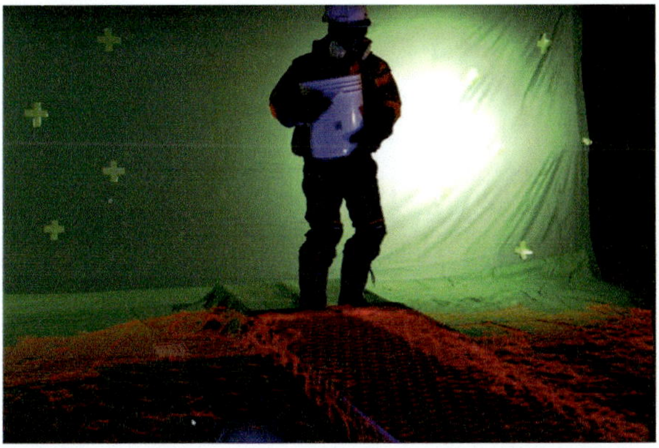

Figure 6.2 *The red cross-hatch at the bottom of the image is the LiDAR scan of the walkway set piece rendered as polygons. These scans help lock in 3D tracking of 2D imagery.*

Source: Image courtesy of Eliot Mack and https://lightcraft.pro/.

Unlike photogrammetry, there is no capturing of the color and the white light reflected off the object, only its shape. This detailed capture of an object and environment is very useful in film production. After a movie set has been built and the filming is finished, some studios do a LiDAR scan of the set before it is broken down just in case it needs to be reproduced later in digital form. Newer virtual production tracking systems use LiDAR in iPhones equipped with laser ranging. We'll examine this in more detail in the lightcraft chapter.

Image-Based Lighting

Image-based lighting (IBL) was introduced in the 1990s by Paul Debevec. It uses real-world lighting captured from 360-degree environmental images mapped to a sphere or dome and used as a light source to illuminate 3D CG scenes realistically. Debevec's work on "Rendering Synthetic Objects Into Real Scenes" (SIGGRAPH 1998) demonstrated the potential of IBL in visual effects and computer graphics.

IBL and high dynamic range imaging (HDRI) are connected for the purpose of creating more realistic lighting in CG. Since HDRIs are 360-degree images, they can be mapped on a sphere and used as a light source (e.g., sky map) that includes sunlight, sky, and landscape.

When an HDRI image is used as a texture for lighting, that is called an HDRI lightmap. This type of light source is precomputed or "baked" and applied to 3D models to duplicate light direction, color, reflections, indirect lighting, and shadows in a 3D CG render.

HDRI Lightmap

Another breakthrough that captured real light so it could be used to synthetically light computer graphic elements was high dynamic range imaging (HDRI). This system was used most effectively to provide lighting for CG characters like dinosaurs interacting with live action. The process worked by shooting the live action plate takes and, when finished, before striking the set, placing a special HDRI camera in the location where the monster was to be. This special camera is designed to photograph an all-encompassing 360-degree view of the surrounding environment that contains all the lighting fixtures used to light the set, along with the set itself, which contributed bounce lighting on the live-action characters. This was often achieved by having the camera lens point into a mirrored half sphere suspended above the camera.

The term *high dynamic range* means that several photos were taken at a variety of exposure settings to capture dimly lit portions of the set along with brightly lit parts. With regular photography, one speaks of a range of stops of light where each stop is either double or half the amount of light. A single camera raw image, for example, might capture 11 stops of light. A high dynamic range image would capture many more.

An example of low dynamic range would be a consumer camera shooting a person against a brightly lit sky. If the camera exposes the person to see detail in their face, the sky will bloom out to an overexposed white mass with no clouds to be seen. A raw image would be able to capture both person and sky for a pleasing photograph. In HDRI, one shot would show the bright sun by itself shot at a high f-stop like F22 that shows only the sun; the objects it illuminates would be dark. This exposure, blended with other f-stops, would yield a file with tremendous dynamic range that comes close to mimicking the intensity of the light on the set.

Once the HDRI is created, the file is used to map the inside of a sphere surrounding the CG character in the animation software. This sphere then contains the panoramic view of the live-action environment, and the image becomes the light source that illuminates the CG character with the same intensity and color characteristics of the lighting instruments that lit the live action. This type of lighting greatly increases the realism of the synthetic creation. HDRI capture did away with the customary guide photograph of a chrome ball and a gray ball on a stick to inform the CG artist where the light was and how it affected the environment. The HDRI did the capture precisely and eliminated guesswork and the simulation of real light using mathematical calculations. While the HDRI is very effective, it can often be overlooked during the rush of production. In those cases, the live action photography itself can be stretched and mapped on a lighting sphere to get an effect that is similar, though not as effective (https://www.lightmap.co.uk/blog/howdoeshdrilightingwork/).

The Reflectance Field

How light is reflected off surfaces is the basis of the reflectance field concept, which led to the bidirectional reflectance distribution function (BRDF). BRDF measures the amount of light reflected off a surface at various angles. The data from the reflectance field is then added to the material properties of CG objects.

Measuring light reflectance off surfaces, combined with a 360-degree light source based on photographic capture of an environment, results in more realistic CG lighting and renders.

Another technique used to light human performers to insert their image onto a CG character was to oversample an enormous number of lighting angles on a human performer so any lighting condition could be manipulated afterward. This idea, called "Acquiring the Reflectance Field of a Human Face," was presented at SIGGRAPH2000 by Paul Debevec, Tim Hawkins, Chris Tchou, Haarm-Pieter Duiker, Westley Sarokin, and Mark Sagar. It consisted of a sphere of lighting instruments surrounding the human subject called Light Stage 1. The initial scan took one minute to capture each individual light hitting the face at all angles. When finished, it allowed complete control of light direction and key-to-fill ratio. The Light Stage 2 version was used in *Spiderman 2* to capture the face of Alfred Molina, who played Doctor Octopus, in order to have a realistic reproduction of his face atop a CG model as it transitioned through several lighting conditions. The film won the Academy Award for Best Achievement in Visual Effects in 2005.

I found this idea a helpful technique on much lower budgets in stop-motion projects where the subject was always still. I used the method in a stop-motion commercial called "Beware the Breadwich" for Togo's restaurants. In it, I shot stills of a miniature street with a key light alone, a fill light alone, the kicker alone, and practical set lights alone. Later, in After Effects, the director, Lisha Tan, could blend each light to obtain any lighting ratio or color combination by merely superimposing each image using the screen blend mode and the opacity control. Paul Debevec and his team's work can be found at https://www.pauldebevec.com/Research/LS/.

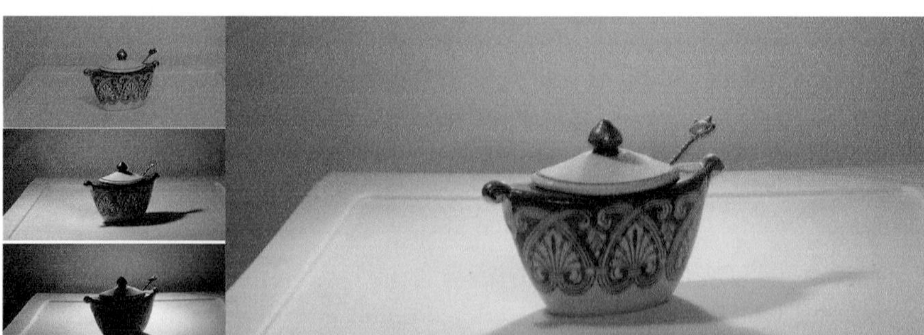

Figure 6.3 *Sampling an object under separate lighting conditions affords the ability to relight in post. Each sample uses the screen blend mode, which replicates double exposure to combine the different samples. The blend amount is controlled by opacity in Photoshop or After Effects. Color correcting the layers can enable theatrical lighting.*

NeRF

The human brain has neurons in layers and learns by receiving input, processing it, and passing it to the next layer, creating patterns that, once learned, don't have to go through the process again. Input can then be judged or acted on faster by just recognizing a pattern.

The artificial intelligence version of this is called a neural network. Instead of neurons, it uses interconnected nodes. Patterns are created by weighting the connections between the nodes. Using very large datasets, predictions or decisions are formed by weighting the connections towards specific outcomes. In this way, an AI neural network can learn how to recognize a dog by analyzing thousands of pictures of dogs.

Neural radiance fields (NeRF) were introduced by researchers at UC Berkeley in 2020 as a method for synthesizing unique views of complex 3D scenes using deep learning.

A NeRF can be trained to create a fairly realistic 3D scene from multiple 2D images by analyzing how light interacts with objects in the scene from multiple angles. This process involves a high number of computations involving data collection, setting up the neural network with 3D coordinates and viewing directions, using simulation of light travel for volume rendering, calculating errors, refinement, and outputting the final NeRF model.

Ren Ng's name comes up again with distinguished researchers Ben Mildenhall, Pratul P. Srinivasan, and Matthew Tancik from UC Berkeley; Ravi Ramamoorthi from UC San Diego. These brilliant minds presented an oral paper in 2020 about the NeRF method. It gathers even more information from the earlier photogrammetry system by tracing along the light rays that intersect at a certain point on the object, thereby capturing its reaction to light from all viewpoints.

The results are stunning as, when the 3D model is generated, it also bakes in the light reflection qualities from all the assembled viewpoints. As you move the model about on the special viewer, you can see through glass, and the object is shown through it with glass distortion. You can see glints reflected off shiny objects appear and disappear as you change your viewing angle. The light field is not so much captured literally as calculated and reproduced using traditional 2D cameras and an array of viewpoints.

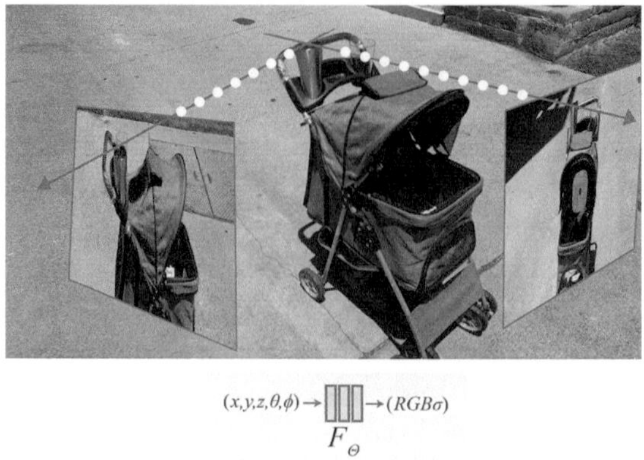

Figure 6.4 *The brilliant NeRF algorithm gathers information on the light values along a light ray from a particular viewpoint gathered from 5D coordinates (x, y, z) and viewing direction.*

Their website, which displays samples of their astounding achievement can be found here: https://www.matthewtancik.com/nerf.

Unlike NeRF, the Gaussian splat method uses multiple 2D pictures taken from multiple angles but does not involve AI learning. NeRF uses nodes and connectivity to consider the volume of the scene and how light passes through it. Instead of nodes and connectivity, Gaussian splats (semi-transparent ellipse-shaped blobs) are created to represent surfaces and textures. The use of a Gaussian bell curve makes the blobs opaque in the center with a falloff in transparency towards the edges. Splats from multiple pictures are then calculated to reconstruct the geometry, texture, and lighting of surfaces.

Because multiple pictures are used, this is an indirect, point-based method of creating objects from surface detail and will not provide exact geometric measurements like LiDAR. This indirect method is for approximating the appearance of objects like color, reflection, transparency, position, and size.

However, for real-time applications, the Gaussian splat method is fast and efficient if high levels of detail and realism are not needed.

Gaussian Splat

No, it's not a new dance craze, but I'm working on it. This technique is another popular variation of the NeRF that uses a point cloud derived from the same multi-sample methods of photogrammetry and NeRF. It claims to outperform NeRF in rendering speed and fidelity. The term *Gaussian* comes from the mathematics behind curves named for mathematician and scientist Carl Friedrich Gauss (1777–1855). The Gaussian function is most famous for creating bell curves of various shapes. In 1991, Lee Alan Westover wrote his dissertation for the University of North Carolina Chapel Hill, called "SPLATTING: A Parallel, Feed-Forward Volume Rendering Algorithm." The Gaussian splat technique uses a variety of image viewpoints to create a point cloud in 3D space. Gaussian functions are then used to convert the points into splats that contain position, orientation, scale, opacity, and view-dependent color information. The splats are then converted into 2D space for rapid rendering.

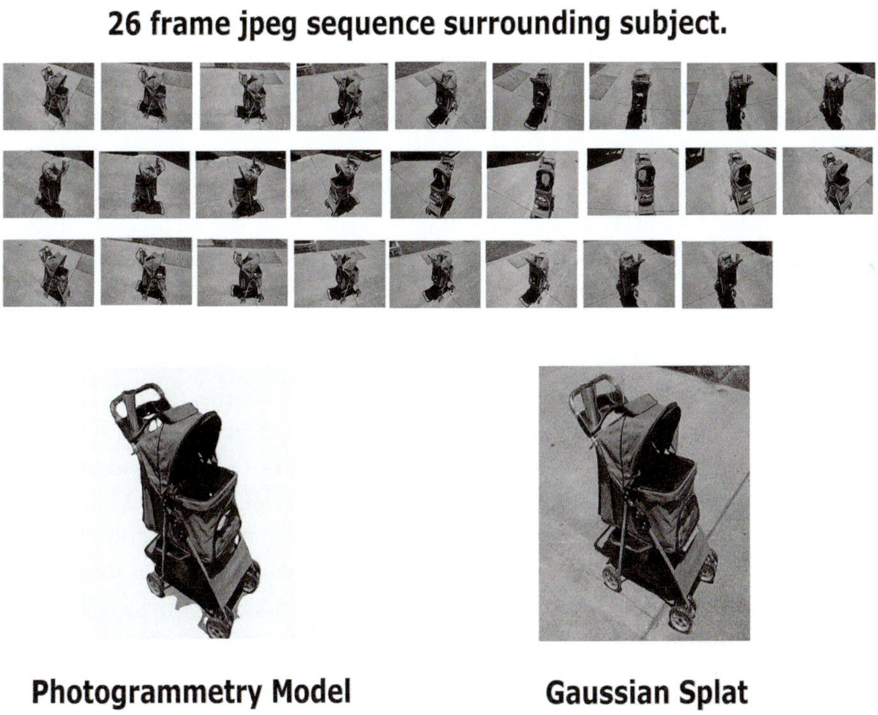

Figure 6.5 *compares models created with photogrammetry and a Gaussian splat. The model on the left had the option of eliminating the background calculated from the positional information. Even though the models were created with the same 26 images at the top of the figure, the Gaussian splat is the superior rendition.*

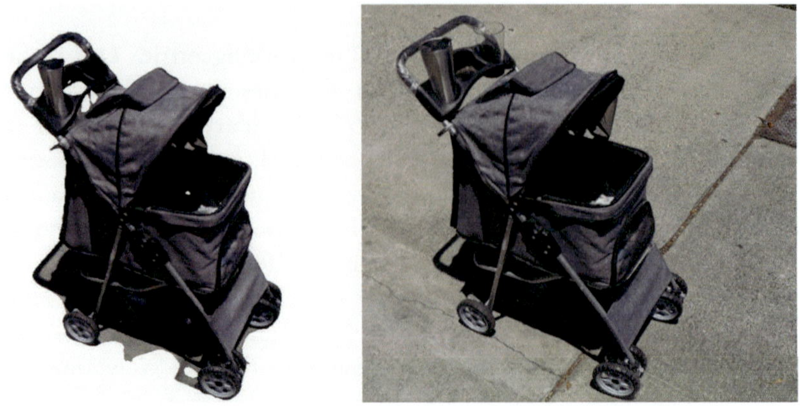

Figure 6.6 *As one can see, comparing the techniques, the photogrammetry model on the left failed to capture the fine netting in the carriage, distorted the chrome cup, and completely missed the glass. The splat captured all the elements and the handle distortion behind the glass. Both models were created using the calculator tools at https://poly.cam.*

These contributors have utilized high-level mathematics to break through the barriers we've had to indeed compute reality. These developments are to be cheered and perhaps feared as they now also apply to the scanning of humans. Apple's machine-learning research group presented a paper on "HUGS: Human Gaussian Splats" in collaboration with the Max Planck Institute for Intelligent Systems, written by Muhammed Kocabas, Rick Chang, James Gabriel, Oncel Tuzel, and Anurag Ranjan. That research can be found here: https://machinelearning.apple.com/research/hugs.

Splats Enter Virtual Production

Unreal and Blender are now accepting Gaussian splat files as part of their environment options. They are a great shortcut option for capturing light effects. With traditional CG models, all renditions of the lighting effect, such as radiosity, reflection, transparency, ambient occlusion, and the like, had to be calculated. Combining all these options can be data intensive, and shortcuts were invented to simulate the effects with less calculation, such as depth map shadows as opposed to ray traced shadows. Depth map essentially calculated where the shadow would be and what it looked like and, in essence, painted the shadow on the floor as a quick calculation. Ray tracing calculated what each ray of light emanating from the source did in the environment to create a more realistic shadow with a lot more calculation. The advantage of the splat is that it captures the actual lighting that existed when the image sequences were captured to create it. Built into the file itself are all the light effects that existed during capture. Windows are transparent and could be dirty or warped, shiny reflections would come and go as the camera moved about the scene.

Companies like Lightcraft are now importing splats to be used as environments for their virtual production software. Inventor Eliot Mack breaks down the process here: https://www.youtube.com/watch?v=J2_LQG8S7WE.

To Be or Not to Be . . . Scanned

During the entertainment strikes, SAG/AFTRA actors made a special push about permissions and rights for actors who were to be scanned. I had heard rumors that extras were hired for a day's work with the stipulation that they be scanned. If you are an extra for your livelihood, having yourself scanned is like selling your soul. Why hire a human being again if you have their perfect reproduction that can be manipulated endlessly? The question comes down to how artists want to create. I assume many directors like to direct live actors on a set for the joy and collaboration of the process. Cinematographers love to find the shot and manipulate light for the best effect. All the traditional disciplines of directing, acting, camera, sound recording, set dressing, and the other unique, hands-on skill sets make a wonderful communal experience in creating a movie. Synthetically mimicking the process in the computer is not the same.

As AI develops, we can turn words written by AI into AI-moving images built from the homogenized and averaged creative endeavors of mankind's entire history of art from the internet. I am happy to have had my career working with people, real sets and lights, and the magic of hands-on, tangible creation. I feel that today's young artists want that too and want to preserve many of the traditions of making a movie with a village of talented people rather than allowing techno lust to destroy the communal endeavor we still enjoy.

I say full speed ahead to splat the pyramids and all the exotic locations that must be preserved and cost-effectively utilized. I'm uncomfortable with the idea of scanning or splatting the actors. Unlike photography, the entire physical presence of the actor is captured to allow the performance of their form to be created by someone else. We have wonderful puppeteers and animators bringing cartoons and puppets to life. Actors in motion capture suits manipulate digital characters and like being inside a creature suit. Having anyone but the actor move their form seems to be the crux of the argument.

I want to see my favorite movie star perform an emotional moment instead of a zombie doppelganger animated by a canned performance capture file. Turning older actors into their younger selves is fair as the actor still manipulates the younger digital form, as in the film *The Irishman*. Bringing the dead back to life for necessity or commerce has been and will be done. The most recent example is the android character Rook in the film *Alien Romulus*, when the actor who performed the android role in the original movie passed away. In this case, permission was granted by the estate of the late actor Ian Holm. These practices championed by SAG/AFTRA provide an excellent guide for traversing our future in this era of deep fakes.

Polycam

For those who want to explore these terrific capture tools, I suggest going to poly.cam (https://poly.cam/tools/gaussian-splatting).

This site offers photogrammetry and Gaussian splat calculation tools for free and subscription. I used them to explore these capture systems. I first tried to obtain a Gaussian splat from some drone footage of my house, but it failed as the take was too short. The nice thing about the calculator is that it suggests why the tool failed and gives tips to improve how you photographically sample your object.

I decided on a whim to try one in very harsh lighting in bright sun with a stroller I had handy. I shot the stills with a locked-off manual focus with a Sony Alpha 6400, shooting jpeg files at 6000 x 3376 resolution at 350 pixels per inch. I went to an alley lit by the bright sun. I walked around the stroller, trying to keep the background road as an even tone for each shot while providing a bit of overlap for each angle. It was all very hastily done by eyeballing the compositions. As recommended, I took 26 stills and loaded them into their file maker. The calculation took only a few minutes to create a 3D object file available to view.

I executed a photogrammetry model and a Gaussian splat model using the same 26 sample images for comparison. I placed a chrome cup and a glass in the carriage's cup holders to challenge the techniques. As I suspected, the chrome cup did not render well and came off distorted, and the glass disappeared entirely. The mesh windows on the carriage also could not be resolved using the photogrammetry process.

The Gaussian splat, on the other hand, provided amazing results, obtaining fine detail in the mesh and the chrome cup. The glass was also resolved while preserving the optical distortions of objects seen through the glass. The site mentions that plug-ins have become available to include Gaussian splat models in the Unreal Game Engine. Using splats of natural environments and light will provide another alternative to fully synthetic CG environments that can suffer from having too much of a plastic look.

Summary

Traditional VFX photography captured a tiny sliver of the light field seen from one unique point in space. Much skill and note-taking was done to ensure that every photographed element was taken from the same perspective with lighting from the same direction to make all elements blend together. Computer graphic models took over from miniatures to a large extent, eliminated photography and storage issues, and allowed for quick iterative change in the digital environment. Photogrammetry brought about more realistic models derived from actual objects and natural settings. The multi-view images of the object were photographed in flat ambient light baked in a flatly lit model from all angles so when a virtual key light was applied, it would provide the same look as a key light striking a real object lit with fill light only.

The Gaussian splat technique captures a true light field and bakes in the light appearance from multiple angles in an environment. Live actors inserted into a splat environment would still need a lighting match, but now the blending would be even more seamless as the subtle lighting effects, such as reflections and transparencies, would change on both the splat and the live light field. In the event technology evolves to be able to record a real-time Gaussian splat of a live performance on a stage. At a later date a cinematographer could position a 2D virtual camera at different points within the splat to recapture the play as a movie. An infinite amount of coverage could be had because the performance and the actors are archived as a digital file.

When I attended USC Cinema, the school acquired takes from the television show *Gunsmoke* so editing students could take this raw material and edit their version of a dramatic scene. The same could be done with Gaussian splats, except that numerous camera angles could be created, just as you would shooting a movie. The issue with a scenario like this is that the lighting will not be optimum for many angles. When shooting a movie using the one-camera technique, each angle would have the lighting adjusted for the perfect presentation (logical or not).

TV sitcom lighting, while brilliant, usually involves flat light from the front, with various areas of cross-key and kicker light components for modeling to accommodate three or more cameras shooting the show and the live audience viewing the performance from one direction. The more cameras you have, the flatter the lighting becomes, allowing for even lighting for all cameras. This technology can move us away from passive viewing, in which the filmmaker shows us what they want us to see, to a world of audience participation in filmmaking.

At the moment, shows like *KOllOK* have successful streaming participation via texting with other audience members during the broadcast, or perhaps, like an improv show, the audience shouts out scenarios to be performed on the spot. It will be the most interesting media world being created today. We hope our book will help provide some direction and insights for you as media evolves.

Chapter 7

Mo-Sys VP Pro – Camera Tracking

Matching a Virtual Camera to a Live Camera

This chapter covers the fundamental concept of matching real and virtual cameras with the live camera driving the virtual one. It is more common to have a live camera drive a virtual camera if only because of the finite qualities and settings of a live camera. If one wanted the opposite scenario of a virtual camera driving a live camera, physical limitations might prevent the live camera from matching. Therefore, it makes more sense to mimic the exact physical specifications of a live camera with a virtual one.

The Mo-Sys company was founded in 2012 by Michael Geissler. His company designs and manufactures advanced camera robotics and virtual technologies for the high-end film and broadcast industry. The Mo-Sys product range includes remote heads and motion control, broadcast robotics, mechanical and optical camera tracking for AR and VR, and on-set visualization.

Since its founding, Mo-Sys has been involved in high-end virtual production and has made tremendous advancements in the technology. Their most recent achievements have been the development of the VP Pro virtual production studio, which incorporates and addresses many of the challenges discovered through real production experience. Here are a few highlights.

DOI: 10.4324/9781003473169-7

Virtual Camera

We touched briefly on the creation of a virtual camera in the Unreal Game Engine. When executing live tracking, this virtual camera has to match to the live-action camera exactly, including all the built-in lens distortions that exist in the real lens. In the past, these parameters were painstakingly added to the Unreal camera. In VP Pro, a special Mo-Sys camera with all these attributes is merely dragged and dropped into the Unreal setting.

Real-Time Camera Tracking

Live tracking of a moving camera has to be accurate within centimeters to keep actors locked to a virtual floor. The calculations to do this are extensive, and the speed of communication between sensors and processors is critical. The company's latest innovation eliminates one of the computing components to enable much faster speed, allowing for much quicker camera moves to keep the tracking in sync.

MoCaptury

Along with camera tracking, Mo-Sys has developed a markerless human performer capture. No suit is needed, and it is sensitive enough to detect fingers and expressions. The system also enables two performers to make contact with each other when their movements drive CG characters.

Invisible Tracking Markers

In the past, VFX artists placed tape crosshairs on green screens to enable post tracking off the live action footage. These tape marks had to be painstakingly erased via rotoscoping. Mo-Sys has enabled tracking markers that appear on the LED wall in between the live action frames so they can be detected but not recorded on the live action.

3D Garbage Mattes

Garbage mattes have been a mainstay in VFX forever. When cameras move, these garbage mattes have to be animated to keep up with the changing perspective of the edges of green screens. A 3D garbage matte is a dimensional equivalent that automatically keeps up with the changing perspective of a camera move.

XR and Focus

XR or extended reality is the ability to add a computer graphic to a live action scene or, in the case of virtual production, a foreground 3D element facing the actor standing in front of an LED wall. In traditional effects this could also be done but if a focus pull or rack focus was done on the live action one would have to animate and match the focus pull in post. Now, in VP Pro an encoder on the real lens sends focus information to the virtual camera to match the focus adjustment along with a limiter to avoid moiré on an LED screen.

Multi-Camera

Multiple cameras on LED walls were problematic as the frustums would collide or overlap, leading to issues. VP Pro allows for multi-camera switching between cameras with no problem. This is done with time manipulation: camera A records during the off interval of camera B, then switches back and forth.

Seamless Set Extension of LED Walls

As I mentioned in the LED chapter, when a background image is photographed off the wall at an angle, the extension will not match in perspective. By turning the wall into a 3D element, extensions are now made as seamlessly as a green screen composite using an LED wall as a background.

Built-in Keyer

VP Pro has a built-in keyer to provide a real time composite as well as the option of using an alternate keyer such as the Ultimatte. Each take can separately record the tracking, background, composite, and raw camera footage for post work later.

Customizable VP Pro Interface

The first iteration of VP Pro as a plug-in for Unreal used many components of Unreal, such as Livelink, Blueprint etc. Many virtual studios have different equipment components, such as outside-in tracking instead of inside-out. Outside-in involves many cameras watching the subject to capture its motion. Inside-out is like the StarTracker: the camera senses its position by looking outside at the stars. The new VP Pro allows for a customizable interface and different tracking systems to send data to its components.

Bare-Bones Virtual Production with a Laptop and Green Screen

The following describes the equipment and procedure for using a live-action foreground actor against a green screen with an Unreal Engine (UE) environment and matching the virtual UE camera to the live camera on the set. The

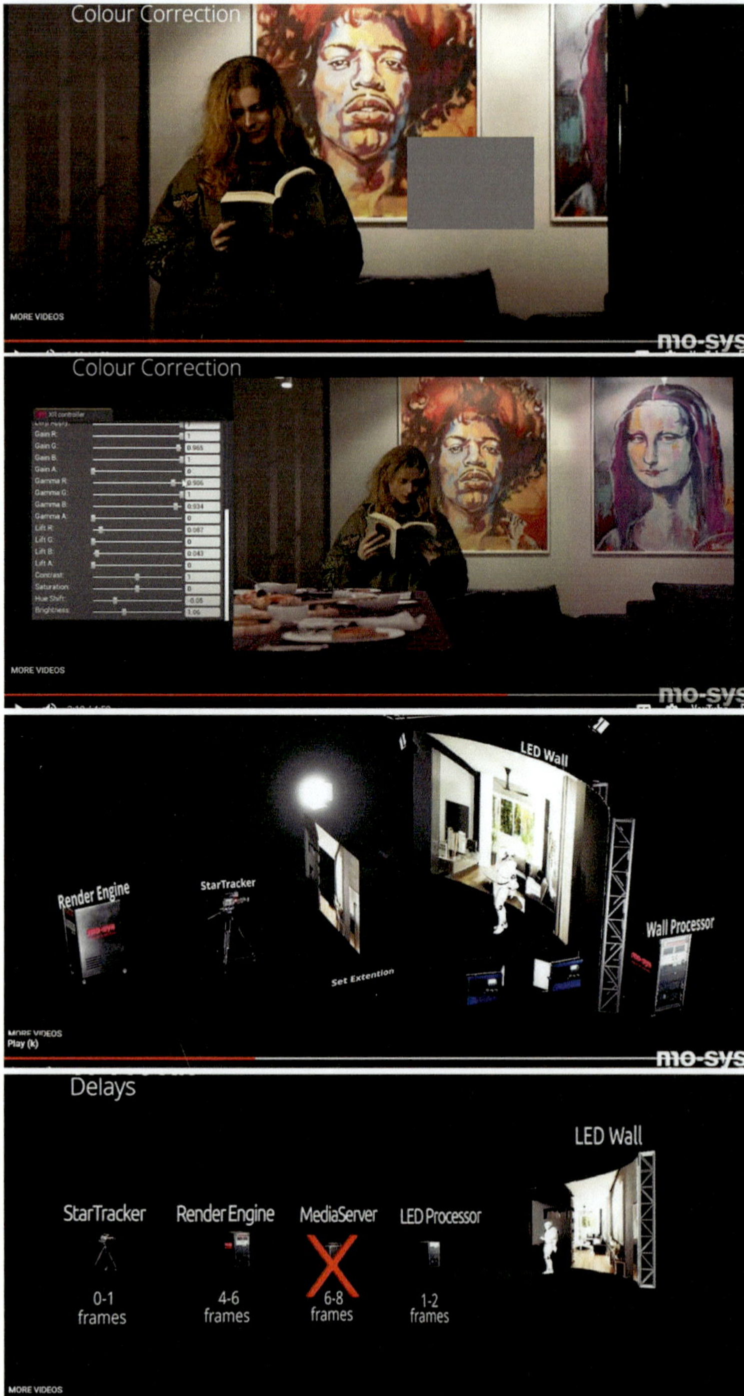

Figure 7.1 *The Mo-Sys VP Pro system. The top picture shows the performer against an LED wall. The end of the wall cuts the hanging picture in two. The next picture down shows the set extension and color correction tool that seamlessly completes the picture with no distortion. You see the augmented reality table foreground in front of the model, also generated in real time by the system. The bottom two illustrations show the layout and breakdown of the delay improvement by eliminating a computer component.*

Source: Images courtesy of Mo-Sys Holding Ltd

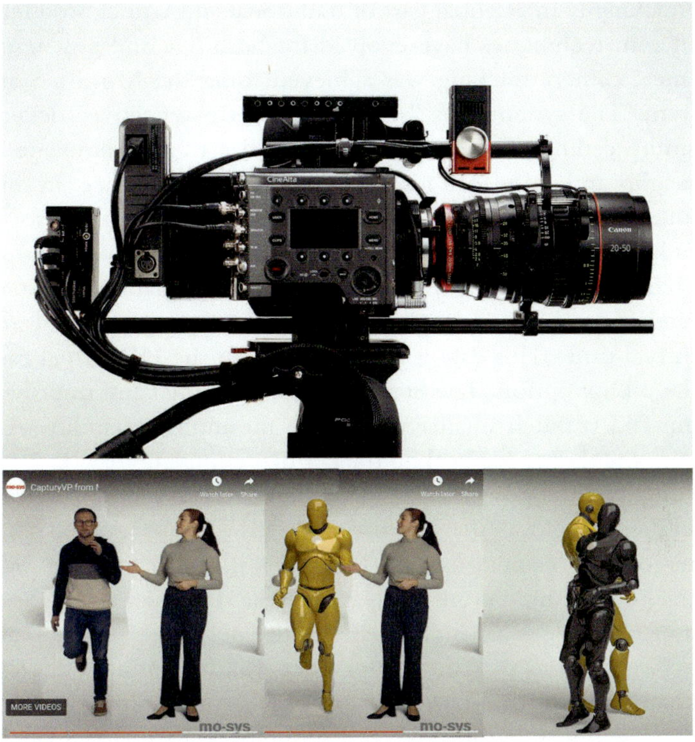

Figure 7.2 *The StarTracker Max is shown in the top image. The star sensor is the partially red bottom box just above the live-action camera lens. The StarTracker's processor is the unit mounted at the back of the camera. Both of these items have the flexibility of being mounted wherever necessary. The bottom image shows the results of the MoCaptury system that amounts to a series of camera sensors focused around the performers detecting their every movement and spatial relationship enabling their avatars to cross in front and make contact with each other.*

Source: Images courtesy of Mo-Sys Holding Ltd

live camera creates a move while the virtual camera is in lockstep, moving simultaneously in the virtual background environment. The original camera green screen foreground footage and the UE-rendered background footage were then composited in a post-production process using After Effects.

For this exercise, we decided to make use of the high-end real-time Mo-Sys tracking software along with their virtual production interface, which they call VP Pro. The Mo-Sys system has been the go-to technology for high-end productions that require flawless live tracking for on-air broadcast presentations as well as high-resolution motion picture production.

Camera tracking is an essential part of traditional and virtual production, and many different techniques have evolved for both live and post tracking. In this instance, camera tracking was achieved using the Mo-Sys StarTracker Max system. The system uses "stars," small retro-reflective stickers placed on the studio ceiling. These stickers vary in size to accommodate different ceiling heights and are placed randomly on the target surface: in this case, a ceiling, though a wall or floor will do nicely as well. A small sensor attached to the studio camera shines infrared radiation on the stars, which are seen by the infrared sensor, creating a star map. This map enables the StarTracker to accurately report the camera's position and orientation to the rendering engine in real time. This data is then tethered to the UE virtual camera via the UE Live Link option. The StarTracker Max is the latest improvement in the system and is much smaller with more mounting flexibility. A brilliant accessory to the device is a backup tracker that completes data in cases where the stars might be temporarily occluded, such as when the camera travels into a car, and the roof blocks the star markers. This accessory, called VisionMax, uses a stereoscopic camera that tracks objects it sees in its path. While this type of tracking has limitations compared to the star system, it is a great boon for rapid production as it handles many of the unforeseen issues that happen in production, such as the cinematographer wanting to move the camera to an area that goes past the stars or in cases of shooting outdoors. VisionMax takes over the tracking data and transitions back to the StarTracker Max seamlessly.

The following was our experience with an early version of VP Pro to create a live tracked composite.

The steps were as follows:

1. Set up the Mo-Sys StarTracker system on the stage.
2. Set up and light the green screen stage.
3. Review and install all hardware and software prerequisites for the Mo-Sys system, including PC, Blackmagic products, SDI card drivers, Nvidia drivers, Bluefish drivers for multiple video source capture, Epic Games Launcher, Bonjour, genlock system, TightVNC, and AJA control panel.
4. Download, install, and set up Unreal's Mo-Sys VP Pro software and VFX license.
5. Configure UE for Mo-Sys and the live-action camera, including UE folder structure, IP address, genlock, timecode, frame rate, tether tracking data and Live Link, UE internal keyer, and UE Take Recorder.
6. Set up the Unreal environment and select a camera position.

7. Rehearse the shot.
8. Shoot the shot.
9. Composite the shot.

Since we were using the Mo-Sys stage, Steps 1 to 3 were already completed because the stage was used for demonstrations and education. Therefore, the live-action camera was already established with StarTracker and a lens profile. (Steps 1 to 3 are well documented on the Mo-Sys support website.) The remainder of this chapter will describe Steps 4 to 8. (Even though most of Step 3 was completed for us, parts are included in Step 4 for illustrative purposes.) Additional information and support is available for Steps 1 to 8 at https://support.mo-sys.com/static/login.html?next=/Step 9 is not covered in detail as it was a conventional green screen composite in After Effects (AE), and there are already many online tutorials regarding green screen compositing in AE and Nuke.

This book does not intend to be a hands-on hardware or software tutorial because this information is everywhere and constantly changing. Instead, it intends to present enduring concepts and fundamentals that all virtual production practitioners should be familiar with, regardless of changes in tools, brands, manufacturers, and versions.

Step 4. Download, Install, and Set Up Unreal's Mo-Sys VP Pro Software and VFX License

Loading the VP Pro Plug-In

After logging in to your Mo-Sys account, find the plug-in with the version number that matches the engine version you're using.

Loading complex software can sometimes cause issues with firewalls. After loading, an error message may appear saying a specific part of the software was determined to be a threat and was removed. So you are safe, but now the plug-in won't run. You trust the provider and realize what was removed was safe, so you have to work with your firewall system, such as Norton; go into settings; and "whitelist" the software you are loading to prevent it from being blocked or deleted. When Epic creates a new version of the engine, a simple update of the VP Pro software will automatically change its version to match the current engine. In many cases, virus protection software such as Bitdefender or the default Microsoft has no issues downloading the VP Pro plug-in. In the case of software such as Norton, the solution was to turn off the firewall entirely for 15 minutes, just long enough to download the plug-in and whitelist the downloads folder. When Norton restarts, you are protected again and have downloaded the plug-in. Be sure to add the VP Pro plug-in to the Mo-Sys blank project so it will always be there when you add environments.

Other Drivers to Install

> **As with any other software,** when installing tracking system software, note that other connective software, hardware, firmware, drivers, and VPNs may be required. Note compatibilities and conflicts.

For the VP Pro plug-in to work, you must install Bonjour software, which enables your system to find the external devices you need, such as the Blackmagic Ultra Studio Mini. You will also need to download the driver for the Ultra Studio Mini.

Bare-Bones Hardware Example

For this virtual production setup, we used the following hardware:

- Juniko's laptop matching specs for UE $$$$$.
- Blackmagic Ultra Studio Mini $.
- Blackmagic Ursa Mini Pro G-2 12K camera pl mount $$$$$.
- Ziess lens 35mm Canon lens 50mm $$$.
- Cartoni Laser Tripod and Fluid Head $$.
- Blackmagic Design Sync generator $.

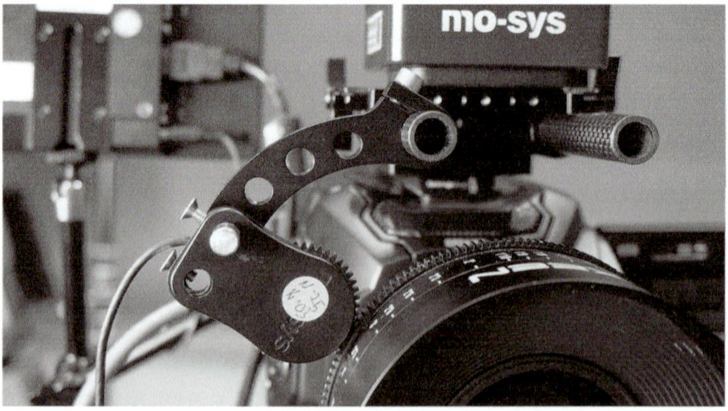

Figure 7.3 *The lens uses encoders to provide focus data to the system.*

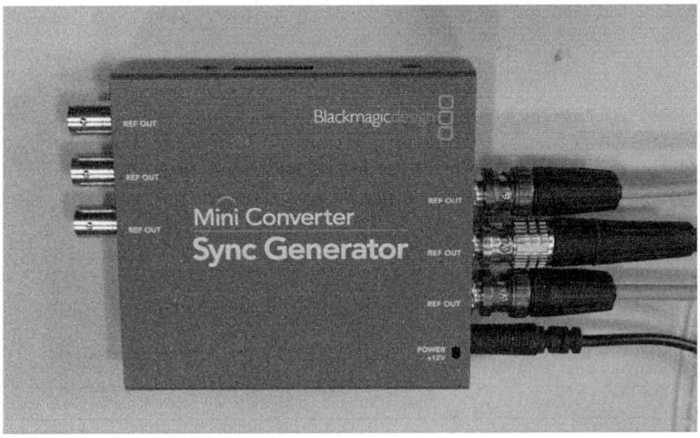

Figure 7.4 *The sync generator provides genlock for all the devices to keep them all synchronized.*

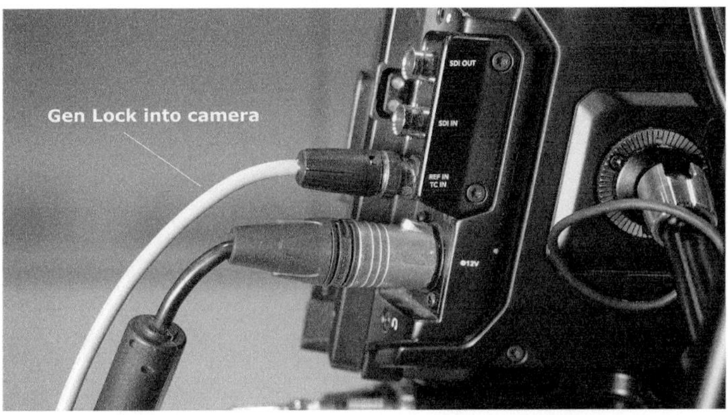

Figure 7.5 *This cable sends the genlock into the reference in the port of the Ursa camera.*

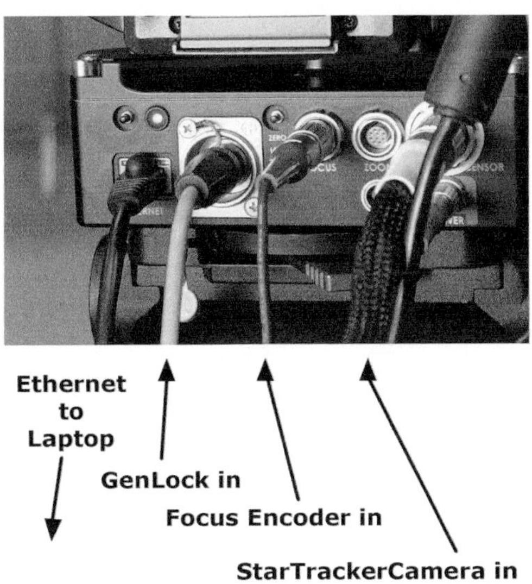

Figure 7.6 *The StarTracker central computer collects tracking data and sends it to the laptop via ethernet. This illustration is from an older StarTracker unit. The StarTracker Max has the same connections.*

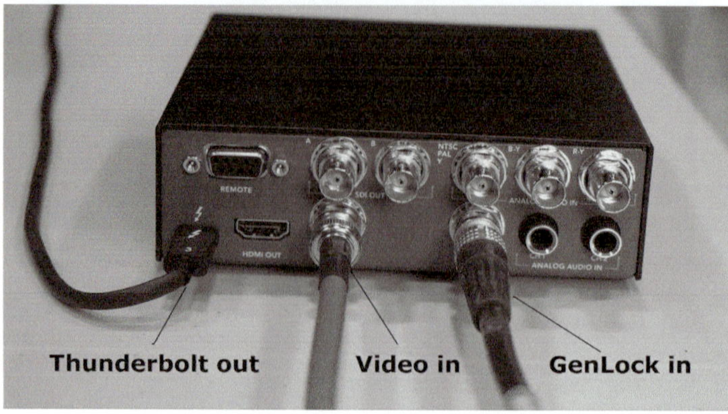

Figure 7.7 *The Blackmagic Design Ultra Studio Mini inputs video signals and converts them into a Thunderbolt high-speed cable that the laptop can read.*

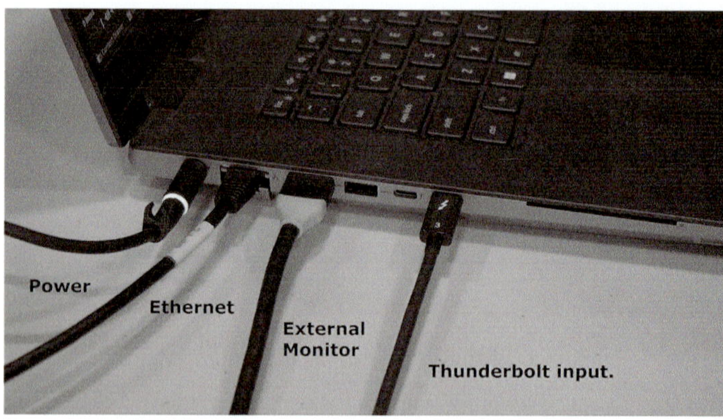

Figure 7.8 *Laptop connections.*

Hardware Pipeline

> **As with any production pipeline process,** test the input, execution, and output first before the actual production. If the virtual production pipeline being used requires post-production (as in compositing), complete that. If the virtual production pipeline does not utilize the post-production process but will livestream broadcast, complete that also.

The basic strategy for the bare-bones method is to capture camera tracking data and video into Unreal and the VP Pro plug-in to obtain a rough on-set green screen composite in real time where the live-action camera and virtual camera are linked so that the live-action and virtual environments are joined, much like shooting a real set. The main difference is that there will not be a finished in-camera composite as would be achieved if using either an LED volume or a high-resolution Ultimatte compositor to generate finished composites in real time, as seen on programs such as those on the Weather Channel. The advantage of this stripped-down method is that the digital camera can record in high resolution 4K, and at a later date, the Unreal background take can be re-rendered at 4K to be composited later in either After Effects or Nuke for maximum fidelity. Because 4K has too much data to handle virtual production in real time, many projects that require 4K are prevized on set in high definition and then composited later at the higher resolution.

Step 5. Configure UE for Mo-Sys and the Live-Action Camera

The Sync Generator and Other Hardware

When syncing or matching a single camera or multiple cameras, there must be a method to accurately determine when recordings start (on what frame) and ensure that frames and frame rates match. Even after they are synchronized, post-production, compositing, and editorial must be able to align all the elements precisely. Ideally, frame numbers or timecodes should match. This is a requirement going back to traditional movie making and traditional analog broadcasting.

In filmmaking, perforations in the film stock allow frame alignment. In video recorded on tape (without physical frame separation), a genlock technique uses a reference signal from a signal generator to "lock" the frames from one device to another. Pixel number one must appear in the same place at the same time throughout the pipeline.

The most important component in our pipeline is the sync generator, also called genlock, which sends out the main beat that keeps all the hardware marching in time. Even though we set the Unreal frame rate to 24 frames per second and our live-action camera to 24 frames per second, and they both run at exactly 24 fps, this is not enough to make the system work. For example, if we go back to early rear projection using motion picture film, we see there has to be a time interval when the film in the camera and the projector stay still during exposure. Ideally, we want the film in the projector and the camera to move to the next frame while the shutter is closed. Even if the projector and camera are running at the exact speed of 24 fps, we must also ensure that the film in the projector isn't being pulled to the next frame while the camera is exposing it.

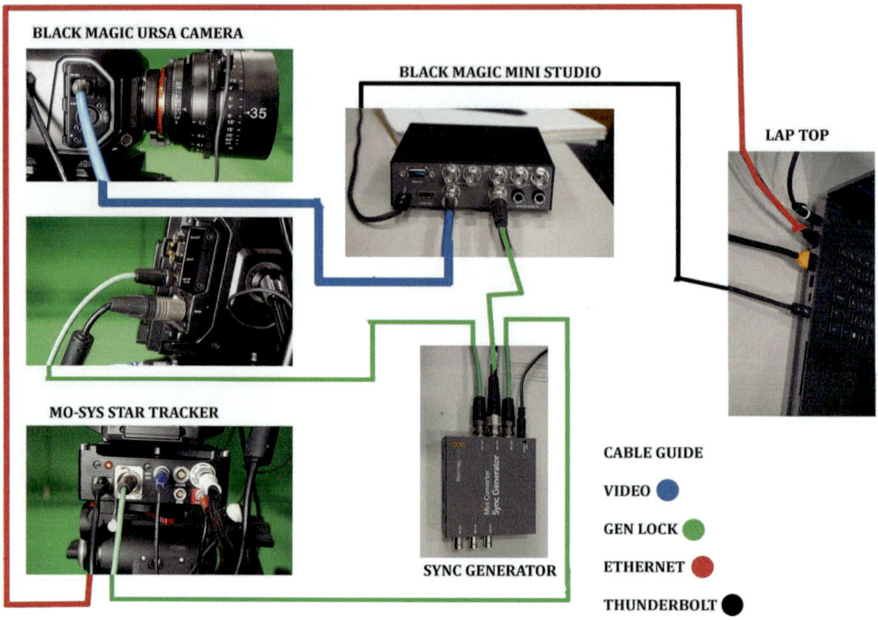

Figure 7.9 *The basic lean-and-mean setup.*

The film position and shutter must be synchronized to have all elements align to the same point in time and repeat that moment of exposure for each frame. In the case of our virtual production setup, we must make sure that during that 1/50th of a second interval of exposure, we are recording the tracking data, the video capture data, and the unreal render data. To obtain this alignment, it is also important to have all the hardware running off the same timecode and genlocked. The other synchronization issue lies in the video signal and the speed at which the data travels through the copper wiring. Because some of the data arrives at the composite point more slowly than the video data, a time delay tool slows down the video signals so all the data hits the finish line simultaneously.

Software Pipeline

Laptop

- Windows 10/11
- Latest Nvidia drivers

Live Camera

- The camera should have SDI output and genlock sync input.

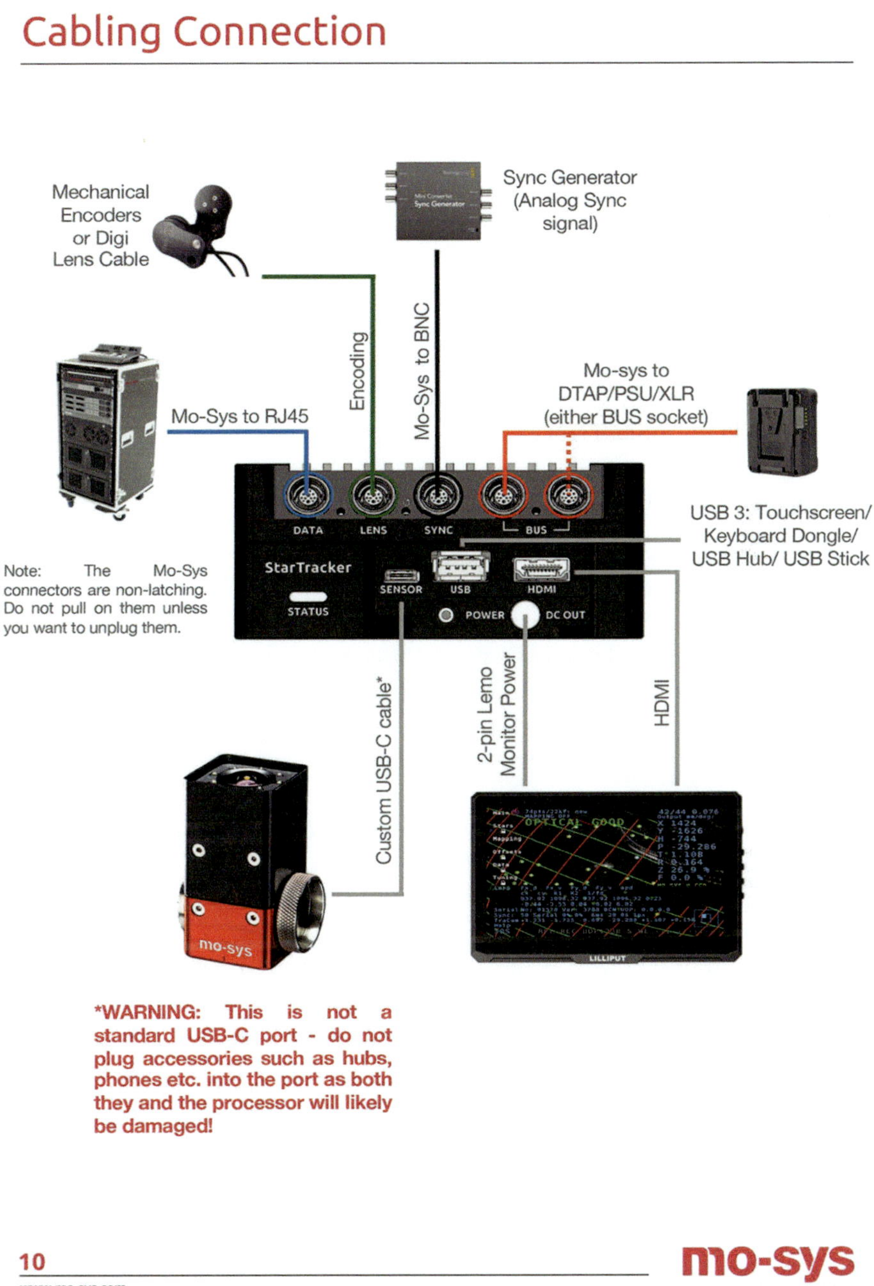

Figure 7.10 *Connections for the high-end LED wall VP Pro system.*
Source: Image courtesy of Mo-Sys Holding Ltd

Mo-Sys

- Install Mo-Sys VP Pro software and VFX license.

StarTracker

- Install TightVNC to access the StarTracker display and control screen via the PC.
- Install Bonjour. This allows automatic detection of StarTrackers and other hardware from VP Pro and its switchboard (allows adding and switching between Mo-Sys devices, like the StarTracker).
- Change the IP address of the laptop to connect to the StarTracker. StarTracker needs to send data to an IP address and a port. The default IP address is StarTracker's.

Capture and Playback

- SDI card driver – standard professional digital video format. This drives SDI signals over BNC coaxial cables. PCs usually send and receive HDMI, but SDI supports higher resolutions like 8K. (SDI card driver options are Blackmagic Desktop Video (minimum v12.2), AJA control panel, and the latest Bluefish drivers.)
- Install Blackmagic Ultra Studio HD Mini software. (The software is for the Blackmagic Ultra Studio HD Mini – hardware with professional broadcast connections. Can send and receive SD and HD video.)
- SDI recorder (hardware like HyperDeck Studio 4K Pro).

Changing the IP address on your laptop to match the StarTracker default removes added setup time to reprogram the StarTracker IP address. If your laptop is only used for virtual production with VP Pro, there is no issue. If your laptop is used for other purposes such as running Nuke, it will have to be reset to its original IP address so your other software licenses will function.

Genlock

The live-camera, StarTracker, and UE must be genlocked (synced) and share the same timecode. (Hardware like Blackmagic design Mini Converter Sync Generator.)

- Set default timecode provider in Virtual Production settings.
- Once the switchboard is activated, it will connect all the devices. Then, go to the UE Blueprint file to plug the inputs and outputs into the

proper places. Export the timecode sequencer 24 fps clock source to reuse.

Blueprint is a node-based visual scripting tool in Unreal. It lets users write scripts in Unreal without knowing a scripting language, which allows them to customize built-in features in Unreal Editor.

Unreal Editor

Used for the virtual camera, virtual environment, recording the virtual environment, and previsualization of the green screen composite.

- Add Mo-Sys files to the Unreal Editor (UE) plug-in folder.
- Create a UE project with the files added to the plug-in folder.
- Upon opening the UE project, log in to your Mo-Sys account.
- Set Mo-Sys to VFX mode in UE.

Live Link Plug-In – Tether Tracking Data From Mo-Sys to UE

- UE's Live Link can stream data from tracking and motion capture systems. Mo-Sys can integrate into UE's Live Link.
- Set Tracking Default Live Link Preset to Mo-Sys.
- Open Mo-Sys starter content.
- Transfer the virtual camera position to the Mo-Sys stage position – use the Mo-Sys virtual camera.
- Match the frame rate of the live camera to that of the virtual camera.

Live Previsualization of the Green Screen Composite

- VFX mode and Mo-Sys keyer – enable Mo-Sys output.
- Go to VP Pro and set a matte key by selecting a bright and dark area of green and fine-tune the result.
- Optional – UE has a native internal keyer.
- Add delay in Timed Data Monitor using Timed Correction.
  - Check the live tracking by observing the composite and panning the camera rapidly from side to side while adjusting the Timed Correction to keep the foreground and background movements locked together.

Sequencer

- Use the UE sequencer to create separate shots.

Take Recorder

- To record and export the UE virtual camera background environment, use the Take Recorder. Set the output format. The shot will be stored on the PC hard drive in the UE project folder. The live camera will record the green screen foreground image on its camera card.
- Set both camera and UE to output ProRes 4444. There is no timecode metadata in. exr format, but there is timecode metadata in the ProRes. mov format.
- Start recording sequentially. Run the live camera, the UE virtual camera using Sequencer, and the Take Recorder.

Post Compositing

- The separately recorded foreground and background footage is composited using After Effects or Nuke.

Planning and Shooting a Shot

The Camera and Other Things to Look Out For

> **When matching a live camera and live set to a virtual camera and virtual set,** traditional photographic specifications still apply. Camera and lighting techniques that are over a century old still need to be considered and have their digital equivalents. Photographic and image output specifications should be consistent or compatible.

For the shoot, I decided to have a character walk into the frame and stop. The camera then tilts up to reveal the figure in front of a desert landscape with a laboratory off in the distance. At the end of the tilt, I added a rack focus to the laboratory. Our camera settings were as follows:

24 frames per second progressive
180-degree shutter
200 ISO
White Balance 5300K
F2.8
35mm lens
Focus from 9′ rack to infinity

Even at 200 ISO, the f-stop was too high, which would reduce the rack focus effect due to an increased depth of field. To open the f-stop, we utilized the

60 neutral density filter in the camera to lose two stops of light, allowing us to shoot at f2.8.

For the file format, we chose Pro Res XQ HD 1920x1080 with 4:4:4:4 full-color space, as this uses the full-frame sensor, as does the camera's 4.6K RAW. One has to be careful here, as other formats obtain HD by cropping the sensor, which alters the effect of the lens's focal length and throws off the lens and tracking calibration. Be sure you're always using the size of the sensor the tracker was calibrated to, or you will get in trouble.

Step 6: Set Up the Unreal Environment and Select a Camera Position

Time and Versions March On

> **When syncing** a live camera to a live virtual 3D environment, note all software versions and match as needed.

The Unreal Game Engine constantly evolves, with the software version changing often. By the time this book is published, the version we are working with will have been superseded by several versions. As an instructor, I have found this daunting when creating lesson plans. I've spent hours creating step-by-step tutorials on my home computer using Unreal version 5.2.3, only to find when I double-checked and troubleshot in the actual classroom that the school's software was on 5.1.2. Most of the button pushes worked, but a few critical ones differed, leading to hunting and pecking. A simple drag-and-drop method created for the latest version might not be enabled in the school's version, for example. For an instructor, it is best to create lesson plans using the actual software and computers used in the classroom. It is also a good idea to have the software set to default settings so all the students see the controls in the same place. Many times, clever students customize the layout for themselves, which results in confusion when others use the software.

This annoying lack of tool stability is the cost of progress. The only thing one can do is ensure that all plug-ins, Unreal marketplace environments, and Unreal engine versions match or are compatible with the current agreed-upon version number. If a student chooses an environment that only works in version 4.6.1 but not 5.3.2, the answer would be to load and run the 4.6.1 engine to complete the project. The best solution is eliminating the variables and making the chosen environment compatible with the taught version. The other advantage of this method is having the students work in teams and take on particular roles for a common project, such as a virtual cinematographer and a set builder.

Creating a Blank UE Project

> **When downloading 3D project data for repurposing**, maintain original source file data. Copy only essential elements as target data on an as-needed basis. Note any file size and data playback limitations.

After you have downloaded the Epic Games Launcher and the Engine version you wish to use, you will be presented with several discipline options. There will be games, film and video, architecture, etc. We will select film and video and a completely blank project. This choice will eliminate as many extraneous elements as possible. This blank project will become our source project, and we will add an environment.

This source project will be our unedited, inviolate project from which we will pick and choose elements to put into another blank project called a target project. In this project, we will have our master environment, which will contain our camera and the elements and lights we choose to add while eliminating unnecessary elements (such as items that will not be seen by our camera).

This strategy makes the data as lean as possible and facilitates real-time tracking and compositing. If you choose a project particularly dense with data, your system may not be able to render it out in real time.

Naming Conventions

We named our project PolarSource. Note that I purposely did not put a space between *Polar* and *Source* just now. The software often detests a space, so one must add an underscore between words or capitalize the first letter of the next word to delineate the words, as I have done here.

Create a New Folder to Hold the UE Source Project

> **Understand all projects' and applications' file organization,** structure, and formats.

Once you have started your blank project, you will notice in the content window that you have the raw beginnings of an Unreal project with two icons. The one that looks like mountains is the map or your main level.

This contains the stage and all the items in the outliner, such as a floor, sky, lights, cameras, etc. The other icon with the cube, called Built Data, contains all the programming code that enables the software. At this point, you will make a new folder with the name of your project. Ours will be Polar_Lab. Once you have saved everything (learn to do this a lot), you can return to the marketplace, find the perpetually free Polar environment, and select Add to Project. All your new elements will now load into your folder.

Examine Your UE Source Project Maps

Understand all the 3D source project elements and data purposes.

Your new map will have many sections that may not have clear descriptions. You will need to open each one to understand what it holds. In this case, the first map shows all the parts of our disassembled set.

The following map shows the environment assembled with dawn lighting; another may be the same with different lighting. Once you choose the level you want, you can see other folders holding textures, characters, etc. An excellent way to explore what things are doing is to go down the list in the outliner and turn the eyeballs on and off to see the elements' contribution.

UE Source Project to Target Project Method

When copying and repurposing 3D data, note which elements require advanced expertise to manipulate and avoid altering if lacking that knowledge. Also, note which elements are memory, CPU, or GPU taxing; if they are non-essential, do not copy them to the target project.

In many cases, the environments you download into your blank project can be very data heavy. Creating a target project will enable you to pick and choose the elements you want from the source project to make a lean data environment. For example, if trees are blowing in the wind that aren't seen in shot number one, you might choose not to add them to the target.

You may also want to eliminate all the built-in cameras to avoid confusion. It may be best to eliminate all the cameras so you will not be influenced by their point of view, and your vision will be the one you use from the start.

Stand-Ins

> **When syncing** or matching live-action to virtual 3D environments, use references to match the scale of humans and objects. Ideally, reference items should be fixed in the real and virtual worlds for quick and easy comparisons while setting up shots.

You can create a basic cube measuring precisely one meter in height, depth, and width for stand-ins. (Cubes are useful as references and to assist in finding critical locations within your map.) The cube can be scaled to simulate the height of a human or live-action object that will be combined with your shot. (For example, in the US, the average male height is 1.77 meters, and the average female height is 1.63 meters.) Another method would be downloading a standard man. fbx file of a static human model as a stand-in. Metahumans can also be used, but you will need a plug-in to add them to your scene.

Finding Your First Shot

> **Scout virtual environments** like traditional movie shot planning and composition. Note physical limitations that prevent matching between the live action and virtual environment: for example, a crane-up that looks good in the virtual environment but can't be replicated with a live-action camera that isn't mounted on a crane.

The fastest way to explore your set is to open your desired map and use the mouse controls to move around and examine the set. In our case, we liked the outside of the lab but not where it was placed in the landscape. We found another view of the valley and created a cube as a placeholder for where we wanted the lab. We made the cube by creating it on top of the lab. We used the transform controls to roughly approximate the dimensions of the lab (like a boxcar) and placed it in the valley. We adjusted our default viewer to be about 200 feet above the valley floor to get our composition, we then used the Create Camera Here option to make a Cine Camera Actor. This camera, which has now replaced our viewport camera, will be a placeholder camera used to help position the Mo-Sys camera that holds the tracking and lens data. We named the placeholder camera PolarCamera to differentiate it from the many other demo cameras in the project.

The UE Sequencer

> **Have a way to save master scenes or sequences** that involve location changes. This borrows from traditional movie making, in which there is a master camera position for an establishing shot in the scene. Within each scene, there are separate shots, such as medium shots and close-ups, used for editing. Once your camera positions are identified, have a way to organize shots within each scene. Unreal uses the Sequencer for this purpose.

Once you have created your first camera position, create a folder called Cinematics, and within that, create a camera-level sequence. Once you have done this, a sequencer window with a timeline will open. You will now add the Mo-Sys camera to this timeline. This will be the master you can always fall back on. After saving as something like Shot_One, the master saves another at these settings as Shot_One version 001. With version one activated, you can plan and make mistakes or change your mind because you can always return to that first master position.

Match the UE Camera to the Live-Action Camera and Save Different Versions

> **When matching a virtual camera to a live camera,** note all specifications. Many of these specifications come from traditional movie making. Sensor size, focal length, and focus limits must match between the real and virtual camera. Lens profiles that include distortion data are very important. Including distortion data in the virtual camera prevents feet from sliding on the virtual floor during a camera move.

Once you have found your general location with your placeholder camera, you will use the Mo-Sys virtual camera that appears in VP Pro. This camera will already have the lens distortion and StarTracker data. Once you begin viewing through the Mo-Sys camera, you will be able to adjust the focal length and position for your shots. The virtual Mo-Sys camera and stage mimic the live-action camera and its position on the real stage floor. In order to obtain the virtual view, you need to position the UE environment so the desired location floor aligns with the floor of your green screen stage. It is a little disconcerting to move the entire environment to the Mo-Sys camera, but once it's there, the Mo-Sys camera can be easily moved to find other shots in your scene.

Save This UE Version to Save Yourself

> **As always in production, iterative saving of data** and recordings is essential.

When starting with Unreal, laddering your saved file is essential. Always save after every milestone and move on to a different version to avoid repeating work.

Lighting

You will want to leave some things alone, such as lighting. With many marketplace environments, you may not be dealing with simple directional light for the sun and a skylight. Often, an enormous number of point lights and specialty lights are put in to make the environment look great. You can eliminate all these actors and start from scratch, but that might not be the most efficient approach.

A better procedure might be to merely manipulate the rotational controls of the directional light to establish your key light direction and leave the rest alone except for adjusting the key-to-fill ratio. In the case of our tilt-up, since the green screen area on the live-action stage was evenly lit with fill light, I decided to place the foreground in shadow to accentuate the reveal of the brightly lit lab. I adjusted the rotation of the sun to place the hilltop in shadow and have good modeling on the laboratory. When the key light was in the best position for this, I noticed that some of the key hit the ridge and caused a flare in the virtual lens. To correct this, we created a plane in UE that we used as a flag to block the virtual sun from hitting the ridge and virtual lens as we would have if it were a traditional movie shot.

Pulling the Key

The VP Pro system has a very good keyer that starts by using two samples of the green screen. One will be a brighter area, and the other will be darker. The system evaluates these two samples and generates a good key at the start that can be further improved to obtain a good composite. Always be aware that this tool will provide a previz key that is not meant for a final composite. It only needs to be good enough to make sure the key components of tracking, lighting, and composition are solid. This key will be rendered on set in high definition, but the footage of the live action recorded in the camera and post rendered environment in UE at 4K will be the high-resolution elements that will be composited in post for final delivery.

Checking the Tracking

The final check before beginning the shoot is to check the tracking and adjust the video delay. The standard procedure is to point the camera at the feet of the subject and rapidly pan in quick jerks to observe how long it takes for the background to catch up to the composited feet. The feet, being the live feed, will move first while the UE image going through the calculation of tracking and rendering may lag behind slightly. Adjusting the delay of the live action will minimize this "catch-up" effect until the tracking is spot-on for conventional camera moves.

Step 7: Rehearsing the Shot

> **When matching lenses** between the live and virtual cameras, lens zooming and focusing data must have a method for accurate sharing and duplication. Encoders often convert physical motion and position into digitally coded output that can be shared across applications.

By this time, final adjustments were made to the height of the camera so that at the end of the tilt-up, the character's head was aligned in the correct orientation of the lab in the distance. Once this was found, the actor's eyeline was located to make it seem that the character was looking at the lab. In this case, a C-stand off camera became the substitute for the lab.

While practicing the rack focus, we discovered how easy it was to accidentally bump the encoder for the focus and have its gear reset at a different point on the lens gear, throwing off the focus tracking. The fix was to seat the gears properly, re-establish the extremes of focus, and reset them in the system by moving the lens to the absolute beginning and end points.

After a practice run, we shot a take by activating the camera record first and then the sequencer recording. Once verbal confirmation was made by saying "camera recording," "sequencer recording," and "action," we executed the move. After ten seconds, the sequencer stopped recording due to some system default.

Finding the Culprit

> **3D environments and software are highly complex** and may have programming or scripting languages. When repurposing such data, editing an unfamiliar but no less important scripting language to execute production processes may be necessary.

Tracking down an issue is commonly handled by backtracking through the software to check on connections and procedures and searching the internet community to see if anyone else has had the issue and what the solution was. In this case, we discovered a built-in recording limit in the Blueprint section of the Polar environment. With many marketplace products, the creators make a showcase reel with cameras stationed around their set. We discovered the time-out limit was because of the showcase code, so it was deactivated. This becomes a cautionary tale when purchasing Unreal Marketplace sets instead of creating one from scratch. There is little consistency with how the marketplace sets are created, so you may encounter roadblocks that must be corrected.

Step 8: Shooting the Shot

Once again, we followed the protocol of the call-outs, including those for sound and shot ID while the camera shoots the clapper which are "Camera Rolling," "Sequencer Recording," "Speed," "Marker," and "Scene One, Take One." The anxious actor finally hears the word he's been waiting for – "Action" – and he forgets his line. Just kidding. All went well, and we could see a live composite preview as it happened while recording the live action on the green screen in the camera and the background alone in the laptop off the sequencer. Both the camera footage and the background had identical timecodes.

A Word About Lenses

> **Lens calibration** is necessary to create lens profile data that can be used to add matching lens distortion to the virtual camera lens. This is the key to having live actors stick to the virtual stage floor. Recalibration may

be necessary if the live-action lens is removed and put back on, as the physical seating of the lens will be slightly different and throw off the calibration.

We used a single fixed 35mm lens for easy setup and simplicity. The accepted practice for cinema shooting is to have an assortment of fixed focal length lenses, such as 18mm, 35mm, 55mm, 85mm, and 100mm, as an example. These lenses are commonly switched out rapidly throughout the shoot to offer different looks to the imagery. Zoom lenses were less likely to be used in the past because, at the time, their quality suffered due to the large number of glass elements necessary for a zoom. Today that is much less of a consideration. The advantage of using fixed or hard lenses today is that it eliminates the temptation to execute the much-overused zoom effect. For virtual production, the better practice would be to use a well-calibrated zoom lens and leave it on the camera throughout the shoot.

The reason for this philosophy is that the simple removal and replacement of even the same lens, be it a zoom or fixed, will throw off the calibration and spoil the tracking, requiring the lens to be recalibrated, which can take from thirty minutes to an hour if it is a zoom lens. This amount of time waiting on a set is unacceptable. I suspect that the rapid change of lenses will continue with any movie that uses a blend of traditional live-action shooting in real environments. Still, for shots on the complex virtual stage, a single zoom lens on a camera system dialed into the tech will be the way to go. It may give an edge to a camera assistant if they are trained on calibrating a lens for virtual production in case a lens needs to be swapped.

While the focus of a lens can be tracked well, there are two issues that come up with both the LED wall method and green screen. When doing a rack focus from the foreground subject to an LED wall, one runs the risk of bringing in moiré patterns if the focus is too sharp on the wall. Mo-Sys has a solution that allows the rack focus but has it stop short before it hits the moiré pattern region on the wall but will continue on the virtual camera, allowing the effect to be seen without distortion. Soft focus on the foreground will appear properly when shot in front of an LED wall. When shooting green screen, there is no issue with moiré patterns, but there will be an issue with maintaining the soft edge of a blur in compositing due to the fall-off threshold of the generated mask. In cases where a good rack focus effect is needed, it is preferable to keep the green screen element in constant focus and create the blur during the composite by adding a camera blur effect on top of the cleanly extracted foreground subject to obtain a properly soft image. This also allows for post manipulation of the timing of the rack focus.

Step 9: Composite the Shot

Compositing was done conventionally using the camera's original output for the foreground at 1920x1080. mov codec Apple ProRes 4444 XQ and the rendered output of the UE background. The UE background output was set to 1920x1080 in. mov codec Apple ProRes 4444. The key light tool in After Effects was used for compositing.

This is an academic exercise and is not intended to be a final cinematic product.

Summary

Communication is key between all the hardware and software used. A well-seasoned Unreal technician on the crew is valuable for addressing the inevitable hiccups, such as the short recording time issue we mentioned. This would require someone familiar with scripts and where they would be located within the system so they can be modified. Going down a checklist of locked-down variables, such as focal length, f-stop, etc., is helpful for real and virtual cameras. Visual lighting match will be needed using the previz facility. To check tracking, it is helpful to observe the composite on the monitor and quickly pan the camera to see if there is lag in the video image compared to the Unreal image. This observation informs the operator how to adjust the video delay to provide the best tracking. Virtual production involving live tracking and compositing is not a plug-and-play situation. Failing to prepare is preparing to fail. Testing beforehand is essential to avoid the plug-and-pray scenario.

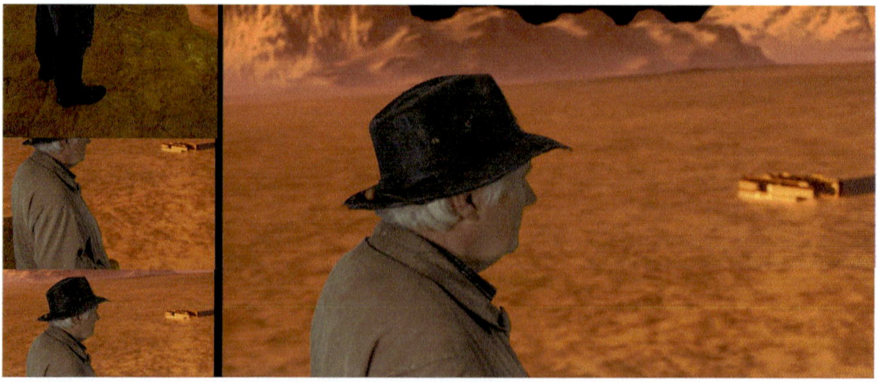

Figure 7.11 *The final composite before the rack focus.*

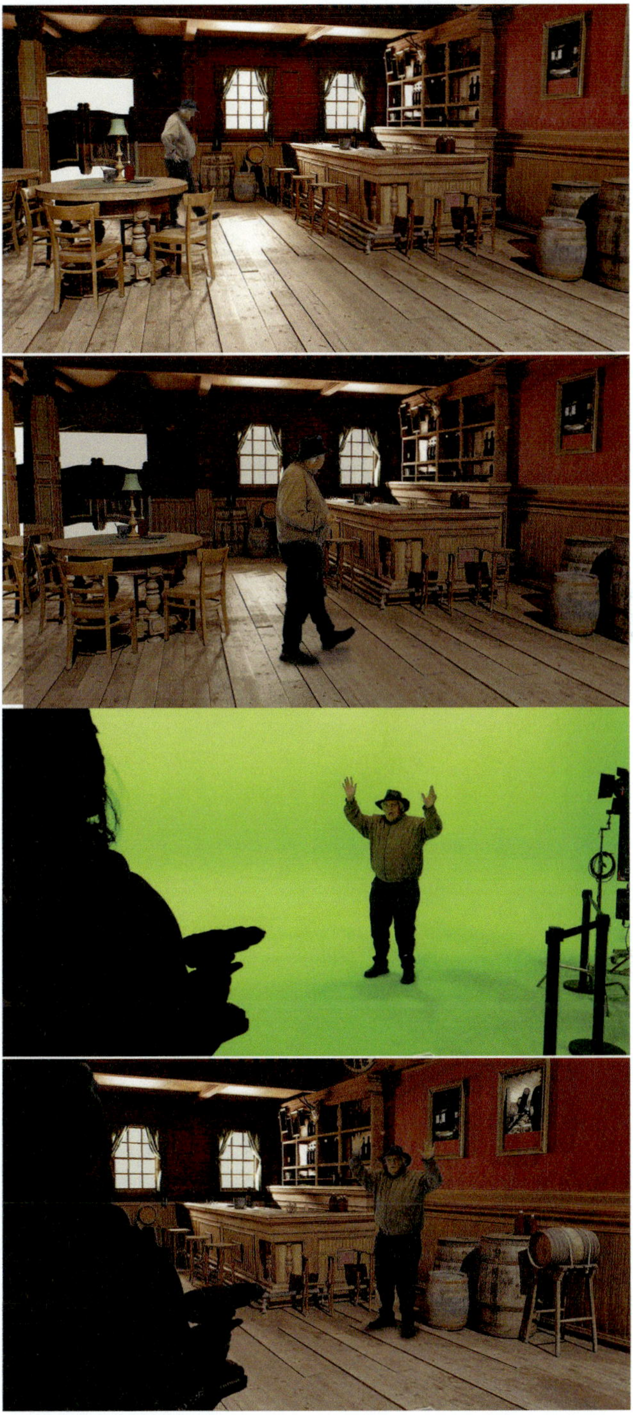

Figure 7.12 *Our second test shot demonstrates many of the advantages of the VP Pro system. The top image shows the augmented reality part of the set appearing in front of me as I enter the scene. The second shot shows the camera panning as I walk across the floor. The precision needed for live tracking has to be within half a pixel of tolerance. The Mo-Sys tracker does this seamlessly. The last two images show the automatic 3D garbage matte eliminating the lighting instruments on the floor and extending the set.*

Chapter 8

Lightcraft

While motion-control camera rigs are still in use today, equipment size/weight and computer requirements are challenging. Also, cinematographers prefer the freedom to create camera moves on the fly. Therefore, post-production camera tracking is in high demand. Recent developments achieve on-set tracking with LiDAR scanning and iPhones.

MIT mechanical engineer Eliot Mack, the lead engineer for the popular Roomba robot, had a passion for movie making and the idea of combining live-action with 3D backgrounds. To realize his virtual production vision, he partnered with Phil Mass and founded Lightcraft Technology in 2004. The first system used fiducial targets on the ceiling that were tracked by a secondary camera attached to the live-action camera to provide location data for a virtual camera inside a game engine. They named the system Previzion. Director of photography Sam Nicholson made fantastic use of the system for the television show *Pan Am* (2011), for which excellent green screen composites of actors were used inside digital recreations of a 1960s-era Pan Am airport with real-time tracked camera moves. Other shows using the system then were *V* and *Once Upon a Time*. Lightcraft won an Emmy in 2013 and filed a patent that same year.

DOI: 10.4324/9781003473169-8

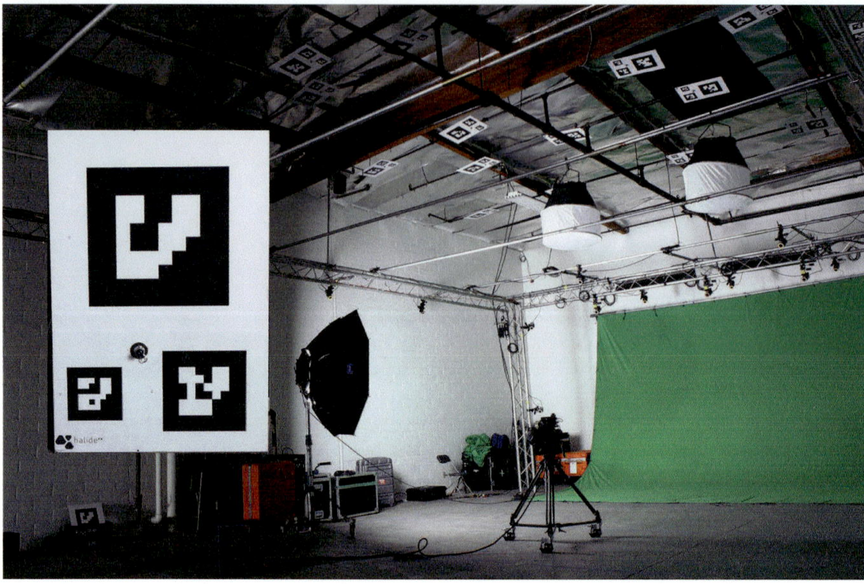

Figure 8.1 *An early version of Eliot Mack's Lightcraft system utilizing fiducial markers on the ceiling for camera tracking.*

Director of photography Emmanuel Lubezki began using LED wall technology to provide interactive light for the actors in astronaut suits in the 2013 film *Gravity*. Although much of this picture was entirely computer generated, the actors' interactive light and visceral performance within the LED light box were groundbreaking.

Michael Geissler founded the Mo-Sys company in London, specializing in remote camera tripod heads and motion control, broadcast robotics, and mechanical and optical camera tracking. This technology provided an important interface for virtual production.

In 2013, VFX supervisor Ben Grossman founded Magnopus, a virtual studio. Grossman worked with Jon Favreau on Disney's *Jungle Book* (2018), in which further use of LED walls as light sources was explored for the green screen stage.

In 2015, Lightcraft launched a new hardware system called Halide to reduce the cost and complexity of virtual production.

In 2016, the Zero Density company out of Turkey released its real-time node-based compositor and reality keyer. It is credited as the first company to use the Unreal Engine in television broadcasting. Its nodes were designed to accommodate several third-party tracking systems, such as Mo-Sys.

In 2019, Bill Warner, founder of Avid Technology and winner of an Oscar and an Emmy in the 1990s for his editing software, joined forces with Eliot to reinvent Lightcraft.

By this time, many more hardware vendors were entering the market, and competition in that arena became increasingly difficult. Lightcraft added engineer Greg Cockroft, who wrote algorithms for Avid, and art director Ben Nowicki to refine the system.

Of great benefit to Lightcraft and virtual production in general was the mission of Rev Lebaredian at Nvidia to use open standards, major new software, and cross-platform tools to transform the use of 3D in a platform called Omniverse. In Omniverse, 3D objects and scenes are in and out of various 3D packages using universal scene description (USD). USD is quickly becoming a worldwide standard and is now built into all Apple products. Because of this, Lightcraft could go from a hardware-based system to entirely software on top of the iPhone and iPad.

Also, in 2019, Jon Favreau's *Mandalorian* was launched and became a magnificent proof of concept for using large LED volumes to create a virtual production show.

Of course, many more companies are involved in VP than are mentioned here. I highlight these firms and individuals because their pioneering efforts laid the groundwork for the general workflow used today, and they continue to be innovators in this form of production.

LIGHTCRAFT JETSET

IPHONES, FREE SOFTWARE, AND OPEN SOURCE SOFTWARE

The iPhone

The following is carried over from the "Democratization of Technology" section concerning the iPhone.

Since 2014, the iPhone has made strides in resolution, lenses, stabilization, and fast 5G speeds. As it continues to develop more and better features, it has become competitively priced against professional production cameras that cost upwards of five digits. When professional directors such as Sean Baker, Steven Soderbergh, Matthew A. Cherry, Zack Snyder, and Park Chan-wook create movies shot with iPhones, they give cinematic credibility to the device.

People who write virtual production applications for the iPhone compound its accessibility by integrating free software like Blender and open-source software like Unreal Engine. The iPhone's LiDAR capabilities integrate well with 3D software and assist in 2D compositing. Now that Blender has compositing ability, there is an option for real-time viewport previewing and cinematic post compositing and rendering. This affordable workflow has laid the foundation to streamline other technologies as well.

Camera tracking has been covered previously in this book, and its importance to virtual production and storytelling is well known. Previously relying on a system of markers, specialized hardware, and software and requiring expert setup by engineers, we will review the concepts behind the iPhone, Lightcraft Jetset Cine, and Blender pipeline, which enables markerless camera tracking and compositing. The subsequent scenario involves compositing a live actor shot against a green screen into a 3D virtual set.

Software

Jetset has multiple versions. At the time of this writing, there are a free version and two subscription versions. Jetset Cine is a subscription version that integrates with a cinema camera, turning the iPhone into a video preview and tracking system. The cinema camera HD output is composited in real time with a low resolution render of the 3D virtual background to generate the on-set Previz.

The purpose of the Jetset Cine and Autoshot workflow is to allow small teams of people to produce hundreds of shots through automation.

Unreal will need to install LONET-2 protocol to send real-time tracking information to Unreal and other game engines.

Calibrate

A lens calibration system creates a profile of the cinema camera lens and includes focal length, distortion, physical offset from the Jetset iPhone, and the angular alignment between the iPhone and the cine lens rig. Multiple captures from different points of view provide enough data to create a 3D solution in the 3D software.

The cinema camera lens overlay shows the lens boundary on the iPhone screen for accurate framing.

The Philosophy

Eliot Mack is free in admitting that his original groundbreaking system, which used inside-out tracking, was extremely hard to use. By the time he won an Emmy for his system, he wanted to build something that accommodated the creative process more easily. In the past, many moving shots had only the image itself to extrapolate positional information, and countless hours were needed to post track objects into scenes. Mack used two breakthroughs to build on. The first was the ARKit in iPhones that enabled the phone to gather data about its location in space along with the addition of an internal LiDAR scanner. The second breakthrough was the Accsoon SeeMo device, which could take an HDMI signal generated by a live-action camera and convert it to an H264 signal that could be read by an iPhone. Another useful development was the open source file for CGI environments called universal scene description or USD. When Unreal or Blender settings are converted into this file format for use inside the iPhone, it is called universal scene description zipped (USDZ) for a more workable file size. With these developments, Jetset has enabled rapid previsualization and content capture while removing a lot of the drudgery of file coordination and manipulation on the back end using his Autoshot software. Eliot sees his system not as a broadcasting tool but as a storytelling tool that enables small groups of artists to create the big-budget imagery we all enjoy on the big screen. Here is a breakdown of the key components.

The iPhone

The iPhone's primary purpose is to gather tracking data and create a live previz composite with data and elements recorded for playback.

The SeeMo

The SeeMo device gathers video from the live-action camera and converts it to a format the iPhone can see in order to directly compare the offset view of the iPhone video and the live-action video. Having these signals side by side enables the Jetset system to calibrate the lens of the live-action camera and create an offset calculation for the off-axis views. The calibration is done with a series of ten or more views of the shooting environment that have a lot of details. If you're shooting on a green screen stage, you would turn the camera around to the stage area and walk in an arc, shooting an area filled with static boxes, tables, chairs, etc. that have easily identifiable contrast points that can be seen by both the live-action camera and the iPhone. These points are connected and resolved to obtain a good scan of the environment and location of the camera. The process takes about four minutes. Once calibrated, the SeeMo is also used to record the Jetset data for the shot as well as supplying power for the cooler attachment for the iPhone.

The Tentacle Sync

Unlike higher-end video systems, the Jetset does not use genlock as the iPhone does not have that feature. The Tentacle Sync sends out a master timecode to the camera and to Jetset. Even though the default frame rate of Jetset is 30 fps and the live-action camera would be 24 fps, the timecode being a consistent signal is utilized to generate a software genlock to keep all the data aligned.

The Cine Camera

The cine camera can be any camera that puts out a pure sensor–size HDMI signal that has no data other than the video signal. The range of cameras is extensive, from the high-end Sony and RED cameras to the lower-end prosumer cameras such as the Blackmagic pocket cinema camera.

The Laptop

The main purpose of the laptop, other than running the software (particularly Autoshot), is to display the synchronization slate that is viewed by both the live-action and iPhone cameras to lock in the start point of the shot.

LONET Software

A plug-in for Unreal that allows it to see tracking data.

Autoshot Software

While Jetset on the set speeds up production time a great deal, Autoshot software does the same by compiling and preparing the tracking data for post. It keeps track of the shots and prepares a ready-made tracking file for the game engine to provide tracking data for the virtual camera to obtain a high resolution render.

SynthEyes Software

In many cases, tracking data works well right out of the gate, especially if we do not see direct contact of people on CG floors. In order to obtain that degree of accuracy, you will need to be within half a pixel of error. In order to achieve this after photography, the SynthEyes program incorporates both the live action and the LiDAR scan of the live-action set. The process is to use AI to quickly roto out a human performer so the live action image of the static parts of the set such as the floor can be analyzed and points can be derived from the 2D live-action image and the 3D LiDAR to essentially obtain a 3D survey of the live action image in order to nail the green screen performer's image onto the floor with no sliding.

The Process

Jetset Pro Version

Jetset Pro allowed us to download the green screen footage from the iPhone for post compositing in After Effects. For our experiments, we used the iPhone 15 Pro Max on the recommendation of the company. The iPhone is a major investment for an individual, of course, but a great entry-level price for someone wanting to try out virtual production. The beauty of the free Jetset is that the iPhone does both tracking and footage capture that are good enough to make student films or sizzle reels for independents. To protect that investment, it is critical to simultaneously invest in a cooler for the iPhone along with the SeeMo device. At the introductory level, the SeeMo provides a long-lasting power supply for the cooler and a holder for the phone to execute hand-held shots. Without the cooler, the phone, while calculating, gets astoundingly hot, which can put it in the range where there are drop outs in the tracking. To be free from worry about this, always use the cooler. Note that the Black Shark cooler has almost no clear instruction on the mounting of the device. There is the cooler and a flat black metal plate. The metal plate is meant to be stuck on the iPhone with an adhesive sticker. If you peel the protective sticker off the back of the cooler itself, it will stick to the metal plate like glue, and any attempt to remove it will peel off the metal plate from the iPhone. To prevent this, there are two thin plastic gaskets that are applied to the back of the

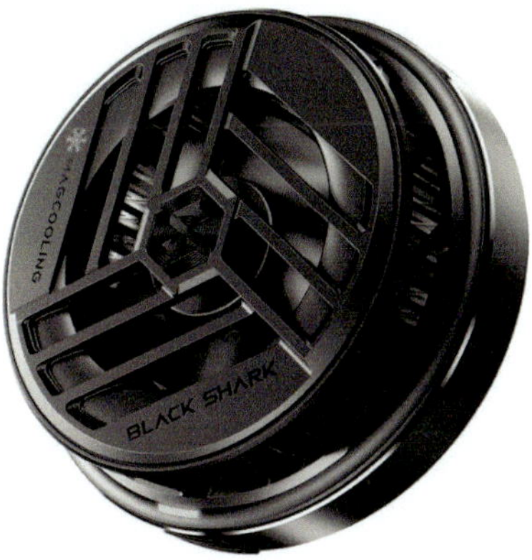

Figure 8.2 *The cooler is a Black Shark for MagSafe iPhones. The Lightcraft company provides links to purchase the exact technology meant to work with your phone.*

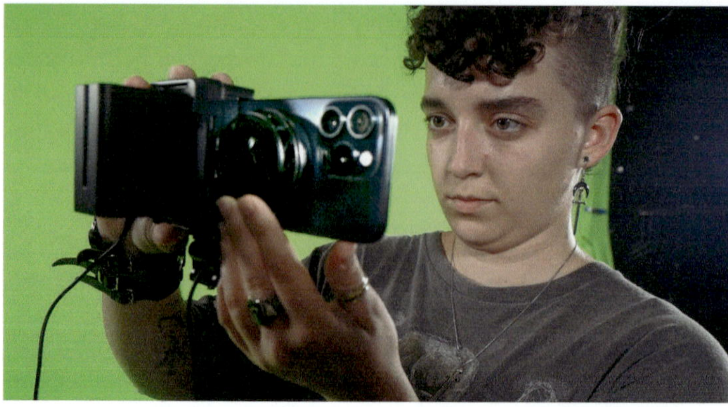

Figure 8.3 *Cinematography student Nova Flagerman shoots with the basic Jetset setup consisting of the iPhone cooler and the Accsoon SeeMo with batteries that provide a nice handgrip as well as powering the cooler.*

cooler to lessen the magnetic pull enough so the cooler holds well but can be removed while leaving the important metal plate.

Finding the Floor and Making an Origin

When you first turn on the Jetset app, you see a view of the space you're in, and while you're moving the camera about, the iPhone is collecting data about the space and the lighting. When you view the space, you will see a grid overlapping flat planes like your floor or a table. The floor is the most critical as that is where your performer will stand, and that surface must match the floor of your synthetic environment. Once you locate the floor, you choose an origin point to lock in your location. This origin point has several arrows showing direction. When you switch to composite view of your background, the origin point will appear on the environment and stick to the floor as you move the camera about. You can record this move and then play it back to compare the live-camera feed and the composite feed of the shot. Below the text identifying the shot is an evaluation of the tracking. If it says Duplicated 0 you are successful as no frames were duplicated during the scanning process. If you are tracking and your iPhone is hot, it may not be able to catch up at points and will wind up duplicating a frame and then picking up the tracking afterward. If you have just two or three duplicates, there are simple post process solutions to mend the tracking.

A Note About Lighting

The iPhone is designed to record not only tracking data but also the room lighting when you pan to find the floor. Jetset uses Apple's RealityKit, which was designed for augmented reality to place CG characters in live-action environments and light them using an AI-generated sphere surrounding the CG model. This sphere has an HDRI map of the lighting environment you are in, such as a picture of the sun and the sky. This image emits the virtual light to light the CG model. This same system will be used to light your incoming background. The system does not support normal CG lights, so if you create a scene in Unreal and light it in a high-contrast film noir style, let's say, that lighting will be ignored, and your set will be lit by your stage lighting. This is an interesting working model as the set lighting would be controlled by the stage lighting. If this is not desired, you can turn off the HDRI function and choose to bake the textures into emissive shaders so it will be seen as displayed in Blender as an example. As everyone adopts their own best practices for these new tools, I expect that users will make use of the HDRI function to quickly see the whole model and perhaps upload sets with the baked lighting to make fine-tuning adjustments to the real light while on set. Further massaging will be done later in post.

Prepping the Background

While the free version supplies backgrounds for testing, it is important to know how to prepare an Unreal Game Engine set purchased from the Marketplace (now fab.com) so it can be used within the iPhone. The company website has great step-by-step tutorials showing this process for not only Unreal but also Blender and Gaussian splat environments. For the purposes of this book, we will abbreviate the tutorials and list the highlights with the assumption that the reader is already somewhat versed in Unreal Game Engine and has a setting already chosen from the Marketplace.

Pick Your Location and Add Scene Locators

When you have an environment loaded in Unreal, it is a simple matter to move about with the default viewer to find cool locations on the set for your movie. Once you have found a spot, you create a basic actor, which will look similar to the origin icon used in Jetset. You will make a number of these scene locators and place them in a folder to obtain your different camera positions. Be aware that the naming convention is very important. In this case, each of the actors will be named sceneloc_, and the description will be something like sceneloc_castle_approach.

The scene locator must be placed exactly on the floor plane of your set with Unreal set to snapping and in object space (not world space). We do this as the orientation of the locator will determine what direction your iPhone is looking during the shot. The red axis should be to the right with the center submerged halfway into the set to set the correct floor height. What we discovered during shooting was that a director may want to reposition the scene locator at the last minute, especially if a figure happens to be standing right on a precipice. Going back into Unreal to add a scene locator will stop production in its tracks. The workaround is to move the camera and subject around to force the location manually, only to find a drastic move may place your subject off the green screen area, requiring the screen to be moved or resorting to post rotoscoping to fix the sudden "brilliant" inspiration. Due to this experience, I think a good practice is to make several scene locators in a variety of orientations to help facilitate sudden changes on set. Another good idea is to reposition a locator to match an origin point on the stage, such as the corner of a doorway the performer walks through, to match a partial real set piece with its CG equivalent. This helps rein in renegade inspiration.

Slimming Down the Data

Once you have found and saved the scene locators, you will begin the process of getting rid of as much data in the model as you can so it can be moved about in real time in Jetset. Much of the data of the model is not seen in your shots, or you only need to see the immediate surroundings to verify you have a good track. When the scene is finally rendered, all the data will be used to create a good-looking setting. To do this, you can select a wireframe view from high above and begin to delete the landscape and other data-heavy objects. You then take the selected elements and move them to a folder that could be labeled USD_exports. USD is an acronym for universal scene description and was developed by Pixar to allow models made from different software packages to be converted to the same language for ease of use. This data is now sent to iCloud with Omniverse exporter to transfer geometry (fast) and textures (much slower). Once textures have been uploaded, they will be slimmed down to run much faster. Once they're uploaded, you can use the Omniverse USD viewer to ensure everything has uploaded correctly. Quite often, you might find you missed a scene locator, for example, and have to add it. So now everything is in iCloud, and we need to send it to Autoshot

Autoshot

The Autoshot software connects to the Jetset iCloud to find the USD model and will condense the model even more by downsizing the texture maps to 512 pixels per texture. After this step, the USD file is converted to USDZ to make it even smaller, and then it is uploaded to iCloud in a version the iPhone can use. This modified map can be downloaded from iCloud via Wi-Fi or directly through a USB-to-gigabit ethernet connector available on more recent versions of the iPhone, such as the 15 Pro.

Doing a Shot

After loading the USDZ model, we can click set origin again and move the camera about to find the floor and set the origin. (You can reorient it after the pick.) You then load the scene locator of the model and slide a ghost slider in between the model and the live action to check your orientations. If you are shooting a green screen, you can choose the color to obtain a key and use the garbage matte tool to detect the edges of your green to create a border that will continue the key outside the bounds of the green screen. Once all this is set, you check for green icons on the lower right that represent tracking, GPU usage, and temperature. If all these are green, you should get a solid track. Now start shooting takes and check the review for frame drops.

Back to Autoshot and Editorial

Once you shoot all your shots for a given day, you synchronize them so the tracking, live action, and model all lock together. The three main files break down into a depth map file, a live-action file, and a composite file. Once synchronized, you can load the composite file into the DaVinci Resolve editor and trim your take to prep it for inserting the tracking data into Unreal. To obtain the in and out frames, you move from the editor component to the fusion section of DaVinci to get that information. After you've edited the clip, you go back to Autoshot, find that exact take, and put in the in and out numbers to prep for processing. With the Jetset Pro, you are using compressed footage directly from the iPhone, whose native frame rate is 30 fps, so for the Pro version, you will be outputting. png files at a Rec 709 color space for speed and simplicity. In the Jetset Cine version, you will use the iPhone to generate tracking data, but the high end camera will be shooting in RAW files with much bigger color space at standard frame rates such as 24 or 23.98. In Autoshot, you now click save and run, and the software creates a Python script that Unreal can read to create and track the virtual camera. Copy the Python script and move over to Unreal.

Back to Unreal

Open the Unreal environment and paste the script into the command console. This will make Unreal generate a level sequence and a camera that will match the live action move perfectly so you can make a composite within Unreal or render the background by itself to bring into Nuke or After Effects to create a final composite. It is useful to do a quick comp in Unreal to check on the LiDAR placement. In the example shown on the tutorial website, we noticed that the tracking on the small puppet was good, but he was submerged in the ground plane. Eliot, who posts his excellent tutorials, made note that the focus distance of the iPhone is derived from the LiDAR data. I surmise that since the puppet was small, the LiDAR must have set the focus at the green screen above his head, placing the focus distance incorrectly and causing the puppet to be submerged. This was solved by manually changing the focus point in Unreal by moving the plane forward, which corrected the situation.

On-Set Practical Takeaways

When trying out Jetset in a school setting, we noticed that the all-important connection to the iPhone was hampered by internet connection issues. Autoshot could not find the phone. We feel the remedy for this is the built-in manual connection that allows you to put the IP address into Autoshot to force a connection. This important connection needs to be verified before a shoot. Lightcraft suggests an affordable private router you can purchase to fix connectivity issues such as this. The other attractive option Jetset has is the AI-generated mask that doesn't need a green screen, only the LiDAR data. This was great for fast run and gun shooting but became a gotcha when the actual live action footage came back with the green screen horribly overexposed or the actor performing outside the green screen, requiring rotoscoping. In their haste, filmmakers often forget to check what the camera is actually shooting. This problem is not new. In the film era, I did post work on a project in which the crew used a video tape connected to the eyepiece that showed what the camera was seeing. It often happened that the iris on the camera was set wide open to get a good image on the video monitor, forgetting that the film behind that lens needed to be exposed at a much higher f-stop. The result was a whole day of overexposed footage. Fortunately, after scanning and digital manipulation, it was saved but at the expense of the quality of the image.

We used the sample fantasy castle environment that comes with Jetset and added a few scene locators to let the system know what area we wanted to shoot in. We then exported a proxy file, converted it into USDZ, and brought that into Jetset. We then picked our scene locators and our origin. We set up the green screen in our living room, shot a couple of shots, and discovered how hot an iPhone 15 ProMax can get when calculating all this stuff. You could fry an egg on this phone! It was hotter than my forehead working on this book. You definitely need to get a cooler for the phone if you are going to do any long-term shooting. After shooting, we sent our files into Autoshot for compiling and then to Unreal for the final render. We did a composite in After Effects and found the tracking to be very good, but the final composite was just okay in that when video is captured by the iPhone that is doing all these other things, the quality of the original green screen file is not optimal. For previz and student work, it is exceptional.

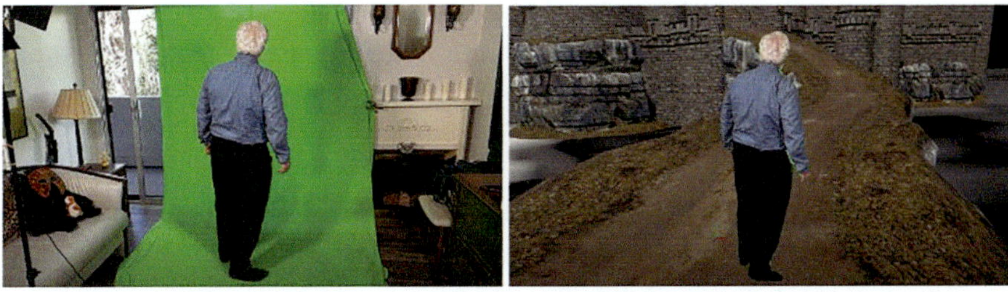

Figure 8.4 *The basic Jetset is so portable that users often set up and shoot with small green screens in their living space. The Lightcraft site also directs you to very effective green screen material and setups for small spaces.*

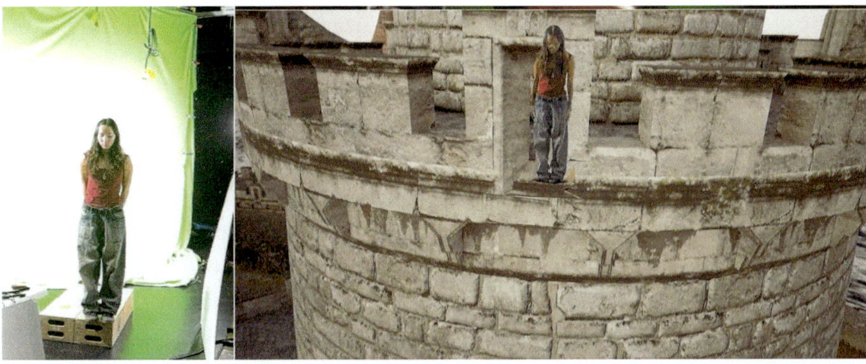

Figure 8.5 *An example of how AI mattes can fool you into forgetting to check what your camera is recording. In this case, auto exposure worked for the subject, but the green screen was tremendously overexposed. A good practice is to point the iPhone at your hand in front of the screen and lock the auto exposure at that point if the green and subject are balanced. Always include the subject for exposure determination, not the screen alone. Student Bela Bandol appears on the brink of a precipice but is merely standing on a green floor. The camera can tilt down into the abyss and tilt up to the sky while Bela remains locked to the stone edge. The composite was achieved but at a tremendous loss in quality due to the overexposed green screen.*

Troubleshooting

If you have issues with a shot such as bad tracking, Auto Shot has a facility to zip a take that includes all the data in a form that can be easily diagnosed by Lightcraft to deduce what the problem is and come up with a fix (https://lightcraft.pro/docs/exporting-takes-for-debugging/).

Troubleshooting Case Study

I did a ghost shot using the Charter House asset in Jetset's sample library. It is important to note that the Charter House is not a mapped Unreal environment but only a collection of object set pieces. Unlike our first fantasy castle test, we could not go back to Unreal and rerender the model as the Charter House did not have a map. As a result, we had to use the previz model that existed in the iPhone and upgrade to Jetset Pro to enable the separate rendering of green screen, in camera composite and environment.

In my ghost test shot, I was able to obtain a good track and previz composite. When we downloaded the take, I found that the green screen element was a much wider focal length and didn't match the size of the in-camera composite. To resolve this situation, I placed the downloaded in-camera composite that worked as a top layer in After Effects and made it slightly transparent so I could see the wider focal length green screen element underneath. I then just scaled up the green screen element to exactly match the image size of the in-camera composite. The most sure-fire way to match size is to turn one of the elements negative temporarily. When a positive and a negative image are placed one atop the other, you obtain an exact match when the image of the performer becomes a silhouette with no details due to the cancellation. It is important to note that you should only use scale to match the elements; any XY transform will throw off the tracking. The iPhone has three lenses that combine to create high-resolution images. Jetset just makes use of one lens and crops in to simulate a tighter focal length. Scaling in post will mimic this original crop. As of this writing, this issue was on schedule to be addressed in a future update. Even after scaling, I noticed the tracking did not match the tracking in the iPhone

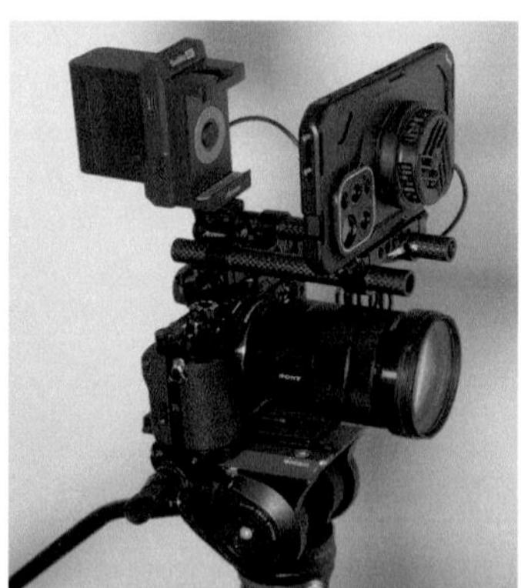

Figure 8.6 *By using a caged camera and iPhone, extension rods can be added to place the iPhone's middle lens (used for tracking) close to alignment with the front of the cine taking lens to lessen parallax shift. In practice, both cameras are pointed at a patterned target on the floor for a few angles. The system then identifies matching markers seen by both cameras and uses that match to align the tracking-data lens to the live-action lens to lock in the track.*

composite, and yet the background was the same size. I deduced that it was a sync issue. If one suspects a sync problem, another technique to match imagery is to check edge geometry. In this case, I drew a mask around the window panes in the comp element previz to reveal the clean background below and discovered the panes did not align. Simply sliding the clean background element quickly revealed the proper sync frame when the planes aligned.

Jetset Cine

The Cine version of Jetset uses the iPhone for tracking data and preview only while the linked high-resolution live-action camera records the green screen element to obtain cinema-quality composites. The process that follows makes use of Blender software and is derived from one of Lightcraft's many excellent step by step tutorials on their site.

Create a Virtual Set in Blender

Set building is a skill that has gotten simpler and faster using free models or kits or model bashing (mixing and matching of parts) instead of building from scratch. There are a variety of kit suppliers. Likewise, there are a variety of marketplaces for Blender and Unreal Engine. Using kits or marketplace resources requires knowledge of and comfort with your 3D software.

Create Scene Locators in Blender

Scene locators are empty or null objects in Blender renamed to sceneloc_* so Jetset Cine can move the iPhone camera position to that point within the virtual set.

In this way, you can have many camera positions within the virtual set that will become a shot list.

Build the Practical Set

Again, it is important to ensure that feet don't appear to slide against the virtual floor. Consider building a practical floor that will be composited into the virtual background. This is where LiDAR scans become handy in helping match the real floor to the virtual floor in the 3D and compositing software. Also, consider adding tracking points to the green screen set floor as an additional aid for compositing. If feet are shown on a real floor, they will have proper

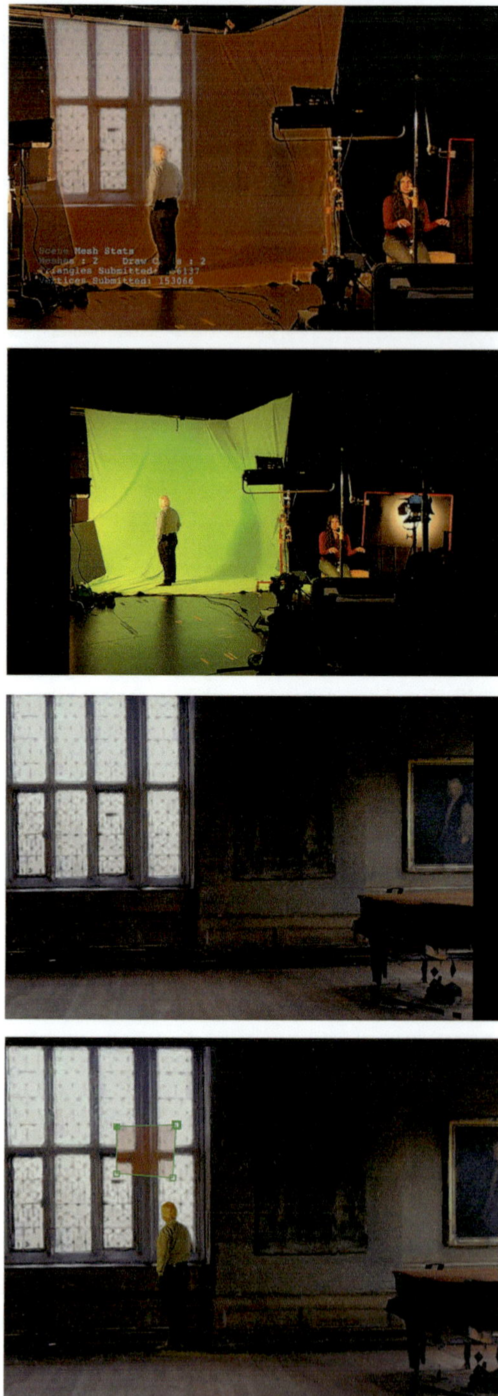

Figure 8.7 *The iPhone tracks and records video using the wide focal length on the iPhone at default 30 fps. The in-camera composite crops the image to the desired look, but the green screen recording must be scaled to match the crop in After Effects. To resolve a sync issue, a window is made in the composite image around high-contrast architecture like the window panes. One can easily see that the panes don't align, but on the proper frame, they will and establish sync. Note that the ghost was shot against black for ease of compositing the transparent apparition.*

shadows with no sliding. If tracking errors do occur, they will appear at the join between the real floor and the CG environment and hopefully become less noticeable.

Hardware

The system makes use of professional cine cameras housed in cages that can be used to mount ancillary devices that enable the tracking and recording of data. A Blackmagic Pocket Cine camera can be used to shoot the live action and will need the following components attached to it:

- An iPhone 15 Pro Max (contains the LiDAR for tracking)
- Blackmagic Pocket Cine Camera
- SeeMo Pro 4K (monitor and recording adaptor for iOS devices)
- A cooler for the iPhone powered by the SeeMo
- Tentacle Sync (delivers timecode to devices Jetset Cine can connect through Bluetooth wireless)
- External hard drive via USB type C (to record longer takes of BRAW camera files)

Tracking and Slate

The real-time camera tracking feed links directly to the Unreal Live Link FreeD plug-in for accurate live camera data. Therefore, an on-set laptop is required to run the 3D software (Unreal or Blender), Lightcraft Autoshot (the file management and conversion component of Jetset), and the digital slate for syncing and matching corresponding shot metadata and tracking info. The digital slate requires a Chrome or Safari browser.

Cinema Camera Output

Autoshot automates EXR frame output from the cinema camera originals. Also included are the most recent codecs, including Blackmagic BRAW, ProRes 4444, XQ 12-bit, and other log formats.

The color space conversions are processed to generate ACES EXR files, in either DWAA or zip compression to save space.

Loading the 3D Virtual Set Into Jetset Cine

Export the 3D model and scene locators from Blender or Unreal using the universal scene descriptor (USD) format. Optimize the geometry and textures for quick previewing on the iPhone to stay within the CPU limits. If in doubt, export without textures. The preview is used mainly for shot blocking, so surface details are less important at this stage. The virtual set will be rendered with final details and lighting before final composite. Jetset has a built-in green screen keyer so you can slide between the foreground and background and see the mixture of the two. The keyer includes garbage matting. Again, the live composite is for preview purposes only.

Scan

Both iPhone Pro and iPad Pro have iOS LiDAR scanning capability, which automatically aligns with the tracking data.

Shoot

After blocking, continue to record the shots. The digital slate will give a unique shot name to each take.

Autoshot, 3D Render, and Compositing

The final textured and lit virtual scene is rendered in the 3D application (Blender or Unreal).

Compositing can be performed in Nuke or Blender. Autoshot can output a Nuke node tree, including the 3D LiDAR scan data in the Nuke 3D nodes.

The EXR frames are included in the correct color space.

Nuke can handle high-resolution EXR files, OpenColorIO (OCIO) color, Z depth data, normal linking, and linking between 3D scene information and 2D elements with fast GPU processing. Autoshot will also output a Blender node tree for compositing in Blender.

Blender 3.5 supports GPU processing for compositing and is designed for real-time interaction. There are also plans for a next-generation real-time render engine for Blender called EEVEE-Next. It is designed for interactive and cinematic projects to produce a higher-quality render for unlimited lights, ray tracing, motion blur, depth of field, global illumination, and faster performance.

The Result

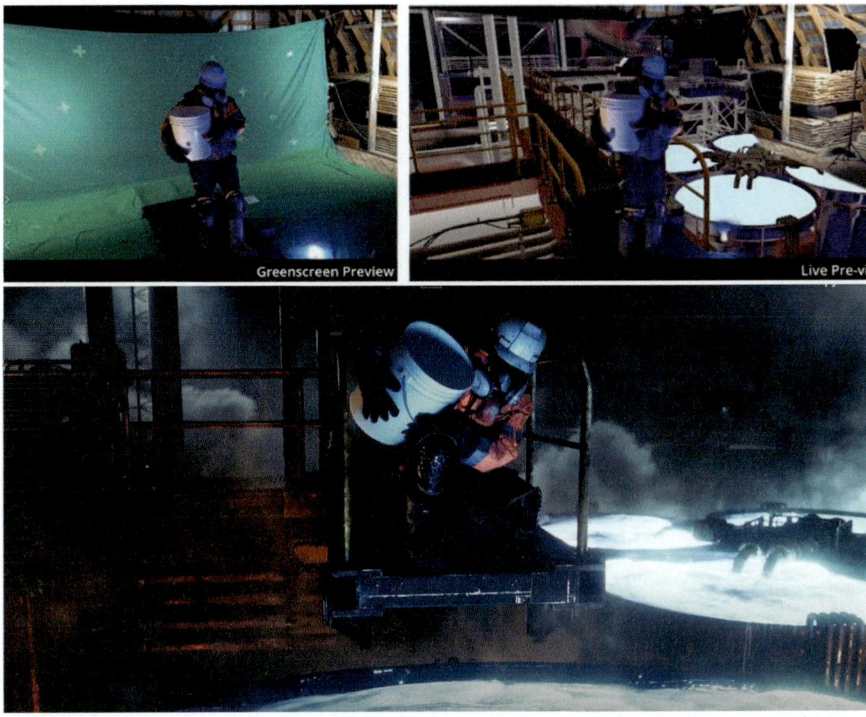

Figure 8.8 *The top view shows the raw live action element next to the previz comp using downsized backgrounds. The bottom shows the final cinema-quality composite with all the bells and whistles post can provide. The character is kneeling on a real grate for added realism.*

Source: Images courtesy of Eliot Mack Lightcraft.com

Summary

Students and independents can benefit from prosumer applications like Jetset that allow previewing composites of live-action actors with virtual backgrounds using markerless camera tracking.

This application stands out for its ability to seamlessly integrate 3D USD files from popular software like Blender, Unreal, and Maya. It lets users drop in 2D or 360 panoramic stills or videos and play back fully animated 3D scenes and characters.

Jetset is primarily used for previewing rather than creating live final composites. Its real-time capabilities allow filmmakers to visualize how live-action footage will integrate with virtual environments during the shoot. This helps make immediate adjustments and ensure that the final composition will look as intended.

While original camera output is possible using the iPhone, image quality and application performance will suffer due to the iPhone's lower resolution and bit-depth output (1920x1080 mp4) and processing speed. To maintain processing speed while previewing, input data needs to be optimized.

While Jetset can provide a real-time preview, the final compositing and rendering are typically done in post-production using high resolution cine camera files and fully rendered environments. This workflow ensures that the final product meets the highest visual quality standards.

The application also excels in capturing and managing production data. It automatically records camera-original video, real-time previz composites, depth maps, and complete camera tracking metadata. The integrated digital slate ensures that every take is meticulously tracked, streamlining the production process.

Jetset's Autoshot system makes post-production easier. It handles data sync and frame extraction, building integrated 2D and 3D shots in tools like Blender, Unreal, and After Effects. This automation allows filmmakers to focus more on creativity and less on technical details. It is also a file format converter and scripting tool.

One of Jetset's most impressive features is its scene locators, which anchor specific parts of a live-action scene to points in a virtual environment. This ensures that the relationship between live-action and virtual elements is maintained throughout tracking and compositing. The integrated, marker-free tracking system supports a variety of shooting styles, from handheld and stabilized shots to dolly moves and crane extensions.

Jetset's keying capabilities are top notch, offering real-time image fusion, blue and green screen keying, AI keying, and automatic depth compositing. This makes it incredibly easy to blend live-action footage with virtual backgrounds for previewing. Faster and more accurate previewing can reduce certain aspects of post-production work.

Jetset offers various subscription tiers, including a free version, a subscription Jetset Pro version with additional features like 4K recording and remote monitoring, and a subscription Jetset Cine version with professional features like cine lens calibration and RAW camera take processing. This makes it accessible to many users, from indie filmmakers to professional studios.

Jetset Cine, the professional tier of Lightcraft's Jetset application, offers several advanced features to support production cameras, enhancing the virtual production workflow. These features include:

- Cine lens calibration to match the virtual camera setting to the production camera.
- RAW camera take processing to allow for higher quality and more flexible post-production work. This ensures that the footage retains maximum detail and dynamic range, which is crucial for high-end productions.
- 4K recording high-resolution footage for professional standards.
- Remote monitoring for the camera feed.

Jetset Cine is a powerful addition to any filmmaker's toolkit, providing the necessary support to integrate production cameras seamlessly into the virtual production pipeline.

Chapter 9

Fuzzy Door Tech – ViewScreen Scout and Studio

Augmented Reality – Beyond Pokémon GO

Augmented Reality

Augmented reality (AR) inserts virtual characters or objects into the real world. It is commonly thought of as more of a gaming, industrial, medical, retail, user experience and design (UX), or education-related toolset. Key developments range from 2000 to 2016 in the form of a mobile AR game, ARQuake; Adobe Flash ARToolkit to design AR applications; Google Glass; Microsoft's HoloLens, and the mainstream adoption of the Pokémon GO game for cellular phones.

Interaction

Up to this point, we have covered how virtual production and the democratization of technology have influenced the way live-action actors are composited into virtual environments, but what about when live actors and partial live sets have to interact and match CG characters and environments? What if the CG characters in this type of scenario wear motion capture suits, are not the same scale as other actors, and have to interact with regularly scaled actors in the same shot? There must be a way to previsualize in real time on the set while blocking shots and creating camera moves. You might think this type of need does not come up very often. Still, franchise sci-fi and fantasy

DOI: 10.4324/9781003473169-9

movies and shows like *Lord of the Rings*, *Planet of the Apes*, *Avatar*, *Jurassic Park*, *Star Wars*, *Alita: Battle Angel*, the Marvel Universe, etc. have this type of need regularly.

However, the equipment for CG live integration with the real world has been prohibitively expensive for independents. Motion-capture body and head rigs, previsualization camera rigs, eyeline markers, stand-in life-size props and set pieces, and real-time depth compositing can all be costly. But what if the democratization of technology allowed the previsualization of CG characters or props on an iPhone or iPad? What if motion capture for body and face did not require markers or suits?

The iPhone Evolution

The authors attended Cine Gear 24 on the backlot of Warner Brothers Studios to get a sense of how things were developing. We had the pleasure of meeting Brandon Fayette, chief product officer and co-founder of Fuzzy Door Tech, developer of the ViewScreen suite of production visualization (ProViz) tools. Brandon has a long history in VFX and was also the visual effects supervisor for the television show *The Orville*, created by Seth MacFarlane.

Mark was surprised that the company chose to demonstrate their product at an outdoor booth in the bright sun, thinking they were late to exhibit. Such was not the case, as Brandon wanted to prove this robust system in the very harsh conditions and heat of the bright sun. It functioned flawlessly. ViewScreen was developed by a visual effects supervisor with input from other visual effects supervisors who understand VFX and the need for speed and simplicity in the creative process. We couldn't agree more with that philosophy.

Fuzzy Door Tech's ViewScreen is a suite of production visualization (ProVis) tools consisting of ViewScreen Scout and ViewScreen Studio to enable filmmakers to see CG characters, props, vehicles, and sets composited within a live-action set or location in real time. ViewScreen Scout and ViewScreen Scout Pro can be used for previz. ViewScreen is a set of augmented reality visualization tools that integrate CG and live action in real time. Scout allows virtual walk-throughs for sets, blocking movement, and visualizing lighting before filming begins. Digital characters can be animated with a joystick via motion capture. It allows collaborative work so a cinematographer can block shots and rehearse camera movements while a director of photography can adjust the location lighting. Assets can be composited into the camera operator's eyepiece for precise action framing.

ViewScreen Scout and Scout Pro

ViewScreen Scout, designed for individual users, is a real-time scouting app for the iPhone and iPad that records digital assets on location or a soundstage and runs on iOS devices such as iPhone 13 Pro/Pro Max and higher or any iPad Pro M1 and higher. ViewScreen Scout Pro, which integrates with Studio and is also sold separately, is a multi-user scouting app with additional features such as shared AR rooms, ideal for collaborating while on full-scale productions. Both scouting apps let you visualize characters, environments, and props on set or location. Studio runs on macOS (Sonoma) and Windows 11 and can be used with any cinema camera. ViewScreen Scout Pro was developed for the TV series *The Orville*, and ViewScreen Studio was used on the TV series *Ted*.

ViewScreen Studio

ViewScreen Studio integrates Scout Pro and includes body and facial tracking recording. LiDAR information and occlusion settings allow the digital assets to interact with the surroundings and other actors. The data positions are streamed from an iPhone mounted on a cinema camera and sent to the compositor on a laptop. Motion is markerless and suitless. The exporter collects and compiles frames, metadata, depth data, and other data from a compositor to deliver camera files at the end of the day. The digital assets are rendered with full textures and lighting in your 3D application and traditionally composited in post. Studio supports multiple cameras synced to timecode.

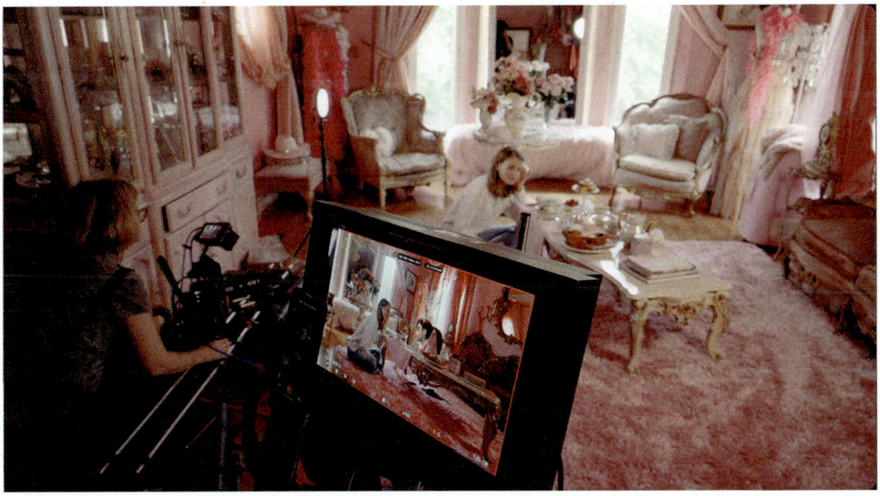

Figure 9.1 *The live camera shoots the clean plate, while ViewScreen composites the character on top of the live feed. The live composite is shown in the camera viewfinder and all other synchronized devices.*

Source: Image courtesy of Fuzzy Door Tech

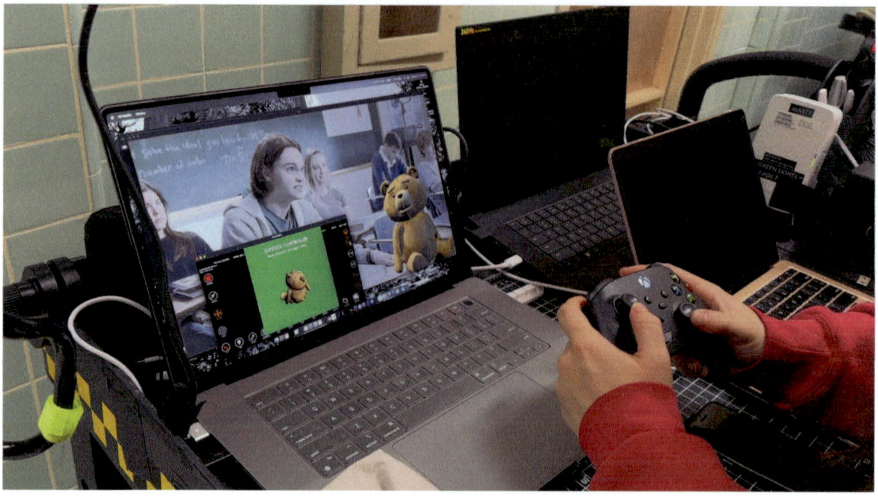

Figure 9.2 *The digital Ted can be manipulated with a game controller.*
Source: Image courtesy of Fuzzy Door Tech

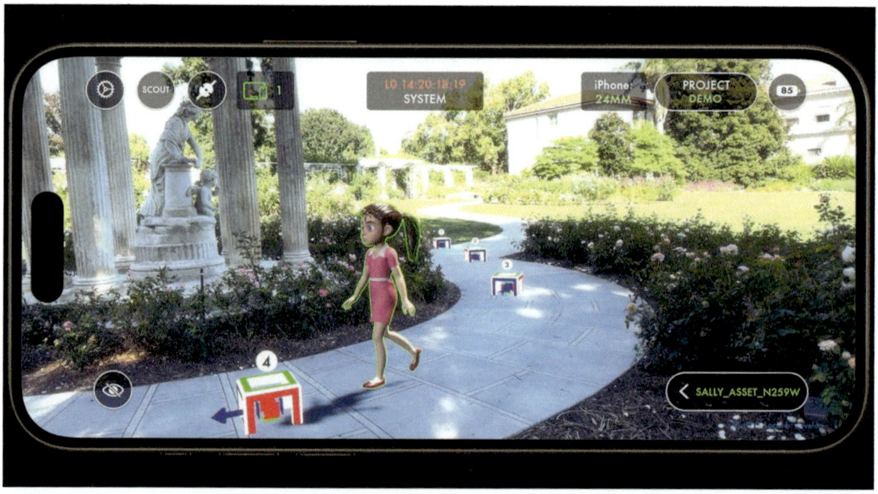

Figure 9.3 *Waypoints can play and direct prerecorded performances such as a walk cycle.*
Source: Image courtesy of Fuzzy Door Tech

Mapping Technology

ViewScreen utilizes seven mapping technologies to create a world version in unity. The LiDAR data supplies information for the geometry and shadow creation. Inertial sensors provide data as well. The data is blended to create the world version of the stage and characters.

Unity renders using its high-definition rendering pipeline (HDRP) format to enable realistic real-time rendering. HDRP uses methods like physically based lighting, linear lighting, and high-dynamic range (HDR) lighting to create realistic imagery.

Timecode Synchronization

The iPhones and cameras are linked with one master timecode. All the different data generators will have different frame-per-second rates. A laptop rendering CG might be running at 350 frames per second, and an Xsens motion capture suit may send 200 frames per second of data. As long as all the devices send out data at a rate faster than the live-action camera at 23.96 fps, the timecode synchronization will lock and hold steady.

Blending Live Capture and Prerecorded Animation

Traditional puppet animation had the advantage of real-time performance interaction that could accommodate improvisation and the speed of creativity from live performance. Digital processes that, by necessity, were executed in post were challenged to capture that real-time magic. ViewScreen blends both methods seamlessly to obtain intimate real-time presentation in the case of motion capture suits used to manipulate characters of different proportions, such as the teddy bear character Ted; hardware and software such as Xsens had tools that could scale the data so a human-size arm could manipulate a Ted-size arm accurately.

One challenge comes with walking. Seth MacFarlane is much taller than Ted's character and covers a much larger area than Ted's legs would move the figure when scaled. To accomplish a match, the CG figure is split into two sections. In the top, the arms and head are motion captured while the bottom is a prerecorded walk whose number of steps will work appropriately from position one to position two. A widespread tool for puppeteering is a game controller. With a few finger manipulations, the head can turn on a dime and look at the person the character is conversing with while the facial capture makes the puppet speak. It's a lovely blending of tools that preserves the actors' and puppeteers' performances and nuance.

Compositing is done quickly for the puppet and its built-in alpha signal, and for live figures that appear behind the puppet, the layering is derived from depth maps generated by the LiDAR function. For human figures that appear in front of the puppet, the depth map and AI trained in human segmentation will draw an effective rotoscope mask in front of the puppet to reveal the human. ViewScreen is primarily designed as an excellent ProVis suite of tools used for pre-viz and production viz. The rotoscope masks are typically cleaned up and refined in post for final delivery.

ViewScreen Scout is truly accessible for independents and students. All the nuance of spontaneous performance can be captured simultaneously between actors, transforming one or more into believable fantasy characters interacting with their human cohorts. The future is quite exciting indeed. ViewScreen Scout is currently in public beta but should be available in the App Store when you read this (https://viewscreen.com/).

Chapter 10

How Did We Get Here?

Independents, Franchises, and Networks: The Development and Proliferation of Venues and Technology

One-Way Transmission – The First Mass Communication

Since the entertainment industry dominates most virtual production technology usage, this book is centered on that industry and its trends, even though other industrial usage exists. Movies, television, video games, live events, and broadcasting have been the main drivers of virtual production technology development; therefore, we will examine these purposes.

> **Mass communication** is the process of sharing information with a large audience. Mass communication is accomplished via mass media – that is, technology capable of sending messages to great numbers of people, many of whom are unknown to the sender (e.g., print, radio, television) (https://www.britannica.com/topic/mass-communication).

Virtual production is built on, if not borrowed from, all the media that preceded it: writing, publishing, radio, and television. This is hardly a history chapter, but as a summary of a concept still in development, some overview of historical milestones, to the limited extent that an active development can be traced, are in order to illuminate the flow of milestones that influences

DOI: 10.4324/9781003473169-10

today's virtual production technology and means of distribution. Although it may appear that today's smorgasbord of media and technology options is just a derangement of unrelated techno-lust and runaway startups, there is a direction and one that has a history. Therefore, perhaps this overview can serve as a compass to consult for context and practical placement to this new realm called "virtual production." As a means of mass communication, virtual production serves many of the tenets addressed by its predecessors.

To be thorough, the invention of the printing press in the 15th century is really the beginning of mass communication. It was followed by the tremendous transformation that took place with the arrival of radio and television in the 20th century.

Networks, Stations, Channels, Advertising, Programming, Subscriptions, and Metrics

Media landscape involves information distribution and contains elements that have a role in managing and measuring how information is accessed and consumed by viewers or users across platforms. The elements include, but are not limited to, networks, stations, channels, advertising, programming, subscriptions, and metrics.

Centre for Media Transition. (2018). *The Impact of Digital Platforms on News and Journalistic Content* (ACCC commissioned report). Australian Competition and Consumer Commission. https://www.accc.gov.au/system/files/ACCC+commissioned+report+-+The+impact+of+digital+platforms+on+news+and+journalistic+content,+Centre+for+Media+Transition+(2).pdf

Radio

After printing, the next form of mass communication was radio (~1900s), which had the ability to reach people faster and could be consumed more easily than print. *Consumption* is the word to use because radio also marked the beginning of marketing and advertising, which built our present-day mass-consumption era. Airwave broadcasting required transmitters and local radio stations, which needed oversight and organization by a conglomerate of national networks. Content like news, entertainment, commercial programming, and advertisements produced by national radio networks organized and controlled the local channels. Affiliate local stations took orders from the networks and blended national content with their own local content.

Network – a group of interconnected stations or platforms distributing across a large area.

National networks (e.g., NBC, CBS) had scheduling techniques so that people living in every time zone could listen to the same thing at approximately the same time. (This introduces the distinction between recorded and live on-air broadcasts). Common content joined the nation in shared experiences that became history, like listening to Franklin D. Roosevelt's fireside chats or other recorded headline news or sensational sporting events.

While broadcasts could be recorded, those recordings were not immediately available to the public for various reasons. Radio transmission was one-way passive listening without any means to respond or interact (unless listeners called in via telephone). At the national level, network executives designed and controlled content and scheduling to gain the largest audience because the cost of production and broadcasting was supported by advertising and marketing dollars. In this way, airwave communication is free to the public.

Station – an individual broadcasting point in a specific region within a network.

Television

Similarly to radio, when television was launched in the 1950s, some networks were already established, and new networks would follow. In the US, the big three (CBS, NBC, and ABC) dominated. As the number of television sets multiplied when they became more affordable, viewership escalated, and the floodgate was opened for the creation of more and diverse content based on niches like programming for housewives or children, cooking shows, recreation, etc. Additionally, the typical genres like news, dramas, variety shows, and live events might be tailored for different age groups or demographics.

The added profiling of demographics needed a way to measure viewership to satisfy marketing and advertising sponsors. Metrics were developed to track potential buyers to satisfy the sponsors. Connecting programs with corresponding ads connected to audience profile became a science. Again, like radio, paid sponsorship made free viewing possible.

Television is still a one-way communication medium. Viewers watch but usually have no direct communication with the broadcasters unless they mail a letter or call.

Channel Expansion – Genres

> **Channel** – a "lane" within a network or platform that delivers content.

Drilling down to define ever-more-detailed profiles of specific audiences, channels increased to reflect these niche groups. Cable TV networks appeared and offered their dedicated content to the public in the 1970s and '80s, for a fee. Examples of channel genres are sports (ESPN), news (CNN), music (MTV), and ethnic and cultural channels. Why would people pay for television when it had been free for so long? Identity and belonging – national identity was, and still is, shifting and fueled by mass media and a cornucopia of options and opinions. Cable TV exists with free TV and a subscription service, which, as a business model, can be more profitable than sponsorship if it is paid monthly, has millions of subscribers, and lasts for years. Producers compete for audience subscribers, and more channels are invented.

Programming – From General to Niche

> **Programming** – the content that is broadcast or streamed on a network or channel. Includes shows, movies, and other media.

In the rush to make money with channel subscribers, metrics loom large. Remember, this is an era without algorithms, but early research may have been an influence. Nielsen Media Research dominated corporate statistical evidence gathering used for program creation, revenue options, and, eventually, subscriber targeting. Evidence dictated timelines as networks and channels planned their shows to air in affinity with their target audience's viewing times, with prime time (evenings) being the most desirable time slot the highest viewership.

Audiences are monitored with set-top boxes that report shows watched and could include ratings, percentages of people in a specific demographic, shares/percentages of total audience watching, etc.

Content Creation and Regulation

The late 20th century is a blooming of new content creation, and this is good for creatives. Writers, actors, musicians, independent producers, movie makers, video and media makers pitch networks, affiliates, channels, and startups to invest in their shows or ideas. Without the control of the big networks, content creation is a Pandora's box of unprecedented opportunity – most of it low budget.

On the big-budget side, costly technology and broadcast airtime are still the realm of the large networks. If anything is broadcast on TV, it must adhere to industry regulation from the US Federal Communications Commission (FCC). The FCC set rules that began with radio broadcasting to ensure that content served the public interest and adhered to specific technical and content standards. In 1949, the FCC fairness doctrine mandated balanced reportage of controversial issues and included granting equal airtime for opposing political candidates who were slandered or libeled. However, since cable and satellite networks did not use the public airwaves, they did not follow the fairness doctrine. The fairness doctrine was also contested on the grounds that it was a violation of free speech (ultimately leading to an abuse of free speech by removing fact checks and balanced reporting). In 1987, the FCC repealed the fairness doctrine while keeping some parts in place until all parts were repealed in 2011.[1]

We exist on a slippery slope regarding censorship, inappropriate material (including pornography and publicized crimes and atrocities), propaganda, polarization, and complications involving freedom of speech. While there were ownership limits that prevented monopolies in the 20th century, regulation of this started to slip in media and telecommunications. This history of radio and television illustrates how we entered a period of risk (to society) and opportunity (for entrepreneurs and special interests), and whoever controls mass communication shapes society (and, by association, politics). This period also exemplifies a reciprocal relationship between commerce, society, politics, and technology. Is it any wonder, then, that technological tools like virtual production and generative AI have a world influence beyond entertainment that envelops the unprecedented means for not just mass communication but mass manipulation?

THE DIGITAL AGE

Two-Way Transmission – The Second Mass Communication

It needs to be mentioned that although the telephone and two-way radio transmission were the first two-way transmission devices, unless the conversations were broadcast, they were not a mass communication distribution system, and broadcasting technologies such as radio and television were still one-way transmissions. The internet is a means of two-way communication that combines telephonic broadcasting with audio and visual immediacy. Developed in the late 1960s by the US military, the prototype of the internet – a system called ARPANET – was invented by the US Department of Defense Advanced Research Projects Agency (ARPA) as a means of communication for military defense in the event of a Soviet attack during the Cold War.

A network that could withstand disruptions, allowing government and military leaders to communicate even if generators were destroyed, was a wartime utility. Later, scientists, researchers, and academic institutions would use it – first at ARPA and then at DARPA – to share discoveries and data, building the foundational infrastructure for the internet we know today.

The World-Wide Web (WWW) was invented by Sir Timothy John Berners-Lee in 1989 at CERN (*Conseil Européen pour la Recherche Nucléaire*, which is French for the European Council for Nuclear Research). Its original purpose was to share information between worldwide academic and scientific institutions.

Alshukri, A. "Website Boundary Detection via Machine Learning." https://doi.org/10.17638/00009453.

Palash, S. M. I. (2021). *Public Diplomacy in Social Media: An Examination of Twitter Use by Foreign Embassies in the US*. https://core.ac.uk/download/475205705.pdf.

Yet another phase of transformation was ushered in by digital technology in the late 20th and early 21st centuries. Streaming services such as Netflix, Hulu, and Amazon Prime Video, disrupted broadcasting by providing on-demand content for viewers to watch what they want as well as when they want, thus offering the possibility to personalize media consumption.

The internet amalgamated the distribution of communication, aggregating networks, stations, channels, advertising, programming, subscription, and consumption from TVs, "smart" TVs, connected TVs (e.g., Amazon Stick), computers, tablets, and cell phones into a digital media ecosystem.

Digital Media Ecosystem (DME) or Digital Marketing Ecosystem

(Note the combination of technology and commerce because this is primarily about marketing and sales.)

A DME is like a business ecosystem but different because it relies on a centralized database with data flow enabled through cloud-based software as a service (SaaS) applications and application programming interfaces (APIs) that allow integration and crosstalk between systems using common platform types like

1. Enterprise resource planning (ERP) – a system for business organization (e.g., accounting, inventory, sales, distribution, etc.).
2. Customer relationship management (CRM) – a system to manage customers, leads, prospects, etc.
3. Content management system (CMS) – a system where users can post content or otherwise freely give marketing tracking information (e.g., blogs, websites, forums, social media, etc.)

DMEs can use enhanced data flow using automated customer tracking with radio frequency identification (RFID) or other means (e.g., fitness bands and smartwatches), devices, AI, and big-data analytics for real-time metrics.

All businesses have some form of DME for customer convenience, data gathering, and marketing and strategizing.

(2024, October). "Everything You Need to Know About Digital Ecosystems." https://www.imd.org/blog/digital-transformation/digital-ecosystems/.

Networks and Stations

Old-style networks that depended entirely on over-the-air broadcasts increased delivery channels via online content and applications by streaming live network broadcasts and providing on-demand programming. Most local network affiliates also streamed their programming via the web, so a wide range of local content – news broadcasts, local concerts, and events – was available from anywhere.

Channels

Even cable channels are turning to the internet with their streaming services such as ESPN+, CNN Go, and HBO Max; subscribers can watch live TV and on-demand content without the need for a cable subscription, but the downside is that now you have to subscribe to each individual channel at a cost. Channels and applications (mini-channels) and platforms and services and so on, are endless because almost anything can be monetized on the internet. For individuals, monetization also allows aspiring entrepreneurs to create income streams or side hustles charging for services or viewership through internet-connected devices like smart TVs, smartphones, and tablets.

Programming

The endless programming on internet-based streaming platforms is consumed as well. Netflix, Hulu, and Amazon Prime Video originally offered only some TV-series programming licensed from studios in the US and abroad, but they introduced original series produced in-house (for example, Netflix's *House of Cards*, Hulu's *Difficult People*, and Amazon's *Transparent*). Thanks to media consumption, users can binge-watch and customize their viewing experiences at home, as well as drawing on their social networks.

Streaming – Real-Time Interaction

Of course, early television and radio used streaming technology over airwaves, so the concept is not new. But the internet's increasing speed and bandwidth enabled real-time interaction in ways that radio and television never could. What changed was that companies like RealAudio in 1995 started offering the public on-demand music. In the late 1990s, Massively multiplayer online (MMO) games like *EverQuest* let thousands of players interact in real time within virtual worlds. *World of Warcraft* (WoW) games went live on streaming media in 2004. In 2007, Netflix provided on-demand video, and gaming features got serious on Twitch online streaming in 2011.

Niche audience engagement is now possible for anyone using dedicated live streaming services (e.g., Twitch and YouTube Live) that enable real-time broadcasting right from your own computer with essentially no barriers to entry: one person can become a broadcasting network if desired. This worked great for e-sports (electronic sports) and other forms of competitive gaming, including audience commentary, instant replay, and multi-camera setups. Streaming services might be employed in conjunction with any public gathering or event, from community happenings to charity fundraisers. Video communication tools such as Skype and Zoom allow for video chat across continents.

Streaming can be live or prerecorded programs. Some live-TV streaming services (such as YouTube TV, Hulu +, Live TV, and Sling TV) fill the gap between cable and internet streaming. Live streaming services use the internet to transmit cable and network shows live, emulating the cable TV experience without the need to have a physical cable.

This can be achieved with a wired or wireless protocol. Wireless (Wi-Fi) uses radio waves to interface with the internet for information transfer without physical wires. However, it is still wired (through a DSL, cable, or fiber internet connection) as it requires a router to manage the data flow. Streaming can be implemented with Wi-Fi (if in range of a transmitter), without Wi-Fi (if out of range of a transmitter that uses mobile/cell networks), or hybrid (switching between the two). Wireless mobile networks can be unreliable. However, there are professional-grade systems such as Teradek that are available to capture high-resolution real-time video with low latency and wireless transfer.

Of course, streaming with smartphones now is the preferred way to watch events and share online broadcasting; iPhones are the preferred mobile devices for streaming as long as you can compensate for the battery life. Entertainment purposes aside, social events like weddings, graduations, christenings, funerals, memorials, and a variety of church services have increased the use of mobile devices to eliminate travel and secure social distancing. EventLive is an example of an online application that ensures privacy and advertisement-free streaming without downloading or registration. Recorded playbacks are also available at any time. If image quality or screen size is an issue, phone streams can be cast to a television using Chromecast, which turns the television into a monitor.

Incidentally, the increased use of augmented reality, 3D models of photos or videos, digital mementos, and streaming technology is revolutionizing the funeral industry, resulting in less need for embalming and the manufacture of caskets, which are practices devoted to in-person viewings. This trend is only mentioned here as an example of how virtual production technology is redefining the practices of many crucial industries beyond general public awareness.

Taken together, what all these streaming options mean is that professional broadcasting tools now have wireless video transmission counterparts that make creating, sharing, and broadcasting high-quality video from anywhere, for any purpose, to any audience more cost effective, more accessible, more portable, and easier to use than ever. Professional parity for the price of a plane ticket, from room to road to any location with sufficient battery power is achievable for most any genre; open this box, plug and play, and anyone can become a roving news crew for less money.

Interactive and Personalized Experiences

The internet has enabled more interactive and personalized viewing experiences. Algorithms on streaming platforms recommend content based on viewing history, and some services offer interactive features like choosing the storyline in shows and movies. Metrics are also contained in viewing history by services to market more accurately. Tablets, computers, laptops, and now smart TVs have seen an increase in the number of devices browsing and mobility in sending and receiving content and interaction.

Viewership and Audience

The integration of networks, stations, channels, advertising, programming, subscriptions, devices, and metrics into the fabric of the internet adds convenience, access, and individual control to the mix. Where once powerful networks held all the cards, today viewers around the world can watch anything, anywhere, at any time. For the virtual producers and independents, the process becomes like that of a network: it must be owned, planned and "monetized" in order to profit from programming.

More importantly, two-way communication has fast interactivity between parties and fueled fandom, especially for science fiction, fantasy, comics, and gaming groups, who found each other online and formed active communities sharing passion and knowledge.

Interactive platforms with email, forums, and chat rooms broke geographical barriers, thereby forming niche communities, including the burgeoning geek culture. People shared their ideas, photos, and videos with the world and got instant feedback. Social media platforms (e.g., Facebook, Twitter [X], and Instagram) transformed the internet into a bustling hub of social interaction, watch parties, and marketplaces. Think of social interaction as viewership, which is another word for an audience. Online activities can translate into income if audience size is increased and monetized through advertising, marketing, sales, or subscriptions.

Virtual Production Integration into Traditional Workflows – Movies and Broadcast Television

In the media landscape, as described here, there are commonalities between traditional television and the digital ecosystem on the internet. Both share elements in content delivery, organization, distribution, audience consumption, measurement, and metrics. For this reason, virtual production technologies may find compatible integration into digital media and broadcast workflows.

Movie making, on the other hand, does not have the immediacy of live broadcast found in the production processes required for television. Virtual production integration in movie production has been compatible as a previsualization tool instead of a mass communication tool.

Virtual production processes seldom output as a live final product in movie making due to the higher resolution of cinematic digital media combined with the complexity of CG VFX. Even if using an LED volume, there is usually some form of post-production manipulation before the final theatrical release. Consider that many blockbuster franchise movies are produced like animation (with less final photography on sets and locations and more CG elements and green screen sets with multiple layers requiring intensive post processes). Unreal renders may not satisfy the cinematic photography requirements of theatrical release on a large screen in real time without substantial calculation.

Examples of integrating real-time rendering into existing movie production pipelines include displaying virtual environments on an LED wall, mainly if supplied by a 3D creation software like Unreal Editor, or displaying virtual graphics on set when there are practical prop displays (like a flatscreen in a living room set). Virtual production techniques can also include live compositing, match moves, and motion capture for previsualization purposes. Virtual production integration into movie making is covered throughout this book; this chapter covers virtual production in regards to live broadcast.

Live virtual production processes in television production can be output straight to the public, either through direct broadcast or modified via live real-time AI manipulation as part of the broadcast process. (AI processes are covered later in this chapter.) Although image resolutions have reached 8K (the 2024 Paris Olympics featured 8K live streaming), for the reasons mentioned earlier, big-budget movies use an offline style of production using live processes for pre-visualization. Therefore, the remainder of this chapter will explore live virtual production integration using digital broadcasting in television studios and on the internet.

Zero Density (ZD) Reality Engine

Zero Density's Reality (software), EVO II (hardware), and Reality Hub (web-based control and automation), combined with the many possibilities of Unreal Editor, allow users to create impressive CG elements and combine them with the real world. This is done with a user-friendly interface and live compositing tools that control how the 3D scene from Unreal is combined with the real world.

The suite of tools within the Reality platform contains a customized Unreal Engine version tailored to virtual production needs. These changes mainly modify the Unreal Engine's post-processing pipeline to ensure it can give all the right data to Reality's node graph for live compositing purposes. This node graph takes care of tracking, lens distortion, keying, and the final composite while allowing users to build completely customized workflows for their studio.

The Reality Hub allows for control over any property from Reality, including the properties of Unreal objects and actors (e.g., Sequencer and Blueprint). This control means that UE graphics and animation can be preplanned before broadcast and run in real time during live broadcasting, but it still allows image or text changes required on the fly.

The preeminent US example of ZD's layout involving UE graphics and HDR footage is the Weather Channel. The Weather Channel uses a large green screen cyclorama set to facilitate live immersive mixed reality (IMR). Their setup is half augmented reality (UE-generated virtual studio set) and half physical green screen studio and fixed studio set with multiple cameras (including a Technocrane with a tracking system that grabs the presenter and then enters that data into a synchronized virtual camera). The two halves are separated by a virtual glass wall that moves to allow presenters to walk into a virtual location. In the physical half, virtual set extensions create more space beyond the green screen set and hide the ceiling and lights as necessary.

One type of studio effect involves a presenter standing on a silver disk inside photoreal footage of a live location that may or may not be augmented. The first example involves a presenter inside an augmented reality of a storm surge. The presenter stood on a disk as a simulated nine-foot wall of water rose around him. Another example was a forest fire with simulated fire tornados. The UE's Niagara VFX system mimics fire, tornados, rain, snow, and water effects.

Static virtual props (rocks, boulders, trees) integrate the live, photoreal location into the studio. The 100-foot monitor, 3D globe, and other graphical props are animated and populated with real-time charts, graphs, and satellite views through data feeds processed by Reality Hub.

The Zero Density system is a great example of a fully integrated virtual production pipeline into a live and real-time television studio broadcast on a daily schedule. ZD is also used throughout Europe, APAC, and MEA (https://www.youtube.com/watch?v=DVuDhJo3nGg).[2]

Expansion of Bubbles

The net converted one-way broadcasting to two-way dialogue and connected more people than radio or TV did by creating a world of "fast talking and fast fighting" that moved more rapidly than any conversational society. The net's two-way communication went significantly beyond email transmission; it converted the whole medium into one that instantly provided informational, intellectual, creative, and involuntary feedback from the world, without delays or contemplation: the free flow of stories, thoughts, opinions, snippets, curiosities, emotions, and know-how without caution, consideration, or restraint. People have taken control of the internet and their television, together with its networks, stations, channels, advertising, programming, subscriptions, and measurements by creating niches of interests and worldviews as a type of subconscious billboard. Interests and narrow worldviews can turn commonality into insularism; echo chambers and parochialism into the cliquishness of our social media bubbles; then from groups to cliques – cults of the identical, alienating all who are outside. What happens when our independent cliques or bubbles grow? We call these historical phenomena social movements.

'What', you may well ask, 'does social movement have to do with virtual production?' If virtual production is a tool of mass communication that serves national priorities such as domination, commerce, and wealth, then associate mass communication with the tall ships of the 17th century (precursors to industrialization), whose purpose was also national domination, commerce, and wealth. In this illustrative analogy, regard social movements as the wind pushing the metaphorical ships in directions unknown. In order to navigate such large ships towards a predetermined point, a keen awareness of climate conditions is crucial.

Impact on Society

Instantaneous two-way communication has a profound effect on society.

- **Empowerment**: Unchecked power. People's narratives and viewpoints become openly shared online and more privately shared among different groups in society. The number of voices in the public sphere increases with less censorship and, hence, more amplified voices with mixed agendas.
- **Echo chambers**: Social media bubbles exclude opposing or new information and encourage indoctrination. Greater community formation created media bubbles. More niches create more closed systems, division, and polarization (resulting in social or political manipulation). More niches also create greater community reach and revenue in networks, channels, advertising, programming, and subscriptions.
- **Sharing of information and data**: Information and propaganda. The internet has evolved into a huge collective knowledge database and a free source of information for anyone who has access to it. However, absence of regulation and censorship meant more and more extremist clusters, misinformation (error), and disinformation (propaganda).

- **Social movements:** Bubbles, niches, and commerce organizing and mobilizing online generate new methods of power for social movements and amplify calls for change. Bubbles and cliques represent fruitful advertising targets according to marketing methods. Thus, bubbles get social currency and credit.

GEEK CULTURE

SPINOFFS, REBOOTS, VENUES – INNOVATION IN BUSINESS MODELS, MARKETING, COMMUNICATIONS, AND TECHNOLOGY

Geek – a person who is knowledgeable about and obsessively interested in a particular subject, especially one that is technical or of specialist or niche interest (e.g., "a computer geek").

Cambridge Dictionary. (n.d.). Geek. Retrieved February 18, 2025, from https://dictionary.cambridge.org/us/dictionary/english/geek

Geek culture thrived online and began to influence mainstream media. Sony Pictures, persuaded by the power of fans and their creative energy, gave *The Amazing Spider-Man* (2012) over to the fanbase to reboot the franchise.[3]

Hollywood (*Transformers*) has also taken note of the "Hasbro effect," in which a fandom's influence on marketing generates big box office numbers, as shown by the success of fan-driven projects, culminating in a platform for limitless creativity at pop culture conventions such as Comic-Con.[4]

Geek culture is no longer marginal – it is now a behemoth in its own right, and it has an ever-evolving virtual production and marketing complex upon which independents can build a blueprint.

Business Model Evolution

Geek Culture's Influence on Virtual Production and Marketing for Indie Creators

Geek culture conventions have the most public visibility and are events where indie creators get exposure, network, build larger communities, market, promote fandom, and are marketed to by entertainment and commercial producers. As large as these conventions can be, for individuals and indie creators, the events are costly and restricted by geography. When events moved online, the need for travel and expensive booth setup was eliminated. Access was democratized, allowing more individuals and indie creators to participate and grow an even more extensive base. Artists and makers could gain exposure to the entire world, reaching an audience of fans and followers way beyond the capacity of physical events.

Live streaming of panels, virtual meet and greets, and QA sessions, as well as finding more fans, were ways in which engagement methods on the online platforms got better. Indie game designers, musicians, and filmmakers are among the many creatives in the indie space. The advent of virtual conventions during the COVID-19 pandemic allowed indie creators to carry on circulating their work and connecting with their public without a physical space to meet in. Audiences sought out digital avenues of production and marketing for the indie creator community to generate revenue.

Expansion of Virtual Production Venues

In progressing from tabletop games to digital media and live events, from an outlier to a mainstream middleman between entertainment and technology, geek culture learned important lessons from tabletop role-playing games: good games begin with engagement, intensive collaboration, narrative, strategy, and world-building. While fantasy and science fiction gaming involves everything from warfare to dungeon crawling. The most popular and enduring games, such as *Dungeons & Dragons* (*D&D*, 1974, a role-playing game) and *Marvel: Champions* (2019, a team-based cooperative card game), not only epitomize geek culture but also continue to evolve in tabletop and digital versions internationally, with current player numbers estimated at around 50 million with a reported value in the billions. Tabletop design also reinforced a similar lesson from group gaming: digital video games, originating with *Adventure* (1975), *Zork* (1977), coming of age with *The Legend of Zelda* (1986), and *Final Fantasy* (1987), became cornerstone genres of the geek microculture because of the collaborative and story-driven experiences fundamental to tabletop games. As desirable franchises with existing fan bases (franchises will be discussed in depth later), both *Legend of Zelda* and *Final Fantasy*, with cumulative sales in the billions, produce income from games, spinoff entertainment, and merchandise.

Tabletop role-playing games (TTRPGs) – *D&D*, *Game Masters*, groups of players using only their imagination to create fantastical realms – entered a new life in the realm of live streaming with Twitch (2011, now a subsidiary of Amazon) and YouTube (2005, now a subsidiary of Google), in shows such as *Critical Role* (2015) and *Dimension 20* (2018), where viewers can watch and engage with performers as they play games. Episodes are often hours long; they can be live shows or shows produced in advance with infinite restreaming of episodes and podcasts; they enjoy multimillionaire sponsors like network television; and the cast of *Critical Role* have equity in the intellectual property; there are spinoffs and adaptations such as comic books, television series, even a film series. Both shows have multimillion views and revenue. By the mid-2010s, interactivity and immersion moved out of gaming to the realm of electronic dance music (EDM) venues at conventions such as BlizzCon (2005), Comic-Con (San Diego Comic-Con 1988), Blizzard Entertainment's annual convention, and Wizard World, where gaming, music, and live performances came together in immersive hybrid models that later became popular streaming media platforms. Community-based activity continued and leapfrogged into new venues that ultimately evolved and became novel and sustainable business models as well as illuminating exactly how long geek culture has been mainstream, not just in the United States but on a global scale – something that clearly traces geek culture as absorbed into today's entertainment world.

Mastering Virtual Production

Gaming Tools and Skills for New Business Models

Video games played a large role in inspiring various technological developments. Playing games such as *Minecraft* and *Roblox* lays the groundwork for sandbox games, fostering design and logical thinking skills. Early access led to joining modding communities for *The Elder Scrolls*, *Half-Life*, and other epic games, where skills such as programming, 3D modeling, and game design would later transfer over to larger professional and commercial tech innovations.

> **Modding communities** are groups of gamers and developers who collaborate and share modifications for video games.

For a number of reasons, video games must be modified. Some gamers want to enhance their experience with characters, features, or modes they enjoy because the games have become too familiar. Aside from wanting to extend the life of their favorite game, they might want to upgrade the graphics with better textures, lighting, or resolution. Mods (short for modifications) permit gamers to communicate with developers and contribute to what can ultimately improve a game. Mods can also function as a career pathway in the gaming industry. Learning languages such as Java and Python is a professional skill.

Gamers discover free software (Blender and Unity are popular) and start creating their own games. Blender is a free and open-source 3D animation suite while Unity Technologies provides quality 3D game engine software. Ultimately, the gamers learn how to do everything themselves: modeling, texturing, rigging characters, building worlds, animating, rendering, and editing movies.

These gaming skills – needed for driving the perpetual chase, cheating death, completing assignments, and navigating graphic user interfaces – are integral to developing countless new technologies, such as those in augmented reality (AR), and virtual production. For example, gamers' experience with 3D layouts and interactivity led directly to innovations in VR and AR by providing a solid foundation in immersive experiences and technology from the Oculus Rift (a VR headset) to Microsoft HoloLens (an AR headset). Furthermore, virtual production techniques for TV and film productions, such as those employed in the Disney+ franchise *The Mandalorian*, are fueled hand-in-hand by expertise in VR-based game engines such as Unreal Engine.

Geek Culture's Influence on Virtual Production Learning for Independent Content Creators

Digital natives find technical advice, tutorials, and tips and tricks on YouTube, Twitch, Discord, and Reddit, as much as they do on LinkedIn. Manufacturers such as Epic Games (maker of Unreal Engine), Autodesk (maker of Maya), and dedicated industry networks such as the Virtual Production Network have all scaled public education to expert use of their products by publishing best practices and usage guidelines. Even Google and Meta (to name but a few) VR and AR training modules offer online courses and certifications.

The democratization of education is a vast topic covered later in this chapter.

Democratization of Content Creation

On-Demand Content

Many networks and channels offer on-demand content through their apps or partnerships with streaming platforms instead of following a set broadcast schedule; viewers consume whatever media and information they want, whenever they want.

User-Generated Content (UGC)

As illustrated in the "Geek Culture" section, the internet allowed individuals to become content creators, essentially network broadcasters, with sponsorships, millions of viewers, programming, and subscriptions. Platforms as networks like YouTube, blogs, and later social media sites like Facebook and Twitter (X) are basically distribution outlets, allowing anyone with an internet connection to become a niche network. This content democratization enabled any previously unheard voices to reach the entire world. No gatekeeper can stop fans or anyone else from blogging; creating forums; posting surveys; making and streaming video games involving reviews and responsive dialogue;

holding watch parties and interviews; thematic collaboration in storytelling; or hosting live events, conventions, speeches, performances, projects, original programs, artwork, and everything else. Although UGC is typically outside established brands, content creators can become influencers whose opinions and brand recommendations are enthusiastically followed.

Independent Producers, Networks, and Channels

> **Machinima** – using game-editing software (like Unreal Editor) to puppeteer characters and add dialogue for animation stories.

One example of a group of people who created an entertainment company based on online machinima animation is Rooster Teeth (RT, 2003–2024, Austin, Texas). It was one of the first companies to produce and distribute digital media. It became a subsidiary of Warner Brothers (WB), which produced one of the longest-running comedy web series ever, *Red vs Blue* (2003–2024, set in the *Halo* universe, gearing for the 16th series), with wise-cracking dialogue. RT produced a number of productions (*RWBY, Camp Camp, gen: LOCK*, etc.), divisions, channels, events, and forums. Warner Brothers shut down Rooster Teeth in 2024 because it was unprofitable. Rooster Teeth turned revenue from website ads, YouTube ads, subscriptions, live events, and merchandise into about $75 million in 2023. WB plans to sell the intellectual property and licensing rights for RT's productions.

The lessons? Maybe don't get swallowed up by a larger corporate entity; maybe you don't have to deal with TV companies and film distributors; maybe you have revenue streams beyond advertising; maybe you speak directly to fans; maybe you keep control of your product; maybe promote a global business.

More recently, HyperRPG has existed as a video production studio producing community content online, founded in 2016 by Zac Eubank (formerly of Geek Sundry) and Jordan Weisman (the creator of *MechWarrior/BattleTech* and *ShadowRun*). Current organizational principals include Zac Lim Eubank, Malika Lim Eubank, Matt Acevedo, and Jo Paloma.

> All the founders of HYPER were either veterans of the gaming or video production industry. With the rise of livestreaming around 2015, we saw an opportunity to gamify audience interactions with narrative experiences. To this day, we still seek to leverage the latest technology to create and promote community-driven content in storytelling.
>
> Malika Lim Eubank (https://www.hyperrpg.com/)

HYPER is a player in geek culture because of their Emmy-nominated series *KOllOK*. They also produced *Power Rangers HyperForce* and *Travels with Malika*, an on-the-road broadcast (https://www.hyperrpg.com/kollok).

Epic Unreal Engine

Epic Games (1990) created the first-person shooter game *Unreal* (1995) and then offered the Unreal Editor for free to individuals and companies making less than $1 million annually. Free use resulted in the now-ubiquitous presence of UE 3D environments and characters throughout entertainment genres and venues and integration with many other applications.

UE's worldwide communities of users and developers are large and energetic, as are Unity's, and the distribution of UE across the types of projects reflects these trends: UE has the high-end gaming work while Unity works on 2D, mobile, and indie game development.

The series *The Mandalorian* (2019) showed LED virtual environment content provided by UE being present on set in a continuously filmed television series.

Sets built by professionals for previz or limited-quality production use are offered by UE Marketplace for free, which can be particularly helpful for productions with tight budgets. For feature film workflow, UE facilitates previz. Directors, cinematographers, and designers can collaborate for storyboarding of camera blocking and sequential narratives in the virtual environments and then add the rough shots to the editorial department/crew to check if the storytelling is effective and approve the take before going to the next shot. This can implement either an iterative process or parallel processing (taken from Agile methodology) for decision-making in the production stage. Also, takes can be saved for post-production and contribute to the flexibility and improvement of the content.

The movie or live television broadcast sets are multi-disciplinary collaborative workspaces of devices and software combining skills in filmmaking, mixed media, game development, editing, and more. The same applies to an internet broadcast set, and post-production may not happen at all, because the mixed technology output is live. UE is a key part of the production workflow on both movie and broadcast sets through its virtual sets, props, and cameras.

Democratization of Technology

The democratization of the tools and toys of production means that devices and hardware that were once accessible only to professionals are now not only available to but also affordable for the prosumer. Smartphone cameras have advanced sensors and even LiDAR for cinematic imagery and 3D scanning to build rapid models. More accurate compositing is also in alignment with the software. Gear manufacturers such as Neewer and Teradek make lighting, stabilizing, and wireless video transmission gear, while manufacturers such as Blackmagic Design and Sony now offer cinema-quality but cost-effective models. Modular and reusable set pieces have also brought down costs and afforded more choices to independent producers. Some of the advantages of real-time 3D rendering, extensive virtual environments, props, and characters (made available through free software such as UE, Unity, and Blender, among others) were discussed earlier in this book.

Virtual production using workflow as a service (WaaS) cuts hardware and software investment. WaaS offers a turnkey cloud platform that allows remote teams to perform pre-production, production, and post-production tasks in real time. Cloud storage is flexible and can be rented. Storage is scalable to manage assets while minimizing costs with solar and battery generators, a real-time rendering engine (UE), and collaborative platforms like NVIDIA Omniverse for workflow management using USD (Universal Scene Description) for asset integration across software packages. WaaS systems have technicians or operators who are trained by the provider, which avoids certain hiring costs.

Other workflow management systems include new versions of Autodesk's Flow Production Tracking system (formerly ShotGrid) and Flow Capture (formerly Moxion). Of course, workflow management systems reduce the number of people needed to run production management, meaning that a small-budget production could run with a skeleton staff from remote locations.

You just need a few people who deal with project management, resource planning, collaboration tools, version control, asset tracking, project progress, and scheduling.

Workflow management systems need to export to creative software such as Maya, 3ds Max, Blender, and UE for rounds of reviews, feedback, approval, and passage into the pipeline. The production managers should be able to observe the status of a project at a glance.

Finally, through workflow management development, small firms can imitate large studios by enabling remote teams to collaborate on large and complex projects. With WaaS, it is possible to create bespoke configurations for production teams to effectively coordinate, visualize, and optimize the scene. Through WaaS systems, consumers and professionals can experience high-end production quality at a lower cost with increased flexibility.

Another production tool is Perforce, the file management tool that is used for UE, providing version control, collaboration, and application lifecycle management for DevOps and development. Perforce Helix Core is a version control software that assists virtual production teams in the handling of the various digital files required for remote teams.

Most of the software in question is open-source use or for use under a subscription or flat-rate model. This affordability, along with the variety of dedicated collaboration software, also means that small teams or a single person can work like a large studio.

Devices, Hardware, and Equipment

Neewer

Manufacturers are targeting the prosumer and social media sector for video and movie production equipment, offering more affordable equipment with flexible, rugged, and mobile qualities to rival those once available only for high-end productions.

Neewer (2011, Shenzhen, China) is the go-to brand for amateurs and prosumers, producing a whole range of budget photo equipment, including a variety of lighting rigs, ring lights, panel lights, RGB lights, and soft lights, as well as competing in the same categories as the more expensive options for camera rigs, accessories, and support.

Neewer has a range of products for prosumers doing virtual production, such as the aluminum handheld Universal Phone Video Rig Kit, with a high stability shooting range and multiple mounting points for accessories, and the Pro 4-Way Macro Focusing Rail Slider, which helps accurately control the position of your camera for industrial photography.

Neewer's line of teleprompters are prosumer- and virtual production-ready, like the X14 Remote Teleprompter, complete with a 14-inch HD beam splitter glass and the ability to be controlled remotely, so you can manage your script with the touch of a keypad for public speeches, online courses, and presentations as a telecaster. The company also provides an X14 Pro model that's suitable for larger tablets up to 14 inches. Both models fold up so they can be easily transported for speeches, online courses, and presentations as a telecaster.

iPhones

For independent creatives, iPhones and tablets are replacing expensive cinematic production–quality equipment like cameras, scanners, custom rigs, camera tracking, motion capture, and even green screens. With the built-in LiDAR technology, everyone can get high-quality 3D scans or tinker with augmented reality. There are apps that flow through the production workflow from scouting, previz, and compositing to editorial. This duplicates the entire virtual production system at an affordable cost – meaning on a student budget. Combined with UE, you also have virtual props, characters, environments, physical effects, and camera.

Lightcraft's Jetset and ViewScreen Scout are iPhone apps for previsualization, part of the established field of virtual production. This book includes both Lightcraft and ViewScreen. The first application in movies was for the previsualization of shots: camera blocking, what goes where in a scene, how to frame it, place the effects, plan the action, and where to put talent, props, lights, and cameras. The second application in movies was shooting them and editing them to see if the shots cut together and supported storytelling. Filmmakers use the first application (visualizing shots before they shoot them) for planning convenience and to help make decisions on shot setup and shot takes. The first application is essential when camera blocking and planning on integrating visual effects. The second application – checking the storytelling through editing – is highly necessary in any movie or media, even without visual effects. Virtual production tools assist in both these applications.

Real-time compositing in apps such as Skyglass instantly blends together live-action footage and virtual backgrounds with green screen keying. AR-equipped iPhones capture motion for animating virtual characters and objects. The iPhone and iPad Pro's LiDAR equipment offers the camera motion with realistic virtual production set matching that enables live and virtual sets to be placed together seamlessly. The iPhone may also be used to monitor the camera feed remotely, allowing directors and crew to see and control the frame from their own devices.

Filmic Pro, for one, brings to the iPhone most of the features of a cinematic camera, allowing for control of white balance, LUTs, color grading, and gamma curves. Audio can also be controlled by levels, gain, and filters, and, whether using internal or external microphones, they too become fully controllable. The very same app, LumaFusion, lets you edit, even when you're on the move, allowing for rapid changes. Cost saving is the reason many independent producers use the iPhone to replace more expensive equipment.

Phone limitations can lead to a degree of image degradation (depending on the specific resolution), especially in low-light conditions. Compared with pro cameras, the available range of lenses is smaller, and creative decisions about focal lengths and depth of field aren't always possible. Hardcore processes such as filming and real-time compositing can quickly drain an iPhone's battery and stop the show. An iPhone heats up when using virtual production tools because the added pressure of processing the graphics and real-time tracking in a green or blue screen environment makes heavy inroads into the processor – both the CPU and the GPU. An overheated phone isn't always reliable. There are peripheral fans and coolers on the market.

High-resolution video files take up a lot of space and require frequent transfers to a computer, unless you want to buy an iCloud upgrade, which may be a requirement for many apps. They also have far less memory than professional-grade devices, so they won't perform as well with tasks such as real-time rendering and complex compositing. Though iPhones are lightweight, they lack the bulk of a dedicated device, so shots will often require more expensive stabilization equipment to make them appear smooth and professional.

Built-in microphones on iPhones are another hardware consideration that might not be as high-quality as those found in professional audio equipment, and external microphones could be required. Apps might be available, but they might not include the type of controls and features (such as distortion) that are offered by professional software.

Such drawbacks aside, the iPhone remains a handy, affordable all-rounder, at least for independent producers using it with low-res video for previz or as a secondary production camera assist.

Software and Platforms

Previously, we covered workflow management platforms like WaaS, NVIDIA Omniverse, Autodesk Flow Production Tracking, and Flow Capture. There are many more cloud platforms, making remote collaboration easier and eliminating hiring and added equipment costs. Even Google Workspace is a well-known tool for creating, sharing, and storage. Beyond the obvious are job-specific tools that deserve special mention because they involve industry standards.

Blackmagic DaVinci Resolve (an industry standard) equips prosumers with a free to affordable full suite of color management tools that support every stage of production, mirroring the workflows of large studios. Color management is covered in this book and is both a creative decision and a quality management check process that starts at the beginning of a project and follows it to the end – movie release or live broadcast. Color management is a process that is often overlooked by prosumers but is standard in professional productions, usually governed by the editorial department. In pre-production, DaVinci

Resolve enables detailed color planning and look development. It is used by both creators and prosumers, first, during production for real-time on-the-spot color grading adjustments and dailies color grading and second, during post-production for advanced color correction and grading to match pre-production shots and images, including HDR support, color matching, and a library of hundreds of look-up tables (LUTs). Prosumers can create and deliver work at a professional level with consistent, high-quality color throughout the entire pipeline.

Processes such as the Academy Color Encoding System (ACES), a standards-based workflow for professionals and prosumers, guarantee scientifically accurate color reproduction across different software suites (e.g., Nuke, After Effects) and budgets. ACES encompasses the full visible-color gamut designed as a workflow that maintains color matching and color conversion from multiple devices across different platforms so that, for example, in Nuke, color accuracy is preserved throughout the visual effects (VFX) pipeline from acquisition to the final output, and in After Effects, color consistency is maintained from import to your final render. The aim is to streamline color management across the production so all producers – big budget or low budget – can have confidence in their product quality.

Teradek

Teradek delivers video solutions for television and film by powering the broadcasters and filmmakers with wireless video transmitters, 4K video encoders/decoders, and live streaming systems. Teradek Core is a broadcast streaming platform that can distribute feeds to multiple destinations. Teradek TV is for production and post-production and connects to a camera or post-production workstation to share high-quality, low-latency video with remote crews worldwide. Large, small, and multiple productions can collaborate during stage photography, editorial, and color timing.

Motion Control for the Masses

While others use iPhone apps that track and record camera movements, prosumers might favor motion-control rigs for more direct control that is repeatable for live action and UE input. Those shooting motion control sequences – such as time lapses and VFX work – want their camera movements to be near perfectly accurate and repeatable. High programming is possible using systems such as Mark Roberts Motion Control (MRMC) with programmable movements, multiple axes, and interface with another professional kit, creating a very stable, reliable result. The intrinsic limitations of an iPhone (sensor size, lens options, stabilization) mean that video of a moving shot may not produce the kind of image quality provided by a professional camera on a motion-control rig. Regarding interactivity, some motion control rigs have remote controllers so camera moves can be made spontaneously.

There is cooperation between Teradek and MRMC. This combination of wireless video transmission from Teradek and MRMC's Bolt Jr camera robot helps provide the best visual quality for productions involving film and photography. Bolt Jr is a high-speed camera robot suited for the film and photographic studio industry that allows fast and repeatable movements. It is specifically made for a range of dynamic shooting scenarios. Teradek's Bolt series adds video transmission from the camera robot to monitors or other video devices. This allows for wireless monitoring and controls. MRMC's robotic precision makes the Teradek Bolt series a powerful tool for professional video production, whether it be for live streaming or monitoring purposes.

Edelkrone also offers a wide price range and scales of motion-control systems, including programmable tripods, jibs, wings, camera heads, and sliders.

Live Streaming Platforms

Aside from Teradek Core mentioned previously, there are many other live streaming platforms. Live streaming platforms built into social media like YouTube Live, Facebook Live, and Twitch may have too many distractions and privacy issues. The trend is to move to more dedicated and secure platforms for better community building, pay-per-view or a variety of monetization options, fewer restrictions, and better engagement: tools like Uscreen, Whop, and Restream. But let's take a look at Twitch's evolution to see how loyalty was built through engagement.

Twitch

What started as a crude experiment in the early 1990s has become a mass medium that is as easy to use as broadcast television. The first live stream was broadcast by a band called Severe Tire Damage in 1993 over a network called the Mbone (the precursor of today's internet). In 1995, RealNetworks unleashed its live streaming software RealPlayer (the first public live stream of a baseball game), and in 2008, YouTube broadcast its first live event. Video game streaming became widespread when Justin.tv was launched in 2007. Justin.tv rebranded in 2011 as Twitch (the dominant video game streaming platform to this day) while in 2016, major social media platforms such as

Facebook, Instagram, and Mixer started to provide their users with additional ways to live stream content of all descriptions.

A Twitch channel is a user or organization's homepage on the Twitch streaming website. A streamer transports some type of content to the audience (viewers) on the homepage. Twitch is known for broadcasting video games, but music, art, and talk shows are welcomed as well. Two features of a Twitch channel are streaming and text chat. Streaming means that a streamer displays whatever he is doing in front of the camera, and the viewers are watching the stream in real time. Streaming live video is the activity performed by a streamer. Text chat is a tool for viewers to communicate with a streaming host and also with each other.

In addition, they can subscribe to a stream and follow streamers to access a stream and donate (mostly in fixed amounts), which generally comes with a perk such as unlocking a fixed image (e.g., emoticon or emote) or removing ads for a certain uptime. Streams can be stored as videos on demand (VODs) and viewed by viewers who missed the live stream. Streamers can decorate their channel with graphics, panels, and other objects that reflect their brand or elements of their own narrative. Twitch channels are powerful tools for narrative creation – not only for the content creator but also for connecting with the fans.

How Much Content Exists?

According to Nielson.com, over-the-top (OTT) digital content delivered via the internet has exceeded 817,000 US programs and is still growing (https://www.nielsen.com/insights/2022/state-of-play/). Currently, the number of OTT subscribers worldwide is estimated to be over 3.9 billion (https://www.statista.com/topics/7527/video-streaming-worldwide/#topicOverview).

While it is difficult to determine how many movies have been created from when the technology began to the present day, estimates place the worldwide count at hundreds of thousands but more likely millions, especially counting episodic television shows and made-for-TV movies (https://www.imdb.com/pressroom/stats/).

According to *Forbes*, there are over 200 streaming services worldwide, with Netflix the leader (https://www.forbes.com/sites/entertainment/article/best-streaming-services/). Netflix had over 282 million subscribers as of 2024 (https://variety.com/2024/tv/news/netflix-subscribers-282-million-q3-earnings-1236181199/).

In the US, the majority of people get their news from digital devices, and many of these rely on social media, while a minority get their news from television (https://www.pewresearch.org/journalism/fact-sheet/news-platform-fact-sheet/).

Clearly, content creation is less of a need than content discernment. With such a glut of available resources created past and present, using generative AI and machine learning, which rely on massive samples to create derivative material, makes sense because of the speed and cost savings they can deliver. However, AI and ML as tools of virtual production demand human judgment to guide the tools towards constructive goals (https://mitsloanedtech.mit.edu/ai/basics/addressing-ai-hallucinations-and-bias/).

FRANCHISE DOMINATION

"**A franchise** is a business model where one party, the franchisor, grants another party, the franchisee, the rights to operate under its established brand and business system. The franchisor provides the brand name, logo, and operational structure, while the franchisee typically pays an initial fee and ongoing royalties to run the business using these resources."

International Franchise Association. (2024, November 21). "What Is a Franchise?" https://www.franchise.org/faqs/basics/what-is-a-franchise.

While games, game tools, and other geek culture products and producers use the franchise business model (as covered previously in this chapter), at the other end of the finance spectrum are the big-budget franchises that range from movies to episodic television shows and even games like *Jurassic Park/World*, *Alien*, *Lord of the Rings*, *Star Wars*, *Avatar*, *Godzilla*, etc. While planned movie franchises have been around since the 1930s and 1940s and included early serials (e.g., *Tarzan*), the Universal Monster series (e.g., *Dracula* and *Frankenstein*), comic book series (e.g., Detective Comics and Action Comics), and action movies for kids that were continued from radio shows (e.g., *Flash Gordon*, *The Lone Ranger*, *Buck Rogers*, and *Zorro*), modern franchises now include expansive universes and interconnected stories, influenced by *Star Wars* in 1977. George Lucas was influenced by old movie serial matinees and space operas like *Buck Rogers* and *Flash Gordon*. The *Star Wars* title crawl was imitative of the text scrolls in *Flash Gordon*.

B-movie serials were cheaply made, cheaply sold, and quick to produce. Made by studios such as Republic Pictures, Columbia Pictures, and Universal Studios, a B-movie was to be shown in conjunction with an A-movie, a much more expensive and much more prestigious film that would star better-known actors. Sets and costumes were reused to save time and money, and stock footage from past productions was also repurposed. The serials were usually aimed at young audiences: children and teenagers. They forecasted many of today's action and superhero films. Franchises nowadays are multi-billion-dollar productions because the high box office yield attracts investors eager for correspondingly high return on investment (ROI). Maintaining high box office yield means maintaining the brand and audience expectations, so there are spinoffs and merchandise flowing at every opportunity, and the all-encompassing fan base is targeted by the convention industry and the theme parks that go with it (*Star Wars*, Marvel Cinematic Universe, Harry Potter).

Because of the high stakes, long production runs, tight schedule demands, and challenge of satisfying and perpetually growing the fan base, franchises have led the way by driving technological advancements in the special visual effects world and, most recently, in virtual production (especially real-time production), designing, adapting, and pushing new storytelling techniques; changing production models and new workflows; and creating new standards for the industry. Franchises impose their own unique needs on emerging virtual production technology and are big enough to develop innovative customizations and new workflows.

Examples of custom needs are international collaboration pipelines and workflows, flexibility, production management and related processes to accommodate incredibly large-scale productions with world-wide collaboration, research and development of equipment and software (including workflows, tools, and processes to maintain visual and thematic consistency and integrity over multiple similar episodes/shows), and developing technology and personnel to create production workflows for a broad array of distribution venues (e.g., traditional theatrical release, IMAX large-format release, streaming, and VOD in games, on mobile devices, and in theme parks). Modern production processes rely on Agile and Scrum methodologies, including software and hardware development/manufacturing, research and development, flexibility, iterative development and production processes, widespread collaboration, continuous feedback and improvement, and incremental delivery.

A short list of the *Avatar* franchise needs were new underwater motion capture suits, enhanced software for simulating wet CG hair and skin, camera blocking and editing in stereoscopic 3D, display for on-set previsualization, and various types of connective software. Expensive customizations ensure that big-budget productions will stay ahead of independent innovation that comes more from unconventional storytelling language and style, niche content, and audience participation rather than the franchise custom needs listed earlier. Some big-budget customizations may seem like extravagances, but when considering that live-action movies are produced like animation features (fewer locations, live stunts, costumes, and extras vs more digital creation), you can see how the blockbuster franchises resemble manufacturers or software developers. In fact, Pixar, being a digital animation studio, created software Presto, RenderMan, and OpenUSD. RenderMan was a commercial standard rendering program for years until competing software like Unity gained popularity. (This also happened with game manufacturers who doubled as software developers, in addition to creative content providers like Epic Games.) Considering that modern blockbuster movies, like animation, have fantasy elements like moving cameras, characters, and props that defy the laws of mass, anatomy, and mechanical physics; supernatural fantasy effects; and have surreal and hyper-real stylized looks, therefore any technology, no matter the expense, that can assist in creating impossible, extraordinary, otherworldly imagery that has to be reinvented and surpassed in every production, is worth the investment.

Furthermore, another distinctive characteristic of contemporary virtual production is its reliance on cross-functional teams. The training in film schools is mainly characterized by narrow skill sets, but heavy dependence on collaboration forces experts across different fields, such as visual effects experts, artists, cinematographers, software coders, and production designers, to work together from the pre-production phase all the way to post-production. All the more reason to draw from a global talent pool. Active participants need to have a sense of how the production process works holistically, so they need to acquire broader skill sets. The side effect is an increasingly versatile workforce. Continuous training via boot camps, workshops, online and expert courses, etc. is always necessary, regardless of the position or level you are working in.

These roles require technical knowledge (hard skills like AI prompting, machine learning, Python, and concatenating data) and the ability to control file-naming conventions, but they need production management soft skills too, so the highly technical integrations from previz to release can be explained and coordinated. Organizational and managerial skill sets are often learned on the job. Virtual production supervisors grow into these roles from other technical disciplines, such as visual effects (VFX), animation, and gaming. Individuals like this already have niche experience that is further enhanced by working closely with directors and supervisors to replicate setups, manage a team, and produce. Such is the case for Felix Jorge, Rob Legato, and Ben Grossmann (Magnopus). Their technical skills are in world-building, visualizing, and environment creation. Likewise, on the gaming side, Kim Libreri (CTO of Epic Games) was the VFX supervisor on *The Matrix* trilogy and worked on pushing real-time rendering technologies for virtual production.

As for large studios, they are franchise dependent; thus, they have larger numbers of employee prospects, are not reliant on using the same technological solutions (since they can mix and match for specialized needs), and thus are not reliant on the latest crop of graduates from the college or university system. They can sift for specialized skill sets as needed. Crews are often built from friendships and alliances from school or past productions. Loyalty and dedication to each other and the project supersedes any HR recruitment. Alien Romulus stayed true to the horror genre by using significantly more practical effects, animatronic models, and puppets than CG characters. The Stan Winston School of Character Arts is an example of what I refer to as a specialized expert school. Indeed, some of these schools are guild-like in that they can offer specialized hands-on teaching, mentoring, community, networking, workshops, and apprenticeships.

Filmmaking is a craft-based profession and, like theater, draws on different types of artisans (e.g., sculpting, painting, drawing, animation, music, writing, acting, photography, set building, set design). While the computer and AI are transforming audience expectations, there is in filmmaking today a nostalgia for a return to craft and crews or troupes. In entertainment, the cliché about getting a job has always been that it's about "who you know." But this entertainment cliché has spread throughout all industries and is compounded by AI and machine learning, which are developed daily to eliminate jobs and save money. Therefore, today's job seekers and career builders look towards a democratization of education that will build craft, crews, and troupes, much like the guilds during the Renaissance that were run by tradesmen and had a master-apprentice progression.

Democratization of Education

Besides colleges and university programs, education for virtual production and VFX is obtainable via a growing number of other sources – manufacturers, employers, gurus, niche schools, corporate training, conferences, communities, technology gatekeepers, and e-learning companies, to name a few.

Networks, employers, and manufacturers publish best practices and guidelines that help train potential hires for employment or jumpstart professional development for established careers. Manufacturers also train technicians to ensure well-qualified workers for their customer base.

This democratization of knowledge is helping a new generation of creators refine their technical abilities and open more avenues for innovation in the mishmash of people and ideas that is geek culture. It also exemplifies the love, vision, and communal spirit that characterize the movement and leans towards the best of virtual production that's open to independents.

In the past, filmmaking crew jobs were primarily blue-collar or working-class roles. In the 1970s, film brats attended university degree programs with expensive tuition that were more theoretical than practical. There were no guarantees of work and no mentors for students after graduation, unless one befriended established professionals along the way. On the other hand, trade schools were more practical than theoretical with less expensive tuition, but in the US, these schools decreased in number when employers required degrees on job applications. Today, this trend is reversing, with more employers requiring lower or no degrees.

Computer and internet technology favors task and application experience.

However, if pursuing a formal education, a technical study (e.g., visualization tools), management (e.g., Agile), or executive roles (e.g., producing and directing), it is still advisable to obtain, at minimum, a bachelor's degree as a solid jumping-off point to develop into virtual production professional roles. The parties who implement virtual production technology and techniques (manufacturers and developers) are taking the responsibility of educating the next generations; for practical purposes, this is centered around their specific hardware, software, or platforms. Manufacturers need publicity and marketing, product diversification, process standardization and best practices, operational competency, integration of peripheral equipment and/or software, customer satisfaction, specialty freelance technicians, and potential employee pools. These skills need to be nurtured globally so a worldwide market can be developed.

Therefore, learning options like virtual production are rapidly shifting to accommodate the continually evolving industry served by continually evolving manufacturers. Another advantage of these commercial courses is that they are better suited to changing industries, both in terms of changeable product knowledge and the changeable requirements of employers. Conventional educational institutions react more slowly to changes in industry and training demands – something that fits poorly in an environment demanding ongoing learning and experience. For that reason, some colleges and universities are sharing programs with studios or manufacturers, where students can work hands-on with an entity committed to rapid information and processes updating.

For the purpose of exploration, we'll use the following categories:

1. Manufacturers
2. Employers
3. Specialty schools
4. Corporate training
5. Expert channels
6. Conventions
7. Communities
8. Technological gatekeepers
9. Online learning and teaching marketplaces

This list is not exhaustive, but it's a first attempt at capturing the new educational and training landscape. Many of the following entries might overlap into multiple categories, but what's probably most important to a learner is that their educational method fills all the desirable guild-like elements: in-person learning, mentoring, community, networking, hands-on workshops, internships, and continuing education. This is about the content of the training (skills and experience) and the mode of delivery (practical hands-on activities and workshops). Specialist schools and courses are likely to follow the guild training arrangement. There's a generalization here, but, in essence, the distinction between trade schools and higher education is that one focuses on skills and the other on knowledge.

The difference between focusing on skills and focusing on knowledge is that skills result in tangible products. Skill sets require practice, and there is no shortcut. There is nothing vague or abstract about the master-apprentice type of training. The desired result is always a product or service well done. This is also the approach used in employee training. Successful training reverse engineers the courses and learning materials from a successful end product or service. However, a review of any number of job descriptions posted by HR departments will illustrate vague, abstract, and confusing mashups of skill sets and knowledge bases with little concrete description of product or service outcomes. These job descriptions are written to lure a mythical "purple unicorn" employee, but mythology is a poor strategy for describing successful products and services when real criteria are expected. The "purple unicorn" job posting strategy contributes to manipulative and devious reactions to something everyone knows is fantasy, overused, and probably not even necessary. For an industry in flux like virtual production, live production observation and experience are the best types of education to learn and practice tasks for a chosen profession – no unicorns required.

Manufacturers

It is advantageous for manufacturers to train operators and technicians to provide a talent pool for their products.

Epic Unreal Engine

Resources for learning VFX and virtual production in Unreal Engine (which offers various levels of expertise and professional needs) are listed next. Unreal Fellowship for Virtual Production is a hands-on learning program for industry professionals from animation, VFX, and film who want to develop proficiency in virtual production, filmmaking, and real-time technology. It's a highly competitive 12-week virtual production program, but even if your application isn't accepted the first time, it has an extensive learning path and a virtual production hub for updated resources. Fundamentals of Unreal Engine, such as integration of models, animation, motion capture (mocap), look development, lighting, cinematic storytelling, etc., can all be learned through Epic's online tutorials and documentation (https://www.unrealengine.com/en-US/fellowship).

The Universal Studios Florida backlot houses the DAVE School, a full-time university for VFX, virtual production, and gaming. It is a completely immersive learning environment that fosters hands-on, industry-focused projects and student and professional inter-relations: "Hardworking students will get first-hand production experience from our VFX industry insiders" (https://dave.nuc.edu/).

For professionals transitioning out of heritage pipelines and into virtual production, the Unreal Essentials for Virtual Production class on Zerply offers the basics of using Unreal Engine. Virtual production professionals will find value in Zerply as VFX and animation specialists are also currently making the move into virtual production (https://zerply.com/).

Moreover, CG Pro provides workshops and courses to the public in several domains, including games, virtual production, and VFX, for novices and experts. The curriculum is suitable for all levels of learning, including intense boot camps and online courses to enable students to achieve their goals in virtual production (https://www.becomecgpro.com/).

Epic Games promotes many user guides and technical tips for Unreal Engine users, such as guidelines for virtual reality performance, user experience, technical details, the native Blueprint scripting language in Unreal Engine, and how to optimize Unreal Engine with profilers, performance tests, and managing scene components (https://dev.epicgames.com/community/unreal-engine/learning).

Mo-Sys Academy

Mo-Sys Academy offers in-person virtual production training in London and Los Angeles with immersive three-day, five-day and full-foundation course offerings. These courses are not free but cost about the same as hands-on facility training. The course offerings are broad in scope and include a range of virtual production equipment and principles, camera tracking, LED volumes, Unreal Engine, lighting, and an opportunity to create a show-reel piece.

Zero Density Academy

Zero Density (ZD) has been mentioned previously in this chapter. They provide free online courses and certification in real-time broadcast graphics using their Reality Editor and Engine, along with other software. Some of their software is free for educational purposes. They have an Open Studio License Program with full access to all licenses of the Reality platform. At the time of this writing, it is similar to Epic's Unreal License Agreement (EULA), which allows individuals or teams making less than one million dollars in gross revenue annually to use the software for free. It is also free for academic institutions to use.

Employers

Some very large employers offer education in some form that can groom prospective employees in the skills and workflow knowledge required for hiring.

Netflix: Learning From Network Guidelines and Templates

Through its extensive educational libraries and workflow guides on the professional website, Netflix offers resources to VFX professionals and vendors working on productions. It guides them to "ensure [their] work aligns with" the streaming giant's "key specifications." For example, the VFX Best Practices Guide defines in elaborate detail what kind of specifications a VFX vendor must provide when working on shows for Netflix. It offers guidelines for image quality, project schedules, and budget. Another resource for VFX professionals is the 2D LED In-Camera VFX Field Guide, which explains how to use LED-based in-camera visual effects techniques. It provides information about the workflow and technical and creative considerations for implementing pre-rendered and plate-based in-camera visual effects.

Further, the Partner Help Center on Netflix's website provides a significant amount of information about the in-studio standards and workflow practices, which is valuable for anyone who wants to work for Netflix as an employee or contractor, as well as for professionals interested in learning about the detailed production practices at Netflix. These resources can equip professionals with an understanding of standards and expectations to be better prepared to work on Netflix productions with the right skills and expertise. While actual practices will depend on the unique characteristics of each project, these resources can be used as benchmarks to assist VFX professionals in getting their visual effects ready to meet the standards set forth by Netflix.

Netflix has another initiative called Grow Creative for upskilling talent. In the UK, the US, and other countries, bridging skills gaps in underrepresented talent in the industry is an endeavor not just for inclusion but to grow an employee pool. Large employee pools mean reduced wages because potential employees must compete for available job slots.

Amazon

Amazon, being a manufacturer and an employer, has a technical apprenticeship program (ATAP) in technical fields, including virtual production. On-the-job training is combined with classroom instruction to develop professionals.

Pixar

Pixar and Khan Academy provide free grade school–level online instruction for the fundamental math and science involved in computer graphics. This site is also an introduction to the environment and workflow at Pixar through employee interviews regarding the Pixar pipeline.

Specialty Schools

Specialty schools are like trade schools and can offer degrees or certificates, mentoring, job application assistance, an alma mater–like community, and continuing education. Be sure to do your research because the schools mentioned here are movie focused, but others may be television and advertising or commercial focused, like finalpixelacademy.com. Commercial advertisement production is highly technical and fast-paced because commercials have a running time of two to four minutes and a short production period. This area can be suitable for those entering virtual production to get experience and build a showreel. Also, commercial television is heavily involved in marketing and sales, two areas that can use AI solutions for rapid content creation. The ethics of generated AI is undetermined and unregulated, so the consequences and risks are also undetermined. Given that AI can be used for both speedy content creation and metrics analysis with few guardrails (considering that the internet model has come to national broadcast networks), is it any wonder that national broadcasting agencies are very interested in generative AI for production, content creation, broadcast, and profit analysis?

Your career objectives should guide your selection of specialty schools. Likewise, explore specialty schools designed for game development training.

There are also partnerships between studios, specialty schools, and traditional universities like the Virtual Production Academy, which is a partnership between studio Pixomondo and Seneca Polytechnic in Canada. The virtual production program is online and can be found here: https://www.senecapolytechnic.ca/programs/workshops/PXO.html.

Gnomon

Unlike most colleges and universities that offer generalized curriculums, Gnomon's curriculum is particular to movie, video, virtual, game production, and digital art. Areas of study include art and design, 3D generalist, modeling and texturing, character and creature creation, VFX animation, games, and virtual production. Degrees and certificates are offered. The age and expertise levels range from high school to college, from corporate training to continuing professional education in groups or individually. Being so specialized, with only working industry-affiliated instructors, the school's curriculum is focused on industry standards, demands, and workflows. There is less theory and more hands-on application with mentoring, networking, and career assessment services offered after graduation. Like a trade school, Gnomon is focused on ensuring its graduates are hired.

Technicolor Group

The motion picture film processing lab Technicolor started in 1915 as an engineering firm that processed film for iconic movies such as Disney's *Pinocchio*, *Breakfast at Tiffany's*, and many, many others. The company has been involved in multiple movie-related technologies like camera design and film printing processes. As digital photography replaced film as a medium, Technicolor partnered with specialized studios to take outsourced VFX shots from large multi-national studios. Specialized affiliate studios include MPC, The Mill, Mikros Animation, and Technicolor Games. These partners have multiple facilities around the world.

The education available from Technicolor Group might fall into the category of employer because there is a connection between accepted and enrolled students and access to job applications with the company partners. For this reason, enrollment is not guaranteed. To enroll in courses, you have to apply with a demo reel, a CV, a questionnaire, and a skills test. Eligibility is dependent on location. If you are not eligible for the courses, they offer a free online set of tutorials through a learning hub called the Technicolor Creative Studios Academy. They post available international production jobs on a career page and provide mentoring to accepted students to prepare them for job applications.

Corporate Training

Actually, many of the sources listed in this chapter might be available for corporate training services if you inquire. Likewise, just because a company says it specializes in corporate training does not mean there are no options for individual learners.

CGPro

Although mentioned elsewhere in this book, CGPro is a Premier Unreal Authorized Training Center (PUATC) and offers live online computer graphics training in Unreal Engine, Blender, Perforce, Generative AI, and virtual production for professionals and creatives. The target students range from production executives to beginners in virtual production. Coaching and payment plans are available. CGPro might also fit into the specialized school category, with multiple types of training, including public, private, and custom. Corporate clients include universities, NASA, NBC Universal, Microsoft, and CNN. Certificates of completion are offered. Because the courses are live online and international, there is much opportunity to ask questions and troubleshoot real-world issues.

Expert Channels

Expert channels may be individual professionals or a group combining their specific skills to create a comprehensive VFX and/or virtual production curriculum. The big advantages for learners are the relatively low cost of these options, using tutorials that result in showreel samples for beginners with no production experience, and the variety of skill specializations available. Some expert programs provide software licenses while learning for Nuke, Maya, Houdini, etc.

YouTube channels

Today's monetized YouTube channels include many expert-owned channels. Some of the more popular and prolific experts include Matt Workman (Cine Tracer), Jordy Vandeput (Cinecom.net), William Faucher, Jonathan Winbush, Brandon Clements, Ryan Laley, JSFilmz, and Alex Coulombe.

LinkedIn

Noah Kadner is a virtual production editor and author *(American Cinematographer Magazine, Virtual Production Field Guide for Epic Games)*. He's also the founder of VirtualProducer.io, an expert community offering many consultation services.

RedefineFX

Jesse Pitela started RedefineFX in 2018. His website focuses on simulation FX in Unreal using Niagra, Chaos, EmberGen, Torque, and tyFlow. Simulations are particles, cloth, fire, smoke, explosion effects, liquids, or any physical, natural, magical, or supernatural effects. There is a paid and a free introductory course. The tutorials result in showreel samples or effects that can be used in your projects.

Fxphd

Fxphd is a monthly membership that provides access to various specialty courses taught online by recordings designed for professionals by expert practicing instructors. Software licensing for Nuke, Maya, Houdini, and others is accessible through a private VPN server. Progress is self-directed. Tutorials can result in showreel samples. The tutorials have high-quality footage to practice with. The vast number of specialties involve job roles like editing, color grading, audio, pipeline and system administration, digital VFX, animation, design, 3D modeling, simulations, rendering, look development, terrain creation, broadcast effects, materials and texturing, compositing, and programming. Just about everything connected to digital and virtual production is included.

Rebelway

Rebelway is an international online program for aspiring VFX artists with a pay-per-course curriculum. Payment can be made via PayPal if credit installments are desired, and financial aid options are available. Costs are below those of specialty schools. Both individual students and corporate training for groups are accommodated. Certification of completion is provided, and the roll-out of classes is handled by scheduled modules that unlock every week. This is because instructors and technical assistants moderate the courses. Instructor feedback can be requested weekly. Once purchased, there is lifetime access to the materials. The program is focused on beginners and has a quiz to assist in selecting courses, along with a student assistance team. Job roles covered are VFX (Houdini, Nuke, Python), beginner courses (Houdini, Nuke, Unreal), and working artist (Houdini, Nuke, Unreal, machine learning and basics of AI, senior artist, technical director, continuing education, and community). There are also many free courses. The website has a job board featuring international studios with mostly Houdini roles, and job placement services are offered. Software licensing is purchased via discounts.

Conventions

This category includes professional membership organizations that promote knowledge and tools for their industry.

CineGear

The CineGear Expo offers yearly seminars, panels, and master classes from industry experts in virtual production. Their website has recorded on-demand seminars, which are free of charge for registration. Attending the annual conventions held in multiple cities in the US is an education in new technologies, demonstrations, and networking. If you are attending in Los Angeles, the expo is usually held at a major studio backlot (https://www.cinegearexpo.com/).

International Broadcasting Convention (IBC)

IBC is a good reference for tutorials and papers regarding how generative AI is used worldwide. Because of the speed at which broadcast productions are created, it behooves the television industry to make an effort to update and keep in step with the tools as they are rapidly developed and to hold conversations about the practical use and ethics of generative AI. Therefore, there is a difference between the tools and usage by consumers for social media and broadcasters (www.ibc.org).

NAB

The National Association of Broadcasters (NAB) is both a trade association and a lobby group representing US broadcasters. In addition to convention presentations, they offer courses, podcasts through NAB Broadcast Education, on-demand websites, and other certification courses to members for a per-course price, such as AI training and certifications, boot camps, and summits. NAB Amplify is a digital hub offering free educational articles and videos on current television projects, technologies, and global media, including virtual production and artificial intelligence. See their AI topics (https://www.nabshow.com/trends-and-topics/artificial-intelligence/). This is a good resource, even if you are not an NAB member.

SIGGRAPH

ACM SIGGRAPH (SIG [for special interest group] GRAPHics) is a volunteer-staffed international organization in the field of computer graphics. It was started in the 1960s. It has a global membership and conducts regular lectures, presentations, and papers at an annual event, as well as on its membership website with a full digital library, parts of which are open to the public. As a special interest group, it covers the publishing of proceedings for conferences, education, courses, research, and related information for those interested in computer graphics and interactive techniques across the board, not necessarily only entertainment. This means it is an organization covering research that can be tapped by any school. It also has a digital arts community for artists' work to become known, and artists can also collaborate with researchers (https://www.siggraph.org/).

Communities

The concept of virtual production is still evolving, so there are not yet many communities accessible to beginners, and social media groups are not numerous at present. Of course, established software users like the Epic Developer Community have activities surrounding virtual production techniques, which have already been mentioned in this chapter.

ReadySetStudios in the Netherlands is attempting to create a community on Discord called ICVFX to share technical knowledge and post questions. To date, this is a small group numbering in the hundreds. Numbering in the thousands are members of a Facebook public group called the Real-Time XR and Virtual Production Community, dedicated to extended reality (XR) and virtual production. Communities seem to be sorting content and focus.

There are communities through overlapping social media interests and professional membership communities. Your choice of community is based on where you are professionally and what interests you. LinkedIn is a good source for professional virtual production groups. There is a Virtual Production Education group for film educators and filmmakers, as well as other forums.

Visual Effects Society (VES)

VES is the Visual Effects Society, an honorary international nonprofit society and professional trade association that offers educational resources to practitioners – a peer-to-peer mentorship program; presentations; internships; employment resources; and diversity, equity, and inclusion resources. Their membership requires an applicant to have "attained a senior level of achievement in the art and/or science of visual effects and have been recognized by their peers for at least five years" (https://www.vesglobal.org/).

Technological Gatekeepers

Technological gatekeepers create, sustain, and update various national and occasionally international technical standards from time to time. In the US, there's an example of a self-governing, technology-oriented professional society: The Institute of Electrical and Electronics Engineers (IEEE) which is by far the largest technical professional society. It is relevant to virtually all aspects of modern US civilization, including electrical and electronic technology (their original focus) as well as computing and a number of related fields. IEEE was founded in the 1840s and is related to world communications.

ACES

The Academy Color Encoding System (ACES) encourages this work through the community by making open-access guides and documentation available, like the ACES Primer, which is an in-depth look into the history, use, and importance of ACES for understanding and applying it into production workflows.

It is also, more importantly, an open, workflow-agnostic, device-independent color-management system. "Academy Color Encoding System, a free, open, device-independent color management and image interchange framework. ACES enables complete, standardized color management for moving images, from image capture through postproduction, presentation, and long-term archiving" (https://community.acescentral.com/uploads/default/original/1X/6ad8b74b085ac8945c1e638cbbd8fdf687b7f60e.pdf).

Common access for all leads to commonality of practice across the industry and, therefore, to a standard of production we can all trust.

Furthermore, ACES also promotes community participation and industry collaboration through ACESCentral.com, a website where users can obtain downloads and information, participate in forums, discuss the merits of different ACES tools (or others), and share the knowledge they've gained by using ACES with other ACES users. ACES was, and is, developed collaboratively between scientists, engineers, and end users, all under the Academy of Motion Picture Arts and Sciences. It is a priority for its designers and architects that ACES be usable in industrial color-management applications, so it does follow-up educational outreach at industry events and workshops to raise color-management awareness and communicate the benefits of adopting ACES's use in their production environments. In this sense, ACES has become an industry-shared reference system for color management in entertainment (https://acescentral.com/).

SMPTE

The Society of Motion Picture and Television Engineers (SMPTE) is a membership organization that was founded in 1916 and developed hundreds of standards, best practices, and guidelines for film, digital cinema, television, and internet video. The standards are recognized globally as it is accredited and recognized both nationally and internationally by the American National Standards Institute (ANSI), the International Standards Organization (ISO), the International Electrotechnical Commission (IEC), and the International Telecommunications Union (ITU) (https://www.smpte.org/).

Regarding virtual production, there is an initiative to offer foundational education on tools and implementation through events and subject matter expert discussions and workshops and webinars. There are virtual courses on imaging systems, high dynamic range (HDR), and cloud-based media production. There are free video resources and courses on SMPTE+ (plus.smpte.org) and the main website (smpte.org).

Online Learning and Teaching Marketplaces

Commercial online e-learning platforms, hubs, and learning marketplaces are numerous. Often significantly lower in cost than traditional schools, they are a convenient option for beginners, people in career transition, or continuing education. These offer gap-filling mini-courses for the ever-changing virtual production landscape to get a better perspective on the field. Some of these options also fall into the expert channel category because individual experts might use the built-in advertising and fee or subscription collection with the marketplace.

The following are some notable efforts at public education for virtual production.

- Udemy
- Skillshare
- Coursera

- LinkedIn Learning
- Teachable
- Thinkific

GLOBAL NETWORKS

MACHINE LEARNING – AI

This chapter would be remiss if it did not mention the astoundingly rapid development of generative AI.

In a nutshell, AI is the ability of computers to act like human brains using a neural network to solve problems. Machine learning is a subset of AI in which specific mathematical models are trained with and learn from structured data sets. Deep learning involves adding layers within a model to accommodate increased complexity. A neural network is created in which multiple algorithms replicate human brain processes.

This section is an attempt to categorize AI applications in use today. It is intended to be an initial birds-eye view of the shifting AI virtual production and broadcast landscape. Any categories used are for sample purposes only because the applications may use more than one type of AI technology. Applications can be complex and overlap. This is not a scientific document but a general broad-stroke illustration for laymen.

Generative AI or GenAI produces original images, videos, speech, text, music, or code from text prompts. The combination of open-source AI and the use of generative AI code-writing assistance has accelerated AI tool creation.

Prompt writing, prompt engineering, or prompt design is essential in getting the desired results from GenAI. The smallest unit in a prompt is a token, which is a piece of a word. Prompt tokens are analyzed by generative pre-trained transformer (GPT) models (large language model or LLM), and the model predicts the next sequence of tokens, which generates the original text, images, videos, speech, music, or code. Tokens in = tokens out.

Prompts can be combined, like scripts, to create autonomous agents (AI agents that act on their own).

There is also AI assistance to help write prompts.

One might say that democratizing content creation, education, and technology also involves machines. Because new and cost-effective, time-saving, and simplifying AI tools are continually being created for public and professional use, it is helpful to look at how AI content is already being used. Computer evolution has evidenced a divide between the humanities and abstraction. Artisans tend to lean towards the practice of tangible, hand-made, skilled craft while computer activity stays in the realm of mathematical abstraction. With the proliferation of AI, the divide between the love of crafts and the humanities, evidenced in human talent, and the utility of mathematical abstraction for the sake of simulation of life, production, cost-effectiveness, and higher profits may create a giant chasm that only human benefactors can resolve – unless AI becomes both the content creator and the content buyer.

Autonomous AI are systems operating with little human oversight and focus on tasks that humans can perform. They include multiagent systems (software programs or robots), large action models (frameworks for decision-making, like algorithms), machine customers (businesses, services, and consumer interactions), humanoid robots (human-like presence in assembly lines, customer service, healthcare assistance), autonomous agents (self-driving cars, vacuum cleaners, trading systems), and reinforcement learning (machine learning).

While there is concern about deep fakes and disinformation, broadcast entities rely more on the workload assistance that AI promises because of the overwhelming ocean of content that needs to be analyzed daily by newsrooms and networks. Quantities of data and content creation, processing, consumption, and archiving are unprecedented in the history of humanity. Increasingly, all industries are looking towards general artificial intelligence to help manage an ocean of data. As listed in the applications and the categories that follow, these are tasks traditionally performed by humans. However, the speed and quantity of today's content necessitate live instantaneous processing.

A trusted indicator of technology phases and lifespans, the Gartner Hype Cycle maintains evidence-based data to plot emerging and established technologies over a three-to-five-year span of time. Subscriptions to Gartner Research exist to help businesses decide which technologies to purchase or invest in. The plot covers five phases of emerging technology and includes the rise, peak, trough (disillusionment), slope, and plateau. The plateau marks an established technology and signals widespread use.

Phases of Artificial Intelligence (Oversimplified)

AI – Narrow skill sets
AGI (artificial general intelligence) – extremely intelligent human performance with a broad range of skills
ASI (Artificial super intelligence) – what everyone fears: sentient machines.

Although the hype continues, AI has passed the Peak of Inflated Expectations. This means we are approaching the Trough of Disillusionment, in which practical implementation and full-scale deployment uncover challenges affecting long-term viability. Media enterprise discussions will most likely center around resolving challenges to integration and scalability rather than human versus computer issues.

The following are some current applications and use categories.

Tagging Content and Metadata

Authenticity

As AI becomes more photoreal and harder to distinguish from real life, it's necessary to have technology that can validate an image. The 2021 Washington, DC–based non-profit Coalition for Content Provenance and Authenticity (C2PA) and its partner organization, Content Authenticity Initiative (CAI), support open-source formats to trace media origins and manipulation for publishers, creators, and consumers. The CAI was founded in 2019 by Adobe, assists in authorship tools for creators, and helps consumers determine media origin. Equipment manufacturers, software developers, and television and film media entities are encouraged to align purposefully. Another partner, Project Origin (2019), was founded by the BBC, CBC Radio Canada, Microsoft, and the *New York Times* to confront disinformation in digital news and track media to ensure integrity (https://c2pa.org/about/about/).

In addition to tracking image manipulation software, digital camera footage's original metadata is instantly created. The Sony A9 III has content credentials. The Sony A1, A7S III, and A7 IV require firmware updates. Leica M11-P has content authentication based on the Content Authenticity Initiative (CAI) and C2PA standards. Image manipulation software (Adobe Photoshop, Lightroom, and Adobe Camera Raw) supports C2PA and CAI. The generative AI application Adobe Firefly uses content credentials to indicate the use of AI.

Real-Time Content Analysis

Live Content Moderation

The IBC Accelerator Project (2021), founded by Al Jezeera, AP, BBC, Reuters, RTÈ, Entertainment Technology Center (USC), and Multichoice, aims to use automation to detect, measure, and flag bias in news reporting to maintain neutrality, fairness, and transparency. AI-driven metadata for video flags inappropriate content while streaming on news and social feeds https://show.ibc.org/

While fair and honest reporting is becoming increasingly impossible to legislate and regulate, AI-driven real-time fact-checking is being explored as with Factiverse Live Fact-Checking and Checkmate, a fact-checking system developed by news organizations. These systems provide journalists with real-time detection, cross-references, and databases for instant verification. Although automatically detecting misinformation and cross-checking facts against verified sources, selection of trusted sources and final decision-making still relies on human judgment. In general, there exists AI use for censorship and fact checking, however, usage tends to be customized per entity rather than designed per national standard.

Sports Coverage

During the Paris Olympic games (2024), AI was used for tagging descriptive metadata and auto-clipping to help journalists find specific content, provide transcriptions, translate interviews, and create real-time captions and subtitles. Biometric and other sensors supplied viewers with live information (https://ttms.com/how-was-ai-used-at-the-paris-2024-olympic-games/#4.-how-does-ai-support-judging-during-the-paris-2024-olympics?).

Intelligent live video streaming analytics are also used with action recognition tracking athletes to ensure they adhere to regulations (https://www.strong.io/blog/ai-for-real-time-video-streams).

Highlights Creation

OBS introduced the Highlights Generation system for the 2024 Paris Olympics. It used machine-learning models trained on numerous datasets of previous Olympic footage to recognize patterns and events such as record-breaking performances or finishes to repeat highlights without delay (https://tmbroadcast.com/index.php/obs-2024-paris-olympics-challenges-solved/).

Ads

Contextual Ads

Fewer people use cable TV, and many are using internet streaming options instead, but internet privacy rules are moving away from third-party cookies that track user activity, so marketing strategy is now focused on tracking programs people watch instead of people and their habits. This is called contextual ad placement. For example, if the program is a cooking show, ads will reflect cooking products and food that might interest the audience. AI tools analyze the relevance and appropriate moments for ad insertion. NBCUniversal and AdSmart have a cross-platform ad system displaying on televisions, mobile devices, and desktops using streaming-connected TV (Fire TV, Apple) https://blog.kargo.com/tag/digital-advertising

Personalization

Recommendations

If you sign up for a streaming subscription, personal information capture for the purposes of personalization is not technically a violation of privacy, especially if disclosed or made transparent to members. Netflix uses AI-driven personalization and recommendation algorithms, with a system powered by machine learning algorithms, to analyze user data, including viewing history, ratings, and interactions. By continuously learning from user behavior, Netflix's AI can suggest relevant movies and shows to viewers (https://link.springer.com/article/10.1007/s11042-018-6323-8).

AI Dubbing

Multiple software developers are competing for network and studio dubbing jobs. Especially desirable is dubbing for translation to multiple languages. The traditional method of hiring actors and rerecording the audio track to match the lip sync is time consuming. Some AI dubbing systems promise a library of like-sounding voices, translation length control when languages are longer or shorter, context awareness to match emoting, natural speaker–sounding translations, and live streaming.

There are AI uses that go beyond dubbing: for example, speech synthesis is used for narration. Speech synthesis can also provide assistance for people with disabilities. Speech synthesis is part of computer interfaces, so commands can be spoken, and the computer can respond in voice. Podcasts, broadcasts, and meetings need to be transcribed and edited, and programs need closed captioning. So let's not forget text-to-speech and speech-to-text usage for everyday purposes.

Here are just a few applications in no particular order.

- ElevenLabs
- Dubformer
- Neurodub
- PlayHT
- Checksub
- Dubverse
- DeepDub
- Descript

AI Color Grading

The link provided is an AI color editor that uses a neural network film emulator to apply cinematic LUTs to footage. It is ACES color managed and simplifies the color grading process. Maintain color consistency throughout your project with the current de facto standard: teal-orange LUT and palette (https://fylm.ai/).

Remote Video Sourcing

App.stringr.com (https://www.app.stringr.com/) uses a vast network of videographers and AI tools to source, produce, and manage video content in real time. The footage is automatically tagged, metadata is generated, and voice narration is added as needed for on-demand news content worldwide. Clients such as local TV stations, national news networks, and digital media companies place orders through a remote application that sources cloud video from the over 120,000 videographer network. The stringr.ai feed platform accesses events, weather, traffic, financial market information, and real estate sales information without sending out a news crew. AI tools also enable automatic transcription, captioning, translation, editing, and collaboration.

Content Creation

When speaking about generative AI, most people will be focused on image creation and simulation of humans. There are unbelievable advances in this area and by the time this book is published, no doubt, the tools in this category will have been increased tenfold. Some tools here may be replaced by better tools or versions. Since this is probably the fastest-growing use of GenAI, the following is a very abbreviated list of categories and popular tools intended to be a good starting point for illustrative purposes.

Real-Time Generative Performance Tools

In the Robert Zemeckis movie *Here*, Tom Hanks and Robin Wright were de-aged in real time using Metaphysic Studios AI system to preserve the actors' performance and personality without makeup or post-production effects. This is different from CGI replacement because it is real-time face swapping reacting to a live performance that goes beyond the type of face-swapping filter found on smart phones. As the actor turns his or her head or hair interacts with the face, the generative image matches. Metaphysic Pro is a platform that has a movie-quality digital asset library of actor samples collected with actor permission so performers can receive fair compensation for use of their digital likenesses (https://metaphysic.ai/studios/; https://screenrant.com/here-movie-deage-technology-ai-explained/; https://www.fastcompany.com/91033193/metaphysic-ai-most-innovative-companies-2024).

Generative Imagery

• Midjourney Website	https://www.midjourney.com/

The website is a more friendly interface than the Discord server. Perks are given to loyal users with thousands of images created and/or a year of subscribing.

• Canva	https://www.canva.com/
• Microsoft Designer. Accesses DALL-E 3.	https://designer.microsoft.com/
• DALL-E 3	https://openai.com/index/dall-e-3/
• Adobe Firefly	https://new.express.adobe.com/

Generative Video

• Lumalabs	https://lumalabs.ai/dream-machine/
• Elai	https://app.elai.io/
• Runway	https://app.runwayml.com/
• KlingAI	https://app.klingai.com/

Generative Lipsync

• Lalamu Studio	https://www.canva.com/your-apps/AAF5prtvncA/lalamu-studio
• PixBim	https://pixbim.com/lip-sync-animations

Generative Humans

• Synthesia	https://www.synthesia.io/
• Colossyan	https://www.colossyan.com/
• DeepBrain AI	https://www.aistudios.com/

Generative Writing

• ChatGPT	https://chatgpt.com/
• Grammarly	www.grammarly.com
• Jasper	www.jasper.ai

Generative Chat

• ChatGPT	https://chatgpt.com/
• Gemini	https://gemini.google.com/
• Perplexity.ai	https://www.perplexity.ai
• Claude.ai	https://claude.ai/

At this time, Perplexity.ai has integrated the Chinese R1 model, DeepSeek, so that servers in the US and EU can explore the model without exposing data to Chinese servers.

Generative Translation

• Google Translate	https://translate.google.us/?sl=auto&tl=en&op=translate
• Notta	https://www.notta.ai/en
• Interprefy	https://www.interprefy.com/

AI and Entertainment

During the writing of this book, Disney created a division devoted to AI and XR technology. This move is expected to cut costs in post-production and VFX, possibly adding to ongoing layoffs, not just at Disney but in the overall tech sector. Some say that as Disney goes, so goes the entertainment industry. In fact, today there are multiple incentives to form partnerships between

AI developers and studios that may not have the Disney-like resources to create their own division. The partnership between Lionsgate and Runway is an example that could be followed by other smaller studios (https://technologymagazine.com/articles/how-disneys-use-of-ai-ar-impacts-the-entertainment-sector; https://runwayml.com/news/runway-partners-with-lionsgate

GOING FORWARD

Frightful concerns about disinformation and propagandistic AI are being voiced and addressed worldwide and nationally. As regulations are formed and consequences enacted, these restraints will no doubt further affect technology for entertainment use (as mentioned earlier in the Global Networks section). Most organizational and governmental bodies are mandating transparency in AI usage while both organizations and the public demand data security. The following are some examples of organizational responses.

AI Governance – Globally

AI Governance Alliance

The AI Governance Alliance, an initiative of the World Economic Forum's Centre for the Fourth Industrial Revolution, assembles CEOs from leading industries and governments, experts from academia, and civil society leaders. The goal is to promote transparent, inclusive, and ethically accountable artificial intelligence systems. They want to govern AI development in the global community, ensuring that development benefits society as a whole (https://initiatives.weforum.org/ai-governance-alliance/about).

International Association of Privacy Professionals

IAPP maintains a website following global and US AI laws, policies, and governance (https://iapp.org/resources/article/us-federal-ai-governance/)

AI Governance – Nationally

BBC

The British Broadcasting Corporation (BBC, 2024) has published online how AI tools will be used in generative AI pilots regarding changes made to existing content, audience experience, and better efficiency. They promise transparency and responsible use of AI tools (https://www.bbc.com/mediacentre/articles/2024/update-generative-ai-and-ai-tools-bbc). This is a good first step towards transparency in ethics, tools, and purposes.

FCC

In the US, the FCC (2024) has proposed transparency standards that would inform viewers when a political ad is created with AI. It does not prohibit use, but only demands disclosure for political ads and not generally (https://docs.fcc.gov/public/attachments/DOC-404389A1.pdf).

AI Governance – NGOs

It has already been mentioned in the Tagging Content and Metadata – Authenticity section how manufacturers like Adobe, Sony, C2PA, CAI, and other non-governmental organizations (NGOs) are handling disinformation and attempting to support information integrity and ethics. However, the list of NGOs dedicated to the ethical development of AI is long and includes established organizations like the Rockefeller Foundation, the United Nations, UNESCO, and many universities. The World Economic Forum (an international cooperative of public and private leaders formed to shape global industry agendas) has a platform called the Centre for the Fourth Industrial Revolution that contains sub-technological domains, of which one is the AI Governance Alliance. Their mission is "Committed to fostering inclusive, ethical, and sustainable AI, the Alliance drives significant change across industries" (https://initiatives.weforum.org/ai-governance-alliance/home)

Here is an introductory list of AI organizations: https://www.aiethicist.org/ai-organizations.

Insurance Concerns

While the US seems to be lagging behind regulation initiatives compared to the some other parts of the world, US insurance companies are not standing still and are anticipating a landslide of lawsuits.

As generative AI reshapes Hollywood, it is upending not just creative norms but also established notions of authorship and intellectual property (IP). The industry is now witnessing lawsuits over unlicensed training data – ranging from a recent one by the *New York Times* against British photo agency Getty Images' complaint against Microsoft over its use of copyrighted content. Courts are discussing how existing copyright laws might apply to AI-generated material, and legislative efforts – such as the proposed European Union AI Act – aim to impose new transparency requirements on AI developers.

Legislative reaction to deepfaked material – AI-produced footage that makes people appear to say or do things they didn't – has been slower to materialize in the US, although bills like the NO FAKES Act are still in the works (https://www.sagaftra.org/sag-aftra-applauds-introduction-no-fakes-act-house).

Meanwhile, the US Copyright Office has been looking into how AI-made works fit into copyright law, specifically that current policies limit protection to works made by actual humans, something that Hollywood studios fear could undermine copyright protections for films and TV shows that increasingly rely on AI for production and post-production work. They are due to issue new guidelines later this year (https://variety.com/2024/biz/features/hollywood-ai-concerns-legal-challenges-1235973275/).

As generative AI has come to be a reality, it has created new opportunities but also new types of risks for the global media, film, TV, and entertainment industries, says Ros Breese, managing director of Tokio Marine HCC's entertainment industry risks product. The new risks that have arisen include a need for the industry to determine how and when generative AI might be used safely to create content – especially as it relates to IP, she notes. OpenAI, the creators of the viral text-generating AI program GPT-3, has been hit with a lawsuit by the *New York Times* over copyright protection.

Breese points out that managing these risks will entail adopting new ways of tracing ownership of content and establishing a chain of responsibility that will be key to future legal cases and thus to how insurance will develop.

Moreover, since the beginning of the COVID-19 pandemic, consumption habits have changed from long to short form (for example, from cinema to podcast and documentary), which requires different risk management, mostly concerning clearance of the permissions and the rights of the archival footage, which remain a major issue for documentary producers (https://www.insurancebusinessmag.com/us/news/breaking-news/generative-ai-presents-eando-risks-for-media-and-entertainment-firms-493253.aspx).

Marketing and Sales

AI and machine learning are probably the fastest-moving technologies in human history. We have touched on AI use in movies and broadcasting, but another purpose that is fueling the logarithmic accent of this technology and should not be overlooked is internet marketing. Technology serves commercialism, and if there is a way to position oneself ahead of others with new, highly desirable tools, then development will be rapid. Combine these realities with open source, and that creates a type of feeding frenzy driven by dreams of high profitability with hundreds of thousands of developers working on new tools daily. Already, since the 1990s, there is advertising by sophisticated AI algorithms, customer tracking and targeting, predictive analytics to anticipate customer behavior, and more detailed customer personalization. Chatbots and virtual assistants reduce the need for live human customer service, which means reduced hiring for that role. But the most impressive and visible advancements are in content creation, and this is where there is overlap with entertainment.

Beyond writing for ad copy, scripts, blogs, websites, and other forms of sales material, there is visual and audio generation. Text-to-images, text-to-video, voice pattern recognition for voice searching, and talking synthespians for presentations are all time savers, allowing ads and marketing campaigns to be created faster and include still more microbusiness startups and internet entrepreneurs (especially helpful since we are facing the "end of work" scenario.) Social media includes streaming, so it has the same content creation and distribution needs as TV broadcasting, but now, almost anyone can be an influencer on TikTok, which is a type of celebrity status.

Internet marketing is a double-edged sword. It allows everyone to become a microbusiness (although many internet business claim to have six- and seven-digit profits), but it is widely unregulated, and claims are unaccounted. It is a wildcat business (meaning potentially financially unsound), and there are visually more people selling applications and courses on internet marketing than are possibly making a living income from internet marketing. However, the fact that more people attempt to own internet businesses and more people fill the need to help those attempting to own internet businesses shows that there is an increase of knowledge on the side of both predators, who prey, and the prey, who know they are being taken advantage of and are demanding accountability. Therefore, both predator and prey are driving the industry and technology further and faster.

Keeping Up

This short synopsis does not pretend to be a predictor or even a thorough summary of everything available today. If you are feeling the urge to update daily, here are some reliable sources to start your deep dive.

- https://www.gartner.com/en/topics/generative-ai – categorized for research and advisement.
- https://www.futuretools.io/ – categorized for utility.
- https://www.futurepedia.io/ – categorized for utility.
- https://www.artificialintelligence-news.com/ – news and explanations.
- https://www.technologyreview.com/topic/artificial-intelligence/ – reporting and explanations.

- https://sr.ithaka.org/our-work/generative-ai-product-tracker/–categorized for academia.
- AI trackers or AI search engines. (Like Google but specifically for AI tools.)
  - https://theresanaiforthat.com/
  - https://theresanai.com/

"Fasten your seatbelts, it's going to be a bumpy night."
Mankiewicz, J. L. (Director). (1950).
***All about Eve* [Film]. 20th Century Fox.**

Notes

1 Stefon, M. (2024, November 22). *Fairness doctrine United States policy [1949–1987].* https://www.britannica.com/topic/Fairness-Doctrine.[0]

2 Blondin, Andy. (2020, July 2). "The weather channel's new studio brings immersive mixed reality to daily live broadcasts." *The Weather Channel.* https://www.unrealengine.com/en-US/spotlights/the-weather-channel-s-new-studio-brings-immersive-mixed-reality-to-daily-live-broadcasts

3 https://variety.com/2015/film/news/why-sony-called-in-marvels-big-gun-to-reboot-spider-man-1201429540/

4 https://investor.hasbro.com/news-releases/news-release-details/hasbro-announces-plan-grow-profit-50-over-next-three-years#:~:text=The%20Company%20expanded%20on%20its%20major%20new,upcoming%20CGI%20feature%20film%20in%20summer%202024

Chapter 11
Teaching Virtual Production

Teaching any technical subject is particularly difficult if the technology is progressing rapidly. University-level faculty can have a particularly tough time if they have a full class load and are expected to be up to date on the latest and greatest. I'm noticing that many schools are hiring technical software assistants to assist faculty in instructing students on the often-complex software to allow faculty to focus on the broader concepts of history, practice, and aesthetics. Many schools seek out working professionals as adjuncts to try to keep current. I am one of those teachers and had to learn a great deal from my academic colleagues regarding proper syllabus and curriculum preparation, course objectives, and grading criteria for artistic projects. I am most certainly not a high-level academic professional, but I do have years of experience teaching students visual effects and have found certain methods that are effective in the school environment. I'm sharing my process to provide some ideas and inspiration for the many fine instructors who teach at film schools and engage in corporate training.

Hands On

I find it is most important to ladder up the education starting with basic concepts that gradually become more complex. I will do an introductory

DOI: 10.4324/9781003473169-11

overview lecture on the history of effects and the basic principles of the camera and lens. I regularly get taken aback when I query my students to find they often don't know the range of f-stops, focal length, or the principle of the inverse square law. I suspect that our cell phone society has done a great deal to dummy down technology, where fun things can happen with the push of a button on an app. This can create the illusion that students know more about software than they do. If one is to make a career in virtual production or VFX, all those basic principles will need to be understood. I cover the concepts of f-stops and depth of field by explaining the idea behind a pinhole camera. I choose a student from the class who wears glasses and is nearsighted to demonstrate how they can see without glasses by peering through a tiny hole formed by curling one of their fingers in front of their eye and peering through the tiny gap in the center of the curl. For those who don't wear glasses, I build on this by explaining that the tiny hole amounts to the nodal point inside a lens where all the light rays converge. As I explain in the first *Filming the Fantastic* book, panning or tilting on this point allows a glass shot or miniature close to the camera to stay locked together with the background it is blended into. I demonstrate this by having the students hold one hand in front of their eyes and position their thumbs and forefingers as if they are a giant hand crushing my head. As they peer through their fingers aligned to my head I tell them to turn their head like they're panning a camera, this will make the hand and head misalign. Panning around the center of your eyeball will more or less keep the hand and head together demonstrating the concept of nodal point. This builds to include lenses, focal length, and sensor size. After the first lecture, the next class gets a hands-on demo.

In-Camera Foreground Miniature

One of my first demonstrations is to composite a small statue or model into a park setting using forced perspective. The camera is also set on the nodal to allow for a pan. To lessen the technology, I try to use a camera with a small sensor size to make it easier to have a large depth of field. This helps put the focus on composition, lighting, blending, and camera movement. The result is fast and fun, and the students begin to develop an eye for what to look for in lighting, contrast, focus, and composition. The foreground miniature is the first precedent for in-camera virtual production, dating back to the silent era. The big difference today is that the synthetic computer graphic set or Gaussian splat is not a miniature but a full-size element composited with our live action with a camera that can execute any kind of move. The early nodal system only allowed for pans and tilts. The students see this demonstration and are given a project in which they choose their own prop element to create their own forced perspective effect.

Introduction to Data Management

After the forced perspective introduction, I give a lecture regarding matte painting and the birth of post-production. For this lecture, I showed an early 1980s *Movie Magic* episode on matte paintings that I was proud to take part in as it showcased the Illusion Arts studio I worked at under Bill Taylor, Syd Dutton, and the Oscar-winning matte painter Albert Whitlock. After the screening, I lecture on the importance of taking note of camera position, lens angle, and the rest pointed out in Chapter 1. I have the students understand that these notes enable the same in-camera effects to be broken down and shot as separate elements for post-production. In other words, with a foreground miniature, the background, miniature, and camera are set so the effect is seen all at once. If you keep all the positions for the camera, miniature, and background the same, all you do in post is put a green screen behind the miniature, and there is no difference in the effect. For this hands-on demo the class takes notes and photographs a student standing full figure on one side of the frame in bright sunlight with a shadow. The objective will be to photograph the same student in the same way the next week, only this time in front of a green screen while keeping the camera and lighting the same to create the effect of a double.

Green Screen Demonstration

For this class, I demonstrate one of the harder lighting situations to replicate, which is harsh direct sunlight. To have a proper demonstration, you will need a good-size stage that will allow plenty of room to replicate the distance of the camera to the performer as used in the background plate and enough room to have a large green screen at least 10 to 20 feet behind the actor to eliminate green spill. The actor will stand on a riser or several apple boxes placed together to make a small stage. A large light providing the daylight will need to be positioned at least 10 feet or more away to obtain even lighting with a sharp shadow. The inverse square law can be demonstrated practically during a lecture by standing close to the light and walking 5 feet away to show how quickly the light falls off when close. Then walk 20 feet away from the light and repeat the 5 foot walk to demonstrate that there is very little or no fall off in the light. Raising the student on a platform informs the student that modifications need to be made to the data from the data sheet as the performer's feet are now higher by an apple box above the ground plane in the photographed background. The actor is shot on an apple box and then shot in the same place but standing on a shiny board that reflects the screen around their feet. This technique is great for surrounding the actor in green without green spill but has the problem of eliminating the shadow. The last two takes have the actor standing on green and then just the green floor and background green with no actor. All this is shot during the first half of class. After break, all the footage is put into the computer lab where compositing lessons will take place. I like to have them shoot these tests in a good format like Apple ProRes 4:2:2 or 4:4:4 to obtain the best green screen element. I also repeat the exercise having them shoot in a compressed MP4 format to see the difference in difficulty if shots do not have enough data.

Compositing

Simple composites are done in After Effects using a Key Light green screen keyer. We do a straight composite matting the top of the apple boxes and the figure into the background. The shadow will not continue past the boxes, of course, but the preservation of the shadow or creation will be visible. The next composite is done with the shiny board, which will make a good composite with no shadow. A false shadow is made by copying the green screen masked element, plunging the brightness to zero to create a silhouette of the figure, and using transform tools to rotate and distort the matte to appear as a long shadow in the composite. Transparency in the shadow is done by adjusting the opacity controls in transform. The next composite is to try to pull a shadow off the green, which will be very difficult with poor results. After this designed "failure," I demonstrate the use of the clean plate (green screen by itself) to generate a tool called a difference matte to inform the computer what the subject is and what is green. The shadow will pull nicely, but you will inevitably have holes in the subject. This will not matter as the figure without the shadow will be above the difference layer and will cover the holes.

Camera Moves

Pan and Scan

At this point, the students have observed the fun of forced perspective with a camera move and the frustration of a good-looking composite that had to be "locked off." We now discuss the historical remedies for creating moves with locked-off elements. The first approach is to create a composite such as a twin shot or a forced perspective lock-off shot in 4K resolution. After the composite is made, the student brings the oversize shot in After Effects and scales in and does a pan or tilt using a high-definition (1920x1080) extraction off the 4K. This will allow the same freedom of movement as a nodal point shot. In this case, you have the advantage of pushing in as well, but it will have the effect of a zoom instead of a dolly move as there will be no perspective change.

Introducing Unreal

By now, the students have been exposed to how to combine real imagery with real imagery using traditional methods. The ultimate goal for the photoplay, of course, is to have a living camera that combines the real with synthetic creations, like the settings in the Unreal Marketplace. The Unreal software is quite daunting, and there are whole animation programs in film schools devoted to it. My classes are designed for filmmakers and directors who want to know the concepts but not necessarily to pursue the high skill set of being a certified Unreal technician. For the filmmaking student, all that is needed is to show them how to open the software, build a simple set of planes and cubes, make a light, make a camera, animate the camera, and render out a movie. Those are the basic components they need to make a film. The first project does that and then adds a ready-made highly detailed set from the Unreal Marketplace, where they place cameras and find their shots. If they want to add people to these sets, the fundamentals of lighting and data collection have already been taught. The virtual cameras created in Unreal have f-stops, sensor sizes, and positional information such as tilt. To measure this information within Unreal, you create the universal cube that measures one meter in all directions and can be scaled to any size. This means you can make a placeholder of a person within the Unreal set and measure how far they are from the camera along with the camera's focal length, height, and tilt. On the green screen stage, you reproduce those positions and focal length with a real camera and shoot your performer on a green stage to match, just like the students did with the twin shot. Before delving into these measurements, I find it best to have the students find the position of their actors by eye using previz.

BARE-BONES VIRTUAL PRODUCTION

Even for schools that do not have access to the Unreal Game Engine, there is a way to introduce the technique using screen grabs of permanently free game engine sets from the Marketplace. Using stills from the sets is a limitation, but in a good way, as the students can concentrate on the basic principles of matching the camera and lighting when shooting their performers against green.

Find a Background Image

Have students browse sets that intrigue them and pick several stills into which they want to put an actor. This is more challenging than one would think, as many of the stills are done from high camera angles that can be hard to match. Having a student pick an angle that is difficult to shoot in live-action cements the concept that both live and virtual cameras must match. Once the screen grabs are taken, you will notice there may be crosshairs or other graphics in the middle of the picture that must be painted out in Photoshop. This becomes a simple gradable exercise of cloning surrounding imagery to paint over unwanted graphics. Discussions can be made about where the light comes from and whether it is soft, hard, or both.

Deduce the Focal Length and Camera Angle From a Still Image

The screengrab will have no metadata that tells you what focal length, tilt, or distance was used for the lens. In years past, production designers and VFX supervisors could extract camera data from the picture itself. This technique was often used if one had a historical picture that did not have any information about how it was shot. A copy of the stills was placed atop a large sheet of drafting paper you could draw on. Typically, if you had a picture with an image of a building, the process was to find a structure with two faces at right angles to each other. Lines were projected from the tops and bottoms of walls or windows until they met at a point. This vanishing point detects the horizon line key to working out the data. Various other processes ensue based on these points that allow you to deduce the camera's focal length, height, and tilt.

A detailed step-by-step process can be found in the 1963 *Journal of the Society of Motion Picture and Television Engineers*, Volume 72, in an article called "Elementary Motion Picture Design Perspective" by Wally Gentleman. This process of connecting imagery with the real world is still used today by production

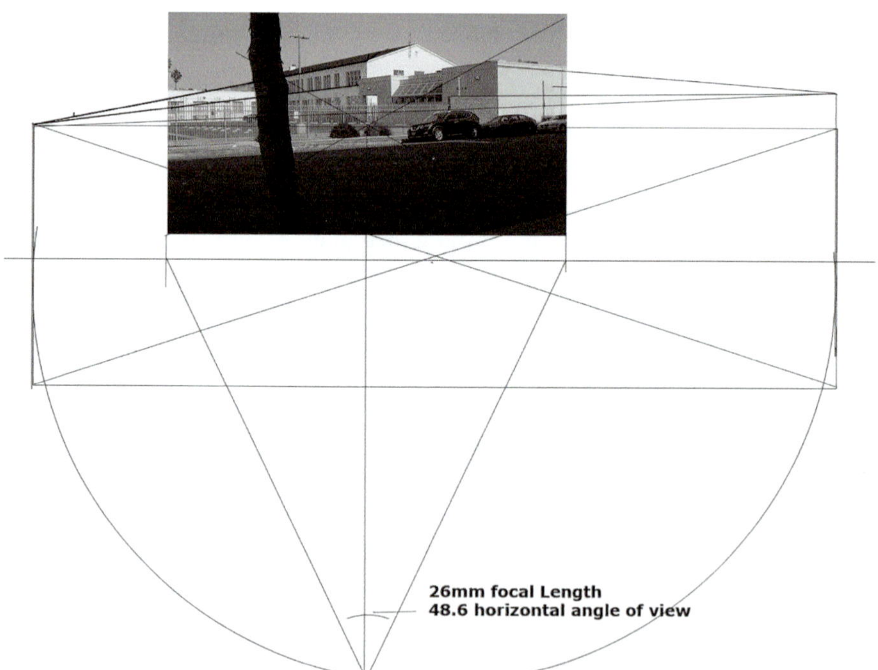

Figure 11.1 *Manual drafting method for determining focal length from a picture. This picture was taken with a 26mm lens with a sensor size of 23.5 x 15.6. After drawing out this diagram using Photoshop, I verified the angle of view by using a Canon field of view calculator.*

designers who design and build sets for motion pictures. I mention this process even in this high-tech age when computers can tell you the focal length of a lens. After Effects, for example, can take a motion picture of a pan or dolly and analyze every frame to derive and create a matching virtual camera. The computer has an easier time with this as every frame of movement is different, and by comparing points, it can come up with a solution even though it cannot recognize objects in the image. This particular tool cannot create a camera from a still image because, as yet, the computer cannot recognize a building, a person, etc. This is why, when browsing certain protected websites, you have tests to see if you are a robot by asking you what pictures have bicycles in them. That being said, artificial intelligence may have learned to see and understand as we do by the time this book is published. In that case, the mention of this process of camera deduction will serve as a testament to the talent and ingenuity of those who came before us.

(https://www.usa.canon.com/pro/electronic-range-calculators/angle-of-view).

Finding the Angle Through Previz

Live on-set previz can be achieved with a video switcher or Dragonframe software that contains a camera live-view chroma-key tool.

For my classes, I don't expect my students to painstakingly reproduce the Gentleman method. Still, I use it so they can appreciate perspective and better understand lenses and how they affect camera placement. I use previz to have them find the focal length empirically. For my green screen classes, I use the Blackmagic ATEM mini switcher ($) to hold still images and combine them with live action against green using a crude chroma-key. This switcher can take both SDI and HDMI inputs, so it can use both high-end and low-end cameras. Once the camera is engaged, I have the students pay attention to structures in a set, such as a table. I then have them place a table on the green stage to composite alongside the background image of the table so they can compare how much of the top of the Unreal table is showing compared to the real table.

Using this direct comparison, one can quickly find the height and tilt by moving the camera about while simultaneously viewing the composite. An apple box can also be a good comparative subject. If an actor stands in one place and does not move forward or back, the illusion will hold, even if the focal lengths

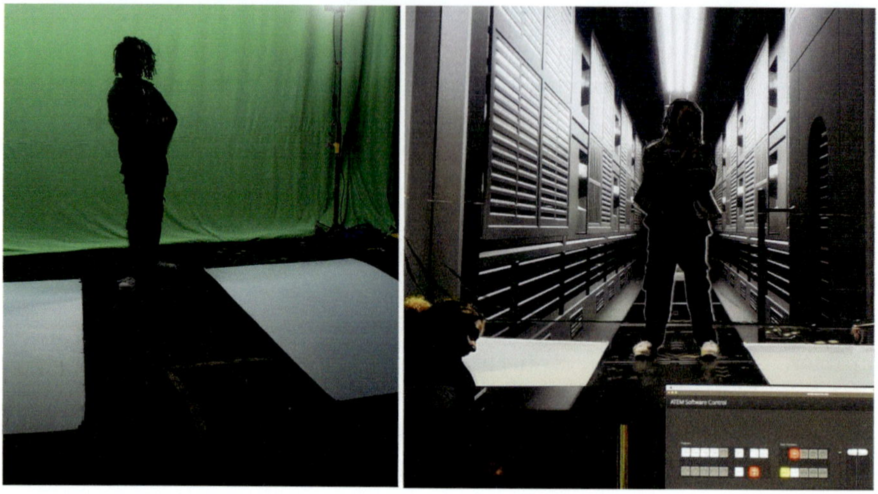

Figure 11.2 *To help find the focal length by eye, foam core sheets can be laid on the stage floor equidistant from each other. When the previz comp is viewed on the monitor, the camera's focal length, height, and distance can be adjusted to match the perspective of the CG hallway still picture. The Blackmagic switcher control on the laptop can be seen in the lower right in front of the monitor, showing the composite.*

do not match. To get the proper focal length, I have them tell the subject to move towards and away from the camera and have the students compare the size changes with the environment. An example would be walking to a door in the distance. If the subject shrinks to be smaller than the doorway, the lens is too wide. If the subject stays larger than the doorway walking to the back, the lens is too long. Adjusting the zoom lens during these trials will quickly find the proper focal length.

Finding the Light Direction and Ratio

The best way to match lighting is not to look at the light hitting the objects in the background image but at the shadow that is produced. For a standing figure, you start with the key light height and tilt to obtain a shadow that matches a similar shadow in the background image, perhaps from a box or a chair. Close-ups are more forgiving, and you can look at the shadows on the face cast by the nose or brow. As far as the lighting ratio or the relationship of brightness between the key light and the fill light is concerned, judge by eye and compare the amount of shadow detail that exists in background objects and matches them. One process I'm particularly proud of is the use of an apple box and its virtual twin. One can place both the real and virtual apple boxes in the same shot and easily adjust either the virtual or the practical light to match the other boxes' shadow and direction. I'm proud to say that, unofficially, a Mo-Sys engineer, upon learning of my technique, now refers to their studio's apple box as the Sawicki box.

Another Previz Tool

Another inexpensive option for schools and indies is the use of a camera that has live view capability, such as a Canon EOS camera, and Dragonframe software. Dragonframe is a stop-motion software with a built-in keyer to composite stills and movies as a background. A Canon 5D, for example, has a live view function that works with Dragonframe and can shoot video as well. So, with a laptop running Dragonframe hooked up to a Canon with a USB interface, you can find your position and focal length by using the chroma-key tool and, once done, use the camera to shoot your green screen elements and record on the camera card.

Later, use After Effects to load the stills from the Unreal set and the green screen footage for final compositing. Using rotoscope mattes, the subject can also appear behind objects in the background image. The main value of these exercises is to serve as a primer in teaching how to match perspective and lighting for more advanced classes. A Canon camera will cost $$ while the Dragonframe software costs $.

The Moving Camera

> **A static live-action camera element** can be post tracked into a virtual camera move rendered in Unreal. As the live action figure lacks perspective change, being a flat image, the method has the best chance of blending if feet are not shown against the virtual floor, where the mismatch is most noticeable.

Many schools don't have the resources to afford an LED volume or a live tracking system. The following concepts and techniques are ones I have used when all I had was Unreal, After Effects, a camera, some lights, and a green screen. These are actual case studies from three personal films I've made with limited resources. Some of the elements will be made available on our companion website for the book.

Inserting a Static Green Screen Element Into a Virtual Dolly Shot

I shot my live-action character with a locked-off camera from one vantage point using the same height and level camera as the virtual camera. To make this work, I had to eliminate perspective change on the character as much as possible, as the character's image is essentially a flat paper-doll cut-out that will be locked into a point in space in front of the After Effects virtual camera. To

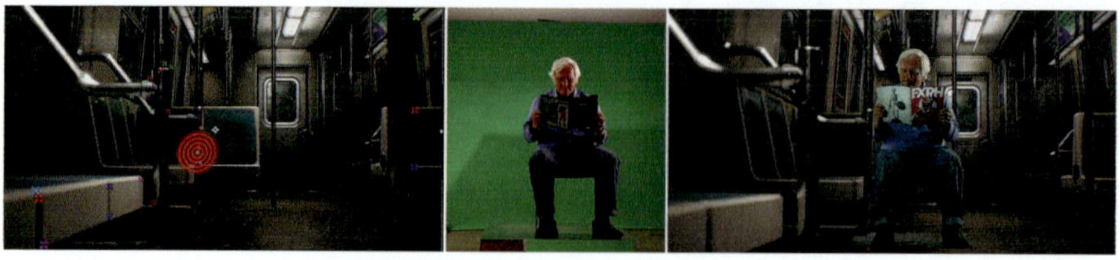

Figure 11.3 *This post-track move with a 2D image inserted into a 3D image with a dolly worked as I chose a start and end camera position that minimized perspective shift on the chair, where the flat paper-doll cut-out of my image was stuck to the tracking target bull's eye. A rotoscope of the foreground chrome bar helped the illusion by placing the bar in front of me at the start of the dolly.*

make sure my dolly shot moved straight into the seat, I found a camera height that kept the edge of the seat flat to the camera throughout the move, meaning that as the camera came closer to the seat, you would never see the top or bottom surface of the seat, just the edge of it, throughout the move. When the character is tracked to the edge of the seat, they stay locked into the scene.

Changing the Live-Action Format to Improve the Resolution

When the Unreal Engine rendered the dolly move, every frame had the exact resolution of 1920x1080. When I shot the live-action character with a fixed lens and a static position, that image was locked into a fixed size. If I shot the live-action character head to toe horizontally, then the character's height would be locked at 1080 with a lot of unused image area to the right and left of the actor. If the actor is shot this way, it begins to reveal its lower resolution and pixilate as the virtual camera gets closer. To prevent the chance of this happening, I shot the live action while turning the camera on its side so the height of the image of the actor was closer to1920, with a minimal amount of wasted space on the sides. This technique ensured the character maintained a good definition and resolution when tracked in the moving shot.

Feet Resting on Green Without Spill

While having an actor walk on a green floor is seemingly ubiquitous, I avoid that at all costs unless I have proper software designed to accommodate that type of composite. For the sitting figure with feet on the floor, I sat on a wire-frame chair with my legs hiding the legs of the chair and my feet resting on a shiny board that can be as simple as an inexpensive silver poster board from an art store. The beauty of this technique is that the shiny board reflects the green screen behind the actor, which will surround the shoes without casting a green spill on them or the actor.

Lighting the Live Action

I used a fabric green screen from the composite components company digitalgreenscreen.com and lit it evenly with two long KinoFlo lights at 45-degree angles to the screen. The screen was placed about ten feet behind the actor to avoid a green spill. To light the foreground, I merely referenced the practical lighting in the Unreal set to find it was just soft overhead fluorescent lights shining down at 45-degree angles into the interior. I roughly placed two more KinoFlos in this position and adjusted for pleasing facial detail.

Completing the Illusion

After tracking the virtual camera movement and attaching the green screen live-action character to a null object placed at the same point in space as the chair, I rotoscoped the silver handrail to allow it to pass in front of the actor to create a sense of dimension. The key light compositor in After Effects was used to do the composite.

Expanding the Scope

The important thing when developing a story is not to limit yourself. Many student filmmakers work on a script and get stuck in the creative process when the "I can't do that shot" idea comes into their heads. Have them write what they see in their mind's eye as if the movie was already done. Once it's all on paper, they can worry about how to create the imagery and compromise from there.

While scouting, students tend to place the virtual camera in places unachievable in the real world. They match the real camera's sensor size and focal length range of its zoom lens. In the details of the virtual camera actor, they come up with a nice shot, but upon examination, they discover they placed the camera hundreds of meters away from the buildings where the subject was to be composited. They need to measure the live-action stage and ensure that their virtual camera stays confined within the real camera's stage space when shooting in the virtual environment. The following ideas came from a film I made called *Power*.

When scouting locations in Unreal sets, keep in mind the limitations of the live-action stage space. Like traditional VFX, you must maintain the same station point and focal length. Don't set your virtual camera 100 feet away from where your performer will be composited if your live action stage is only 50 feet. The distance and focal lengths must match.

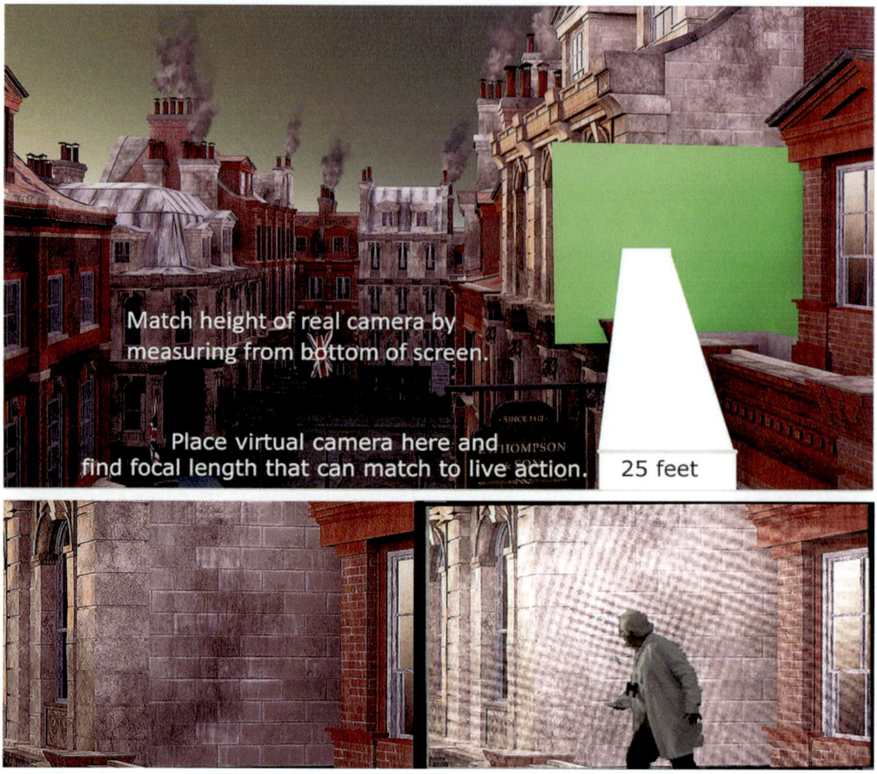

Figure 11.4 *After measuring the actual physical stage and green screen, you can place a virtual camera in the Unreal environment using the exact dimensions. All dimensions in Unreal are in real-life scale. The best measuring tool is the 1-meter cube that can be stretched in one dimension to provide a matching distance. In this example, the meter cube was elongated to 7.62 meters, which equals 25 feet. A matching green screen plane is placed where you want the performer to be. Measuring the camera height from the bottom of the green plane provides the camera's height on stage, even though in the composite, the virtual camera will be many stories in the air. The virtual camera will be animated from the ground to this height to be at the right spot where the virtual and real cameras match. This is the manual method of camera positioning when you don't have high-end tools such as Zero Density, VP Pro, or Jetset.*

Using Photoshop, I captured the area of the virtual set that would be revealed by the green screen. Using a still of this region of interest, I projected it on the crude LED wall available as a positioning guide to provide blocking marks for the performer. Notice the lower resolution and moiré distortions of the LED wall on the lower right compared with the pristine first-generation image on the left. This preservation of quality for both foreground and background is the big advantage of shooting green screens.

> **The 1-meter cube is the universal measuring stick** for aligning virtual and real stages. The cube can be elongated from the floor so that it bisects the virtual camera lens to obtain the camera height on the live-action stage. The cube can also be shaped to match the dimensions of a standard apple box so the key light direction and angle can be matched using the real box and its virtual twin.

Elevating the Camera

As my live-action camera was only on a tripod and not a boom arm or a dolly, I had to find a way to make a dynamic camera move virtually to hook up with a static live-action plate. I found flying over difficult, so I opted to do an elevator-up move from the ground floor to the top of a building where I would appear. To plan this out effectively, I measured the available stage space. I now knew that my virtual camera "twin" could be no farther away than this from where I would be within the real set. 25 feet = 7.62 meters. The screen measured 4.87 meters by 2.74 meters.

I went to my desired Unreal location for the rooftop and created a plane using the exact measurements of the LED wall, then placed it against a wall on the balcony. I stretched a cube to 7.62 meters, placed one end against the virtual wall, and placed the virtual camera at the other end of the cube to match the distance limit of the real camera. I then fine-tuned my focal length and distance until I arrived at a pleasing composition of 20mm. For the camera height, I used another cube to measure the distance from the sidewalk to the balcony floor at the top of the building, 15 meters. Then I moved the cube to the camera position and noted that from the balcony floor to the middle of the lens, I added 1.5 meters. This let me know that my real camera had to be 1.5 meters above the stage floor to mimic the height of the virtual camera up in the air. Many thanks to Michael Geissler and the Mo-Sys company for allowing me to use their demo stage for the exercises and illustrations in this book.

Lighting

Since this was a challenging exercise using extreme angles and I had few light instrument options, I decided to have the film take place at dawn, when most of the settings were in ambient light much like the subway interior. I used one directional key light to provide three-quarters cross-key lighting on the subject to provide modeling in some shots, but with others, I left the lighting as soft fill. In the case of this stage, fill was provided by the general overhead room lights. For starter projects with students, I recommend simple soft fill lighting so there is no continuity concern with lighting. Students have a tough enough time getting their shots composed and matched between the actual and virtual. A more advanced project would introduce mood lighting.

The Composite

In the sequencer, I was able to animate a bright green point light illuminating the base of the building, simulating an off-camera death ray. Then I animated the camera upward to come to rest at the end point using eases for a smooth effect. This elevator move was okay, but it would have been better if I had built in a crane with the camera to match the type of move a live-action camera crane would make. One does have this option in UE.

Running on a Real Floor

We see this type of staging very often in movies where large sets with floors are made with the green or blue screen in the background. In a school setting, an LED screen rarely meets the floor exactly and leaves a dark gap. The proper way to address this is to have a raised platform that contains a real floor so the green falls off nicely behind it. In this case, I did not have the resources to build a raised floor and used a fabric screen to extend the green right to the floor. It worked but left much to be desired.

When students try to composite a situation like this, they struggle with the green spill on the floor, which creates a horrible broken-up and unstable mask

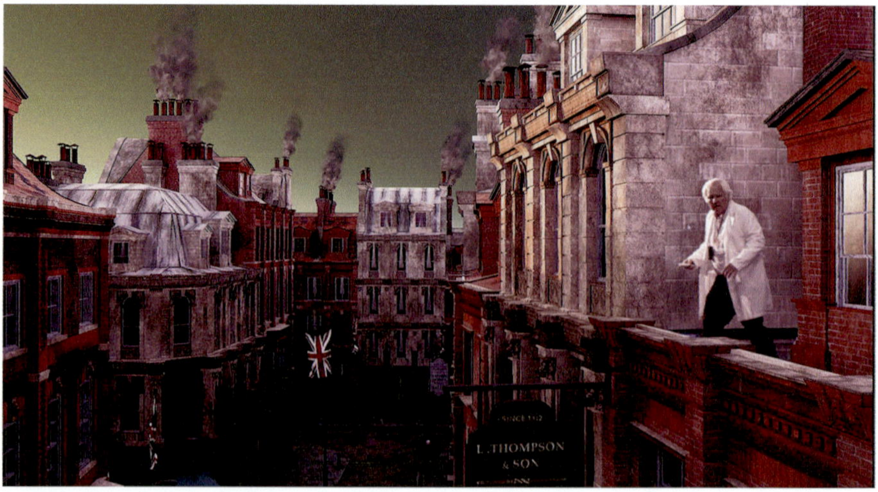

Figure 11.5 *The final shot.*

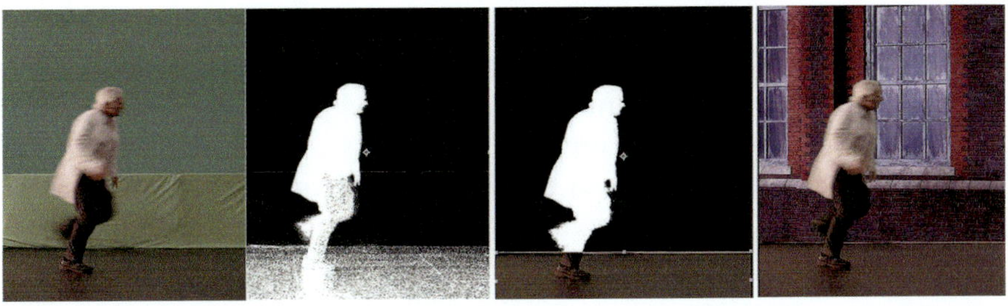

Figure 11.6 *Trying to clean a matte from spill reflected on a shiny floor is a time waster. If you just want the floor and the feet, split it in and add spill suppression. The first matte pull shows the buzzy floor. The second matte pull is good in the screen area in the top half, and the bottom with the floor and feet just uses spill suppression of the raw element with a simple split screen. The composite shows the ease and advantage of the technique when one is not able to put the screen the proper distance away to eliminate green spill.*

in the floor area. The disparity between the brightness of the fabric screen and the reflection precludes having a proper mask for both places. The answer to this is to pull a good mask for the figure in front of the green and use a split screen to add the legs walking on the regular floor while adding a green spill suppression to eliminate the green reflection.

Even though the noise was eliminated from the floor, the odd, unmotivated brightness of the floor in areas where it reflected the screen became an anomaly but not enough to distract from the photoplay. Real floors and performers should be placed 15 to 20 feet away from the green screen. In a tight, cramped stage, this is not always possible. A better solution for getting rid of the green screen floor reflection is to shoot with a polarizing filter.

> **If a green screen is not placed far enough away** from the performance area, you run the risk of green spill and the reflection of the green screen on a smooth floor. The reflection of the floor will be dim and uneven and cause the keyer to try to pull a matte off the reflection, resulting in a noisy, chaotic matte on the floor. The solution is to key off just the green screen area, do a split screen to the floor by itself, and use spill suppression to neutralize the green reflection. The feet on the floor don't need a key.

The High Shot

I was quite gratified watching my students see this shot at our final screening, and one student was notably shocked by how I was able to run down the street of an Unreal set. Most of my students were making their movies entirely in Unreal using metahumans. For the high shot, I did some scouting in the real world and located a parking structure I had access to in the early morning sunrise. I put my Sony A6400 on a sturdy tripod shooting down at the driveway entrance at six a.m. I turned it on and ran down the three floors of the structure and down the driveway. In this case, I took measurements of the height of the real camera and the tilt and focal length, along with sensor size, and replicated those measurements onto a virtual camera shooting down on the Victorian street.

One would think the obvious way to do this would be to have me run on a huge green screen. This would be far beyond my means, and being surrounded by green in this manner would create big issues, such as pulling a mask and eliminating green spill since I was wearing a white jacket. The composite was merely a soft split screen matching the color tone of both the live-action and Victorian streets. I recall that, at one point, one of the instructors suggested I use metahuman for that shot. I instantly rejected the idea as matching my hair, a white jacket blowing in the wind, and my unique movements would have been impossible. The metahuman would stand out just as much as in an old 70s movie when an obvious dummy is thrown off a building trying to match the live actor.

Not everything needs to be green screen. Blending a real roadway surface with a UE street works very well as long as the real and virtual camera positions and focal lengths match. A simple soft split is all that is needed.

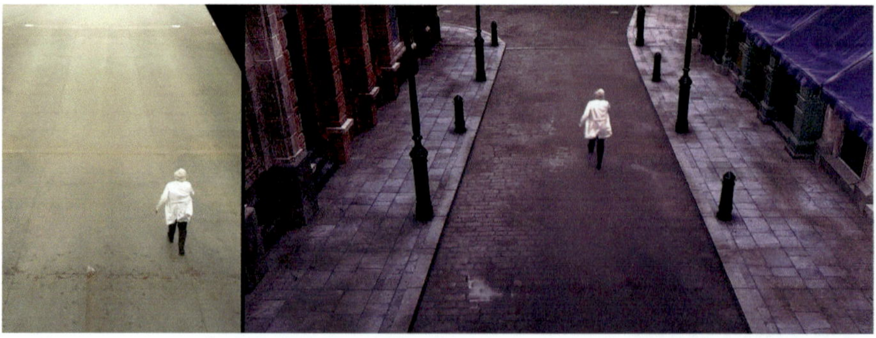

Figure 11.7 *To get high angle shots that are problematic or impossible with an LED wall or green screen, go back to the old-school split technique. The live-action camera height and tilt were duplicated in the virtual space so the background and foreground matched. A soft split and color correction between the element on the right and the virtual set created this shot.*

Shooting Outdoors and Element Isolation

After I had done the *Power* movie, I wanted to explore obtaining added realism for the next virtual production. I wanted to shoot outdoors in natural light for the live-action green screen and have the Unreal set conform to the real on-location lighting. A tall bridge was perfect for an unobstructed sunlight setting. Searching the marketplace, I found the Automotive Bridge Scene supported by UE 5.1. It had a soft, foggy atmosphere, which was nice, but I wanted the scene to be in harsh light to push the realism challenge.

One thing I noticed with the set was that the modular bridge pieces sat in the background without connection, so the bridge supports floated over the rocks below. In other places, the sky map that enveloped the set became stretched and streaky in places, which destroyed the realism. As this was the case, I decided to replace the supplied sky and background with photo backgrounds of the real clouds that surrounded the bridge and decided not to show the base of the bridge at all.

Removing the Background

This procedure involved quite simple thinking with a traditional mindset. To isolate the bridge, I merely made an extremely large plane, colored it green, placed it behind the bridge, and then recorded a push-in camera move. One could, of course, delete the original sky and other parts of the environment. Still, using a large green plane was the fastest and least destructive way to isolate the bridge. Then, the rendered push-in with green was taken into After Effects, and Key Light was used to replace the green with a real sky photo.

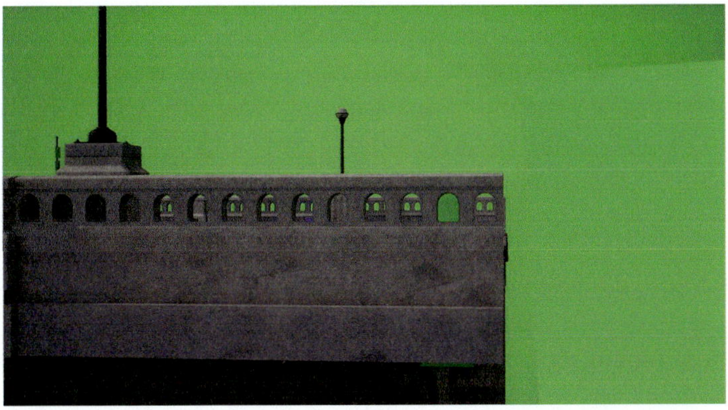

Figure 11.8 *Using green planes within the set was an easy way to selectively isolate sections of it. Note that the one portal hole is filled with green to enable the fly-through. The beauty of placing green screens in a digital environment is that the mattes pull perfectly.*

Lighting the Sitting Figure

For a strong daylight effect with sharp shadows, I needed a light that could cover a large area and bright enough to light it evenly. I used an Arri M18 HMI light with an 1800-watt lamp. This light was super bright and could run off most domestic sockets. The lamp worked beautifully but was hampered by the low ceiling of the set I was in. When dealing with large area lights like this, it is best to have them far enough away to obtain even light intensity throughout the set. In this case, I would have preferred to put the light up higher to obtain distance, but I could only move it horizontally due to the low ceiling. This caused the light to fall off my head as I walked forward and began to move outside the light's cone angle. Fortunately, I decided to dissolve before this error became apparent. Having this large light also enabled me to light a green fabric screen all along the walking path. For the fill light, I used the ambient room light that happened to be lit with daylight fluorescent fixtures.

When lighting a large area, it is best to use big lights far away to lessen the effect of the inverse square law as it pertains to light. The inverse square law, in simple terms, means if you double the distance of a light to a subject, the light doesn't dim by half but dims to one-quarter of the intensity. So if you put a light 4 feet from your head, by the time it reaches your hand, your hand will be quite dim. A big light 20 feet away would have less of an effect because no part of your performer will be 40 feet away from the light, thereby greatly diminishing the effect.

The mapped plane solution is still a compromise as there will be no spatial distortion on the paper doll cut-out 2D image within the 3D set, and the image quality can suffer when used as a texture map. The final composite is best when the original green screen element is tracked atop the move. By shooting a clean plate (green screen without actor), the computer could determine what was a shadow and what was a green screen, allowing for a noiseless shadow below the figure. Animation was also added to the clouds to enhance the shot.

When shooting the performance, I made sure to shoot a take of myself viewing the paper, then getting up to walk across the set, and then I shot a clean plate of nothing but the green screen. This clean plate was essential to provide the data to pull a good shadow off the green fabric. Now, the computer could compare footage with and without the shadow to delineate it from a wrinkle of the fabric or a shaded green area.

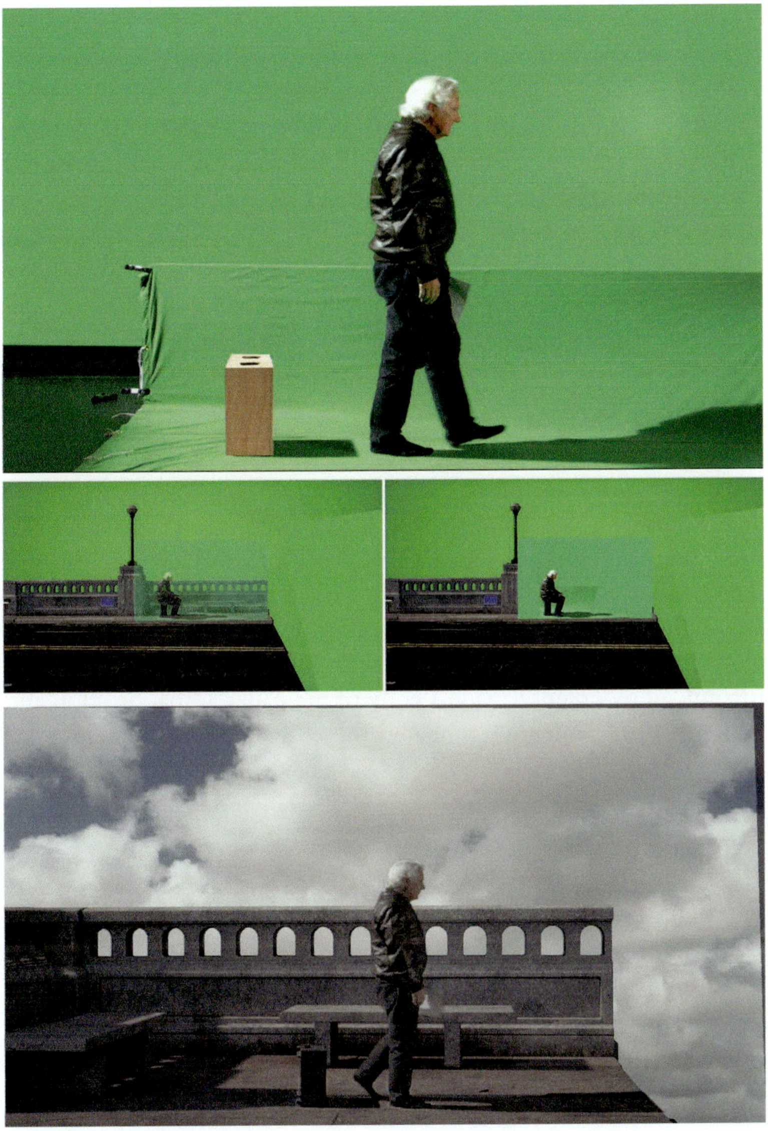

Figure 11.9 *A combination of a green LED wall and a fabric green to walk on. Positioning the sitting figure on the set was done by making the performer's green screen element transparent to enable the figure to appear to sit on the CG bench. The apple box was used to inform the direction and angle of the key while comparing it to the virtual box in the virtual set underneath. A full apple box is 20 x 12 x 8" (51 x 330.5 x 20.3 cm) Another solution would have been to place a plane with the video of the actor mapped to the plane to eliminate tracking errors.*

If you need extra data to pull a shadow off a green screen, it is important to shoot a clean plate of the green stage by itself so the computer can compare pixel by pixel what is different between the clean plate and the take, thereby identifying the shadow area. Developed by Ultimatte in the 90s, the Zero Density system uses this philosophy in its software by having a synthetic copy of the clean green screen stage mapped with a photo of the actual stage to make the comparison (described in *Filming the Fantastic with Virtual Technology*, Focal Press, 2020).

The Falling Paper

For the standing-on-the-edge-of-the-bridge shot, I made sure that the camera was positioned so the platform I was standing on was horizontal to the lens, meaning the camera was looking at it dead on, neither above nor below the platform. Even though I was just a few feet from the ground, the sidewalk would be masked out, and the end of the bridge would continue downward as if I were high above the ground. When I dropped the paper, it fell in front of the green screen and landed on the sidewalk. In the composite, when the paper was surrounded by green, I made a copy of the paper at that position and used it as a "hook-up" element. I animated the extracted still image of the paper

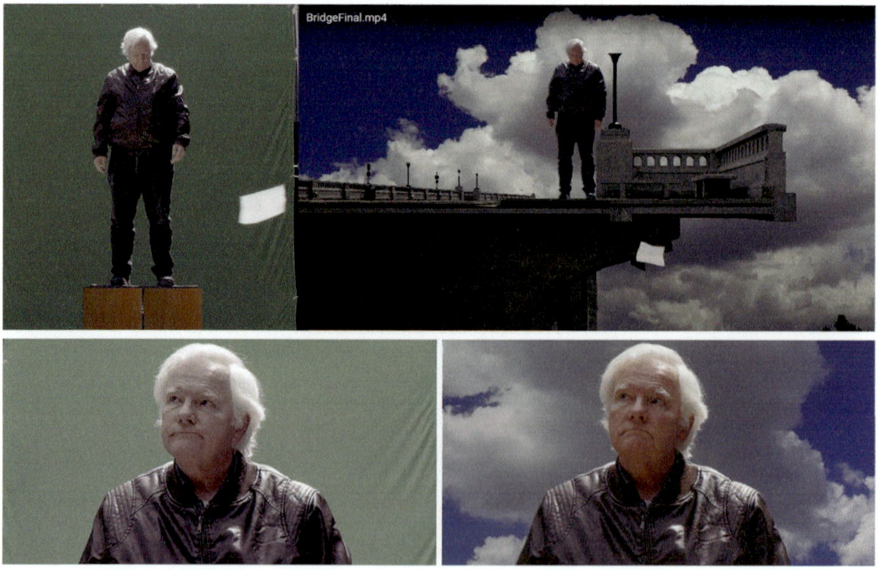

Figure 11.10 *Isolating a still of the real paper and adding distortion and animation, I could switch from the real paper to its animated still counterpart to have it flutter downward out of frame. Excellent results can be obtained with the green screen technique, as shown by preserving fine hair detail when shot properly.*

with the pin puppet tool in After Effects to have it gently fold and travel down out of the frame. The original trajectory of the paper was matted out after the animation of the still took over.

> **For objects that pass beyond the green screen area,** one will have to rotoscope the parts of the object not in front of the green screen by rotoscoping. In the case of an object falling free of the performer, a single frame of the object can be extracted from the screen and turned into an animated element to travel wherever it is needed in the shot while adding distortion to preserve the illusion of a 3D object.

The Final Shot

This was another instance when it was easy to manipulate the light direction in Unreal to match the length and direction of the shadows. Due to time and monetary constraints, I was not walking on green but on the brightly lit sidewalk. Fortunately, I was wearing dark pants and shoes. The top part of me against the green screen was made using Key Light green screen compositing. My legs and pants were done using two luminance keys. A luminance key derives the mask using the difference in brightness between the two elements. I used one set to make a dark silhouette of both the shadow and the pants and another with just the pants keyed with no shadow.

By putting one matte on top of the other, I lowered the opacity of the bottom shadow layer to match the shadow density in the Unreal set. The latter preserved the detail of the pants. A soft split through the legs blended the green screen and luminance keying methods. Since the green screen did not meet the ground, roto mattes were used to erase the dark shadow join between the screen and the sidewalk.

The camera elevation was done in post by creating a taller-than-wide, locked-off composite image of me on the bridge with the clouds. I then simply pushed in on the lower section of the tall image and animated the extraction upward to create the rising camera move. The tall aspect ratio was rendered in 4K to prevent loss of resolution so the extraction had full 1920x1080 resolution.

> **Changing the aspect ratio of a background element** along with its resolution can provide an opportunity for post-camera moves. For films shot in the 1.77 aspect ratio, a background could be rendered at a 2.35 widescreen ratio to enable post pans using this extraction method.

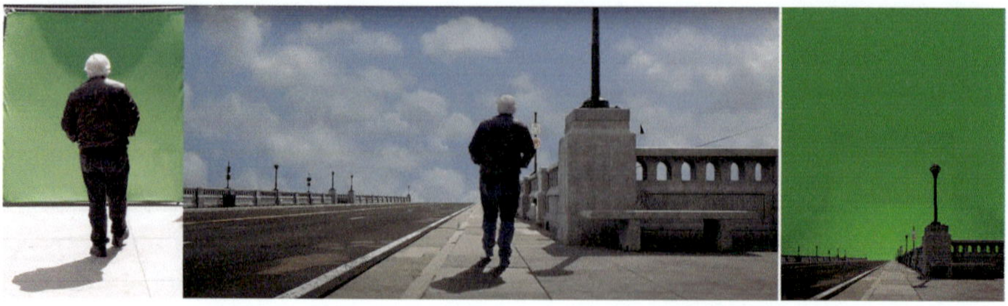

Figure 11.11 *Using the same focal length but rotating the virtual camera on its side provided a taller aspect ratio. Rendering the still on the right at 4K allowed for a close-up extraction 1920x1080 to place the figure on the bridge and boom up without losing resolution. The combination of green screen pull and luma key pull enabled this composite. Rotoscope mattes were used to mask the dark gap between the green screen and the bright sidewalk.*

Virtual Production 2

By this time, my virtual production class will have explored the history of using VFX to combine performers into unique environments and make films that have camera movement. For the next semester, the advanced class will move forward to explore the world of live camera tracking, used for both green screen and LED volume production. Those classes are still in development, but my personal approach would be to introduce live tracking using Jetset Pro, which enables the iPhone to shoot and record a tracked green screen element and the tracked background by itself as well as an in-camera composite done with either green screen or an AI depth map matte, similar to what you see when you blank out the background during a Zoom call. The importance of this is to remove a lot of the heavy technology in the beginning and explore the aesthetic of why you are picking a composition and why you are moving the camera. For this approach, I would use the supplied default environments that have already been prepared for use with the iPhone and just shoot with it. The next step would depend on the resources of the school. If the institution was fortunate enough to have an LED wall, I would focus on learning Unreal or Blender and have students prepare for their final project (executed in the third semester). This would entail working out the shots as a previz assignment using CG stand-ins. Part of the course would involve learning on-stage compositing software such as Mo-Sys VP Pro or Zero Density on the LED stage. In schools that do not have a wall, a green screen stage would be used instead. For schools that prefer a post approach to virtual production, the second semester would continue with the Jetset product but focus on the preparation of Unreal or Blender elements to be small enough to be used as low-res environments in the iPhone along with the integration of iPhone tracking data with a Cine camera such as RED or Venice. Added focus would be made using Nuke and other programs to refine the tracking to lock the performers to the floor during camera movement. For high-resolution in-camera work, I would make use of the Mo-Sys VP Pro or Zero Density with LED volumes or on-set green screen compositing. In the case of Mo-Sys, the live tracking would be locked from the start, and I would highly recommend a brief course teaching how to set up and calibrate the StarTracker. Calibration is critical and provides the student with a valuable skill set during production and when entering the workforce.

Finding Faculty

I have seen employment offerings from some universities seeking unicorns: namely, teachers who have a PhD and years of practical film experience in high technology. Good luck with that. In this author's opinion, virtual production needs to be taught by at least two specialists in this complex discipline. One would be a seasoned camera professional who has had a lot of experience with on-set VFX production, and the other would be well versed in Unreal, Blender, Nuke etc. and have production experience on the computer graphics side of things. In other words, the real and the unreal. Between these two unique individuals, at least one would have a higher-level degree and would take the lead in curriculum development, grading, and academic disciplines. For traditional film schools to compete with the trade education offered by manufacturers that leads to work, their programs need to provide enough faculty who have a hands-on understanding of the technology. Part-time adjunct pools will not service this need. Administration should also dedicate a staff member to maintaining the equipment. Unlike a camera, virtual production involves many technologies that all must work together flawlessly, and it is very easy to have one item in the pipeline fail and halt production. Staff who handle the care and maintenance of cameras, lights, and grip equipment will need the technical knowledge to handle video, camera, and computer communication. It seems obvious that virtual production will continue to be added to school curricula as it is a viable alternative for many aspects of film production. The costs will continue to become more affordable, especially for those who learn how to best make use of these skills.

Chapter 12
Interviews

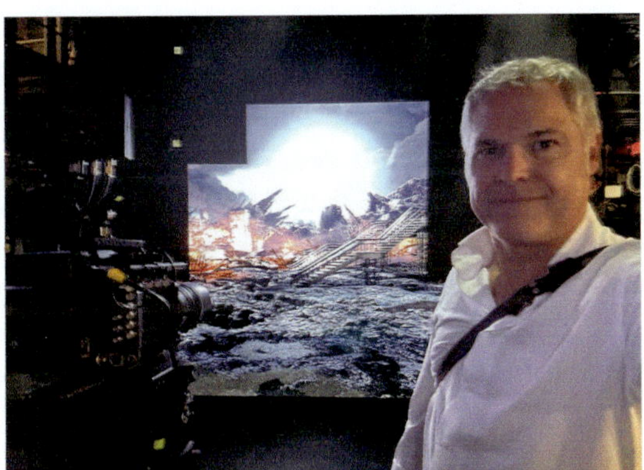

Figure 12.1 *Eric Wolford.*

Eric Woldord

Mark: I'd like to introduce Eric Wolford, who is a very seasoned cinematographer. He's worked in the industry for many years shooting documentaries all over the world, independent films, and we crossed over a little bit.

Wolfie worked with Michel Gondry on some of his projects, and I had the good fortune of meeting Michel on *Eternal Sunshine of the*

DOI: 10.4324/9781003473169-12

Spotless Mind. I'll never forget that. You also shot some miniatures for *Interstellar*, which I assume was done at New Deal Studios.

Wolfie: Lit them. Yeah, I was on the lighting team at that time. I ended up getting really lucky on *Interstellar*. I came in for just a couple of days on the miniature units. They were having trouble timing a solar effect. They had this huge 20K spotlight with no lens, and they wanted it to kind of have a pattern to it, and they were handholding it, and it wasn't moving right and all that.

I had had some grip-rigging experience, so we had it on a 20-foot arc that you could move around so that it would work, but they wanted to kind of hang and do a little, like, bang. So I designed a circular ring underneath, and I put a second piece of speed rail and used that as a guide. And then I had little tape marks on it, and then I could do it to the count they wanted it, to the count of 22 seconds.

So then, I could do a circle, and then I had somebody stand there with the timer. And then I was able to get exactly the effect they wanted. It was a really fun day. I got to add my little piece to the one moment, you know, but it's good. You look at the amount of effort that goes into a movie like that.

And, you know, 20 people there filming, and it's like a second and a half of the spaceship going into the vortex, you know, and the light does that. That's amazing. That was two days, right there, that three seconds; that was two days of work and 20 people. It won the Academy Award for effects that year, I think, and deserved it.

You know, Nolan has such a great vision. When I found out what we were working on, I was like, what's my day today? Yeah, I'm available. Yeah. I want to come work on that.

Mark: You said that the lighting instrument, they don't have a lens in there to get the sharp shadows. Was there any problem? This wasn't an HMI? No UV problem?

Wolfie: It was a 20K sun. It was like a parabolic mirror, and the light gave really clean, beautiful sun, tungsten kind of light. So it had a particular kind of vibe to it. We didn't use those particular lights that much. I'd seen them a couple of times. You'd use them specifically and usually indoors and usually on miniatures.

Mark: Right, right. That was an older Mole Richardson light. Wow. So, you really came in at the right time. I mean, your career and, in a way, it's almost, if I say this, it sounds like you have a nefarious past, but you were a white hacker for NASA. You were a good guy.

Wolfie: Yeah, I was a white hacker.

Mark: And how old were you then?

Wolfie: I was 16. I had a bulletin board system, which was kind of the predecessor to the internet. So I had a Commodore 64. I had a modem. I had a dedicated phone line, and people would call in and leave messages to each other one at a time.

It was part of a bulletin board network that was nationwide. And I was in a hacking crew, and we were doing all the kind of usual teenage hacker–kid things. I knew how to make traceless long-distance phone calls. I knew how to get long-distance calling codes. We're doing all the war game stuff.

And then two of my friends ran afoul of the law. And then, I was like, 15. One of them got arrested by the FBI, made the front page of the *Washington Post*. My dad was like, "Was this your buddy you were talking about?" And I'm like, "Yeah." And I was like, "I'll knock it off." So I went half into retirement.

These have real consequences. And my other friend, he was doing much worse. Kind of stuff [other] than just information, which is what I was doing. But then a buddy got recruited by this company called NEMA. Subcontracted by NASA. And it was a NASA contract. And they needed teenage hackers.

They wanted to see how teenagers would try and crack systems, and they thought they were really secure. So they hired us to be like, Yeah, yeah." The kids tried to get in, and we were fine, and we ate their lunch. We broke into everything they gave us, and we cut through them like butter. I got in first; we were in there within a week, and it was crazy.

Yeah. That's some of the NASA stuff, but [what's] interesting is that transitions into LED wall work because hackers are the same DNA that LED wall people are, right? Hackers are misappropriating technology, breaking it, using it for different purposes, making it work. And, you know, that's what we've done with LED walls.

You know, we've mugged the large-scale screen people for concerts. And had the manufacturers make it smaller and better. We grabbed a 3D game engine from the video game console people. And now, we use that as a special effects engine that [it] was never intended to be used for, with all the constraints that comes with that.

Epic Games has done an amazing job of hearing us. We're a very small portion of what Epic Games does, but they were very kind in adding all sorts of techniques and tools for us to be able to work the wall better.

Mark: Yeah, and it's true. I think this background of yours really made you perfect for dealing with this virtual production that everyone's trying to catch up on.

One thing that I may ask because I was watching your reel this morning. The LED wall has a lot of challenges, of course, moiré patterns. We'll get into that a little bit. But the thing that strikes me most – I read a white paper by Tim Moore of VU Studio, who predicts that virtual production is going to take off now the hype cycle is over.

And we're going to move away from the big LED volumes to smaller screens. Now, the issue I have with smaller screens, which I'm sure you've dealt with in some way, is usually as a cinematographer, you've got your establishing shot, then maybe your twin shot of two characters you want to use, and then the close-up, and then as soon as you do the over the shoulder and move that camera, you run out of the small screen.

It's gone, right? So on your reel, there's a bar scene. That, I assume was done in front of an LED wall. Am I correct in that assumption?

Wolfie: There's several. I just re-edited my reel. So I'm on to a new reel, and I have a whole LED wall reel that I'll have up here in about like two weeks. It was great.

So when people go to WolfieDOP. com, if anybody wants to go see the reels, they can go check those out. I've-I've shot a lot on small walls. I've shot [on] medium-sized walls. I've shot on large walls.

And, you know, the smaller the wall, the more your blocking gets destroyed. The smaller the wall, the more constrained you are. Now, if you have a technique where you have set extensions, and you can use the person on the wall, and it can generate outside of that, but that's a whole other level of complexity.

And I've seen that crash and burn as much as I've seen it succeed. You need a dedicated camera, a dedicated team. You need a really good bad team. You know, it's asking a lot.

Mark: I remember they did that – we were on the stage at Mo-Sys, and they had the extension. It's almost like early Cinerama, where you blur the edges, and sometimes the architecture doesn't quite line up, but you hope that it's going to be so incidental. It's never perfect when you try to blend the LED wall with a perfect—

Wolfie: Yeah. 'Cause you're dealing with pure digital, and then you're dealing with digital as seen through the RGB Rec. 709 color standard or Rec. 2020 color standard, you know? Yeah. It's tricky. Yeah. You're better off if you need, if you need more space and you don't have the wall, I think you do the wide shots on green screen with a green screen floor and get a couple moments that are digital that go by quickly and then get into the close-up work on the wall.

And I think that's a perfectly fine solution. So in the case of the bar scene, you do an over the shoulder. So, in that case, did you move the actors to keep in alignment with this?

Wolfie: Oh, yeah. Whenever you do coverage on the small wall, I rotate the virtual camera, and I have kind of a technique when I light for LED walls. I have kind of a ring of fire, you know; I have large lights with bags on both sides with egg crates and inside and then backside and then high and then overhead.

And I'll just design a rig where, you know, you can rotate them around and then just generate a key light from any of the four or six angles that I need. I can side light. I can back key. I can front key. I can make this the key, especially when you're doing coverage on smaller stages; it's just the way you do it. I just shot Kelsey Grammer for *Liberty or Death*. It's a TV show about the Revolutionary War, and Kelsey came in, and we had, I think it was like 12 setups, and we did the first one. We rehearsed it, and then we did a couple of takes, and then he was like, "Oh, it's not going to be four takes per shot, is it?" And he nailed his lines on the first one, but, you know, it's a technical thing.

And we were using a jib, and we had cues, and you have to line up an LED shot to have the perspective. Just perfect. If you mess up any kind of angle or the virtual cameras a little off from the physical, or he just looks a little taller, and you just use the stand-in that was a hair shorter. So you have to change the marks. We realized very quickly we were going to have him until like 8:30 p.m. We ended up getting him wrapped by 5 p.m., and we had like eight to ten minutes to do a lighting change over on an LED wall and get it all matched up. Now, it's possible, but fortunately, I had that lighting setup.

Mark: You're ready to change the lighting in a heartbeat because you've got the lighting already pre-placed.

Wolfie: Yeah. And for instance, you know, they brought up one of the scenes, and something that was an error. So they're like, "Okay, now we're not doing that. Now we're going to the scene at the end of the day. And we're going to push that one to the end of the day." So it wasn't, even if I had a lighting reset.

Then I'd have to relight and all of that. That's very nervous-making for a DP who might be facing this for the first time. Obviously, your experience has prepared you for that. It would be brutal. It would be brutal. I came up through the ranks, and I did ten years as a grip and then as ten years as a gaffer, and that experience with shadows and that experience with lights, really.

Really drove into me all the tricks of the trade, and I got to work with so many talented DPs over the years that are really, you know, and it's interesting because you need to know Unreal Engine, you need to know cameras, you need to know color science, and then you need to know lighting. It's a very challenging cinematography.

Like a kid who's a hacker at 16 and got a security clearance for NASA. I like a challenge. I work best when I'm a little scared, you know? I'm like, yeah, that's true. I mean, you know, pretty sure we can make this work. And I'm not going to say scout's honor, but I'll take a run at it.

We'll push the limit. Just budget a little extra time for when we have a crash. That's going to be in my pocket that I haven't told you about. And I do know we can make it happen. Even if we have to punt.

Mark: I see. Well, well, speaking of prep, sometimes you have prep, sometimes you, you don't. In the case of virtual, you've got, as you say, have to know a little bit about Unreal. And are you, are you involved in the lighting of Unreal sets before you actually do the shooting?

Wolfie: Yeah, absolutely. Some video game programmer is not designing my lighting setup for my virtual sets. That'll be me.

Ah, oh good. So you've got that. No, the number of times they've been like, oh no, they've already got a pre-lit. I'm like, "Yeah, let's go in there. Oh, so you want me to put a key light directly over camera and wash out all the black colors on the wall?" and the producers like, "Oh." I'm like, "Yeah. So anyway, take the key light, put it back beside, put a fill light here, change it to 12 degrees."

Also, if you looked at the set, there is a wall right down there and I won't have anywhere to put any of the lights. The sun comes from the left. I have 20 feet where I can get a little sunlight over there and get the distance and have the light fall off and not bloom on the actor's face and make it look really studio-like.

Mark: Oh yeah, that's a big one. Usually you don't have head room, but nowadays, you don't even have side room.

Wolfie: Yeah, sometimes you get on a stage, and it's like the wall goes boink, and you're like, I guess I'm keying from the left here. I always look up what the physical can. There's so many issues.

Mark: I remember DP Yuri Neiman wanted to change – he never got this done – but instead of director of photography, it'd be director of imaging. And I think what you're saying about lighting in the virtual space is a prep before you get on to the actual stage, and that is quite a good point because you can't really light. Just like a rear projection, if you light the LED wall from the front, you are going to white it out.

Wolfie: There's ways to do it, but you have to be very careful, and you want that to be a conscious choice, not some guy in India just threw a key light there, and it looked cute on the metahuman, without any consideration of any of the other physical concerns. Right, right. We had a situation on *Europa* where – and this one caught me – I knew it was coming, but I didn't know how badly it was going to hit.

On *Europa*, we have, like. hard direct sunlight onto the surface of this ice planet and we had a, you know, a 30-foot-by-50-foot white snow physical set that the actors would walk around on. And then, Pixomondo did this beautiful job of blending that into the LED wall, and there would be Jupiter rising over the glacial mountains in the background, right?

They had wanted to try some kind of frontal lighting. I'll show it to you, but you're not going to want that on this set. So I had already designed a rear light, and then, so we turned it on, and the light just hit the floor and then blew out the wall completely because you're doing hard sunlight pointed at a high angle down onto the ground, and you had a 30-by-50 white bounce. Blowing everything up at the screen. Completely unusable.

I knew I was probably going to do a little back-edge lighting. It was going to look better anyway. There are these beautiful practical lights on the actor's helmets that weren't reading. And so, you know, everybody was like, "Oh my God, how are we going to do this?"

We're going to make the wall brighter. How are we going to do this? I'm shooting on a Venice 2. One second. I said, "David" – my AC – "David, put it to 3200. From 800 ISO," and he said, "But it's already—" I'm like, "Just do it." So he puts it at 3,200 ISO, and then I took my key light from 95% down to 2%.

The jump from 800 ISO to 3,200 ISO is huge. It's now filming in nighttime mode. Right. And it's counterintuitive that you would want to go higher in ISO when the wall's blown out, and there's light going everywhere. Right? Yeah. But by going to 3,200 ISO, I was able to bring all of my physical lights down 97%.

And then the little lights on the helmet suddenly glowed. At 3200, the glow from the lights created some nice design on the skin tones. And then at 1% and 3%, I literally had my lights down to like 1 or 2%. Light hitting the bounce was way lower, and then you could see the wall fine. It was dark in there, but the camera was seeing it as bright sunlight because we were shooting in nighttime mode. So sometimes your fix is with the camera, not Unreal Engine.

And that's a great example of why you want to bring a cinematographer in early on. You want a cinematographer driving the thing because you want to find the best lever that does the most work with the least amount of hassle to the entire rest of the system, right?

I noticed that's a bit— Sometimes, that's an Unreal Engine lever and, sometimes that's a camera settings lever.

Mark: I noticed at Cine Gear that Sony, for the Venice camera, has an Unreal tool that has a moiré detector and a color alignment tool because color is a big thing with a lot of these screens because I think a lot of people bought screens before they were actually manufactured for movies.

They're more prone to moiré as they were meant for billboards. Color is very spiky. I think a lot of people, [there's] still mortgage on these walls, so you have to deal with them.

Wolfie: You got to get the ROI on it, or you can buy up again. Paul Debevic is amazing. He taught me a lot about LED in manufacturing.

He talks about how the red LED creates a very narrow spike of the red spectrum. It's not a full bodied red because of the nature and cost of how red is created. So that's why you get that kind of lobster effect sometimes on skin tone and the red color. It is just giving a narrow spike of the red.

So it picks out the red dots in your skin and highlights those. So one of the things we do with LEDs is we add – even though the wall will give you some color and some environmental lighting – I'll add full–color spectrum lights to that. So that it fills out the red spectrum. So if I'm using red from the wall, I'll actually put a red light there, even though you may not need it other than the skin is going to blotchy.

And then I'll add full-spectrum red, and then the skin tones will return to normal. When you're doing 20 feet by 80 feet of LEDs, you need to save as much as possible. The colors are getting a lot better. Sony's panels are amazing. ROE's panels are amazing.

You know, everybody's getting better and better. The VP Toolkit's very interesting. We used to have to sit there with the DIT, put the color chart digitally on the wall, put a physical color chart up, have somebody there for skin tone, and dial in a look-up table so it all looked right. And the physical world matched.

Sometimes, like a six-hour process to eight hours; sometimes it'd be faster, but it was usually a huge deal. Now the VP Toolkit has a digital color chart, a physical color chart, and the computer goes in and scientifically scans everything. And it takes 20 minutes, and it's spot on, and you'll walk on set and, you're like, "Do those work with the wall?"

It's like kind of shifting blue. What the heck? Go look at the monitor, and it'll look perfect. Oh, yeah, because the sensor sees the LED wall very differently than the human eye sees the sensor.

Mark: That's right, because I went through that struggle, exactly what you're saying about the Macbeth chart, the real one, and the synthetic one, or whatever is recorded.

And it, it takes forever. And I think a lot of people do fool themselves with that by not looking at the monitor. Now, in the case [that] you don't have that particular tool, I imagine you run into issues where directors are getting their close-up or whatever, and they love the lighting just right, but they're just looking at their performer and the camera position.

And then you're starting to get a moiré. Do you ever have – because no one likes to compromise on their vision – do you just say, "Look, we're, we're going to be in trouble if we shoot it that way"?

Wolfie: There's always a way, moving further away, change of focal zoom, add in a black pearl mist, squirt the air.

Sometimes you just need a hazer, oddly enough, you know, a little bit of atmosphere just kind of makes the moiré go away. I'll deal, I'll deal with a slight change in vibe, [rather] than bad, distracting moiré. There's a technical threshold, and then there's an artistic threshold, and those are two different goalposts, and I will not let a director push me below a technical threshold, where it's, in my opinion, unusable footage or footage that, once seen in the edit, would need to be redone, and I just won't do that.

I hold the line here, but it may not meet my artistic standard, but it meets the technical standard, and the director loves it. And we're in an intense scene, and we're in the person's eyes, and it sits in the edit. I'm not going to fight the storytelling, right? We're there to tell a story.

We're there to capture an emotion, and everything has a cost. I pick my battles to be a day of prep or two days of good pre-lighting. It's my own playtime with the model, the human that's the right size and the right everything in the costumes. And I find out all my problems on those days.

So I carve out time for me to make sure we get past the technical threshold and then reach my artistic threshold. You've got to remember, you're there to serve the story. You're not there to make the most technically perfect example of anything ever of all time. Am I happy with everything I've ever shot [with] an LED wall? No. You know, I'm my harshest critic. I had the honor of lighting Roger Deakins for a still shoot.

Oh my God! And they had full motion lighting because they—they were all these cinematographers that were up for the Academy Awards. Janusz Kaminski and all of that. It was all my heroes. It was crazy. So we lit Deakins.

I mean, he's one of my heroes for beauty lighting, and he's an amazing cinematographer. We asked him, "How do you feel about *Blade Runner 2049*?" They won the award. I mean, it was an incredible, incredible movie and incredibly well lit and across many diverse environments.

And it really was a spectacular use of cinematography and storytelling. And he goes, "Oh, I've seen it 147 times. All I could see are my mistakes." So it's like, as cinematographers and as technicians and as artists, we're always very, very hard on ourselves, but at the end of the day, was it entertaining? Did it not distract from the moment? You listen to Deakins, and he runs into all the same problems all the rest of us do. It doesn't matter how big [you are] and how much money you're making and how big the project is and if it's 300 million. You still don't have enough time; you still don't have enough lights; you still don't have enough prep. The train is two-quarters size, and it's like— looks like a kid's train, like in *Jesse James*. That's the game of it, right? You just make it work.

Mark: I saw him work while I was shooting matte paintings for *Courage Under Fire*, and we were in Texas, and they shot half the scene. The weather's great. And then they get to the close-ups, and it's raining cats and dogs. I thought, "Oh, well, I guess we're calling it a day." But he did this amazing thing. He put a big silk above the performers. They're not getting wet. They're softly lit. He narrowed the depth of field to make the rain invisible, and he kept on going. It was amazing.

Wolfie: Yeah. We're going to finish this day. Yeah. A lot of respect there.

Mark: Yeah. So, I see that Blender and Unreal are competing. Unreal is the main tool for these synthetic backgrounds today. Do you find that? Or is everything interchangeable now?

Wolfie: That's a great question. Blender is great for kind of quick, almost like 2D mockups. I see them used in a 2D fashion, even though it's not fully— It's a rendering engine. It's wired for getting really quick ideas up pitched to a client.

And if it's a short scene, not involving rigorous coverage, you can do a Blender background and then some 3D objects for depth, and then shoot it. And you can get a scene up and running really quickly. So it's one of the tools, and Blender's techniques are very fast, and that's its advantage, and it looks good quickly, but it's harder to build a whole scene that's tracked and does all the things that we [get] from the Unreal Engine.

It ends up being a heavy sketch tool. Like, 99% of the stuff I see is Blender first sketches because people work in it really quickly. But then sometimes, "Oh, it's a commercial; we need a two-second shot of the person going like that." Okay, cool, just render a 2D background from Blender and use that as a 2D plate. And that'll be fine.

Mark: Yeah, the one thing that I noticed when I was learning Unreal was a lot of my co-students— I mean, being a ham actor, I had to put myself into the damn thing. Everyone else just decided to use metahumans. Why? Because everything's in the same universe.

I kind of get a little nervous about that. There is a move to try to capture Gaussian splats of people. They're starting to do that in motion now, but it kind of takes away the— the working. It's like theater never went away, even though movies became popular. (joking) Movies are a fad; radio['s] making a big comeback.

Mark: Because I think people like to do it, like to see it that way. With the coming of AI and [having] the written word all of a sudden generate imagery, it seems to take away the dignity of work of the artists and the technicians that have built up this industry.

Wolfie: The first thing is, the elephant in the room is data set. So these AI models are scraped data sets from artists. It's a huge copyright concern. Yeah. Hey, I just scraped every HR Giger thing that was on an internet somewhere and incorporated it.

And now I can take in Giger does *Dune*, and it scraped everything that Denis Villeneuve has ever shot or Greig Fraser is amazing. And then it marries the two of them together. They're not derivative, you know, so it's like, that's gross.

But beyond that, AI is another tool that's going to be exploited. It's going to be here to stay. My practical experience with AI is that it'll get you 85% of the way there, and then you'll spend 95% of the time getting the last little bit with humans. So it helps in "Do you want the castle to look like this, or like this, or like that, or like this, or like that," and then the director would be, like, "Oh, that one."

That's scary, but modern, you know, you're like, great. They like number 13. So then 13 goes to the modelers, and then the modelers build number 13. So, it helps hone people's visions very quickly. I've used some AI-generated sets; they work better on the monitor at home, and then they kind of break down on the big 80-foot-wide wall.

So, there's some more work to be done on getting those to line up perfectly. But the AI stuff looks incredible faster and cheaper.

Mark: Consistency is a problem with it. I mean, you'll get like 90% of what you want and say, "Oh, do the same thing, but make the tower taller," and you'll get something completely different.

Wolfie: Yeah, yeah, but you know, that's only— that's only a matter of time. You look at where, two years ago, "Hey, AI created a dude, and it's this six-fingered, you know, on acid at Coachella monstrosity with three eyes doing this," and you're like, "That's years away from being usable." And then you cut to like two years later, and I don't know which one of those two was real.

So, that curve on AI, if it continues as it has over the last three or four years, it will be getting terrifyingly good. Photoshop creates a different background, and you see it happen first in photos because it's still image, and it's easier. And then you see it in video where it's a still image done 30 times a second, however long your shot is.

So it's coming. Yeah. And I think AI-generated backgrounds are going to be here faster than we know. They want that [for] video games. They want it for everything. And so many environments are so very predictable.

The rest of the full video interview can be found on the book's companion website.

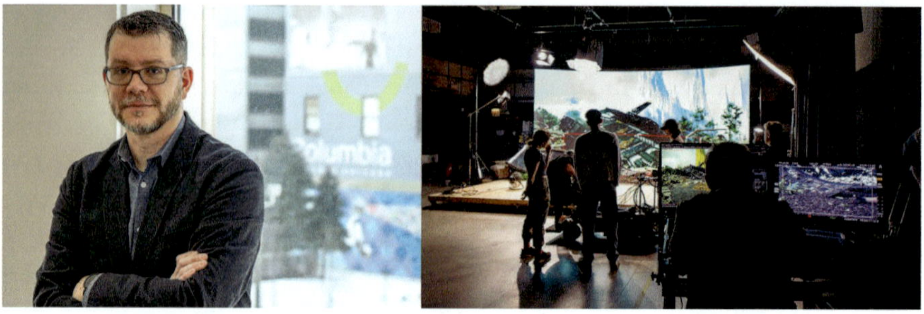

Figure 12.2 *Professor James Brust and the school studio.*
Source: Courtesy of Columbia College Chicago, 2024

James Brust

Epic Mega Grant recipient and Unreal Engine authorized instructor James Brust has more than ten years of experience teaching in the fields of cinema, visual effects, immersive media, and design. As associate professor of instruction in the School of Film and Television at Columbia College Chicago, James was responsible for the design and implementation of their LED volume, as well as developing the curriculum for and launching the virtual production program. Currently, he oversees these initiatives and has the pleasure of introducing students to the world of virtual production.

Mark: You have been involved in media education for many years and were instrumental in creating not only a workable LED stage space for students but also a strategy for instruction. Can you relate your experience on the creation of the student film *What Remains*?

James: Absolutely. This took place in the ICVFX Studio Techniques class, where the objective is to form a functional production team and create a short film or teaser utilizing virtual production. I had the good fortune to work with a very talented group of students with diverse enough areas of interest that they naturally gravitated toward the key production roles needed.

Their first task was to pitch story ideas to their peers and ultimately choose the one they would focus on as a class. Because of the sci-fi setting and concise story that lends itself well to the format, the class chose Hannah Brumfield's (senior) *What Remains*, and she took on the role of director. Jayden Ray's (freshman) story was a close runner-up, and since Hannah was also working production design, Jayden came on as co-director.

Beyond that, students filled in other key roles like producer, DP, gaffer, engine operator, physical art department, and virtual art department. Each student was responsible for their respective roles, and they all went above and beyond to meet the weekly deadlines and recruit talent and additional on-set crew.

This worked, because Columbia also has students in game design, game art, and animation programs that are also interested in working in this field, and the prerequisite course Virtual Filmmaking introduces these students as well as film and television students to Unreal Engine as a narrative production tool. So the mix of experience included both on-set skills as well as a digital team familiar with the asset pipeline.

Logistically, the class only met for three hours each week, but the students did a lot of pre-production work and nearly all the post outside of class. With some innovative work by the production design team, the set made it through four weeks of very tight filming schedules and the footage was handed off to the editor each week. Communication was mostly handled via Discord, which was immensely helpful for keeping everyone in the loop.

Ultimately, it was a great experience for everyone involved. The time pressures mitigated the expansive potential of virtual production in a way that I think worked very well. The students could still dream big but acknowledged the constraints and made effective creative decisions.

Mark: I see you are an authorized Unreal instructor, which is a high honor and accomplishment. I understand that even though environments can be purchased from the marketplace, your focus seems to be on the creation of environments from scratch. Do you have this type of project be a group exercise or individual, and if a group project, how do you determine who does what?

James: Not entirely. For the game art and animation programs in the School of Design, the students are learning to be talented artists in that respect, so there is a fair amount of instruction there, but for virtual production, the goal is telling an effective story, and there is rarely time to do everything from scratch.

They leverage marketplace assets, Quixel Megascans, ArtStation, Sketchfab, TurboSquid, and anything else they can to assemble their scenes fast and cheap. We spend some time on import processes, materials, and optimization, but in a very different way from what the design students are used to.

Due to the interdisciplinary nature of the class, a handful of students are already coming in with that design experience. In the studio class, those students work together as the VAD (Virtual Art Department), dividing the work into scouting, individual assets, and lighting.

In the intro class, it's broken down into smaller individual exercises, and by the end of that, filmmaking students are fluent enough to create high-fidelity previsualizations and can actively participate in scouting and idea generation with VAD later on.

Mark: I see that Blender is becoming popular in virtual production due to the lighter data load. Do you care to share your thoughts on that software? Is Blender part of your curriculum?

James: Blender is part of the curriculum in the School of Design, and as far as virtual production, it is the tool I recommend when there is any asset work to be done. Partially because I know it is capable, but also because it's easily accessible for all students, but there is not specific Blender instruction within the virtual production curriculum.

Once they are part of the VAD, they use whatever tools they are most comfortable and proficient with. Maya is still part of the curriculum in the School of Design as well, so some students use that; some use Blender.

It certainly is the case that more and more students are relying on Blender as their go-to 3D design tool because it has become so widely used, and they don't have to worry about not having access after graduation.

Mark: For the student film, you combine students from two departments to create a film. This is a great template for virtual production. How do you break down the coordination of the complex discipline of virtual production so that all the students have a rewarding experience.

James: Some of this comes from the first course in our program, Virtual Filmmaking, that students take, which is greatly inspired by my experience in the Virtual Production Fellowship with Epic Games. My biggest takeaway from that was, regardless of background, you can not only understand how to use Unreal Engine as a narrative production tool in a very short amount of time, but actually bring full visual concepts to life with incredible fidelity.

It fits very well as an interdisciplinary course because I can introduce sequencer and virtual cameras that are instantly familiar to film students, while the 3D assets and character animation are familiar to the game art, design, and animation students. Pairs and small groups are immediately excited to collaborate because they see the potential, and working with a real-time engine, they can iterate and experiment in a way that is creative, expressive, and develops a mutual understanding of their respective talents.

The biggest goal I have when they get to the studio course is not that they are all masters of Unreal Engine coming in, but that they have created strong bonds with peers across disciplines so that the various roles necessary in virtual production are all treated with mutual respect, and communication is clear from the start.

In some ways, virtual production, particularly ICVFX (In-Camera Visual Effects) and the necessity to "fix it in pre" helps to mitigate the tendency for students to focus only on their area of interest and either overestimate or overlook post processes like visual effects.

As Columbia implements the process for virtual production in student projects outside of the dedicated courses, establishing clear roles and expectations for crew members up front, in line with industry practice, like VP supervisor, engine operator, and virtual art department also helps greatly in facilitating the incorporation of what was previously disparate groups.

Mark: How many virtual productions get to be made at Columbia?

James: Two were created the previous spring when the class was working with a green screen. As the volume was launched, they were able to create *What Remains*, which was produced in the ICVFX Studio Techniques course. However, as of summer 2024, we are finalizing the formal inclusion of virtual production in Columbia's production-planning process, which opens up the possibility for students to incorporate virtual production in any of the nearly 200 productions students at the 250 level and up create every academic year.

Mark: The decision to purchase an LED wall is a big one. Can you share what manufacturer you used and the decision-making process?

James: Higher education generally follows a similar RFP and bidding process, which administrators are well familiar with, as well as their unique institutional idiosyncrasies, so I won't get into that. What I will say is that, depending on the region or institution, this primarily goes out to AV integrators, and based on their experience, history with the school, or simply that the request is coming from an educational institution, there are many ways a proposal for a large LED wall can be interpreted, some closer to classroom presentation or digital signage than a volume designed for filmmaking.

Fortunately, we had done a fair amount of investigation into manufacturers and wrote a very clear system specification, so we immediately recognized which integrators were approaching the project correctly.

Resolution Studios and Smash Virtual have both been tremendous local resources as we built out the program and volume here at Columbia College. Resolution has been iterating their volume for some time, and their latest build used Planar 1.9mm tile to great effect. When we received a proposal that incorporated the same tiles at a price competitive with less established brands at a higher pixel pitch, it was an easy choice.

As far as the processors, we knew we wanted to go with Brompton up front, and not only is the feature set unmatched for virtual production, but it was a clear signal to the vendors that this was not an average LED installation.

Even though we could have displayed the full resolution from a single Tessera SX40, we intentionally split the volume into three, with individual render nodes and three Tessera S8 processors to replicate the way larger multi-node systems function. This also leaves more GPU overhead per node, and is made significantly easier with Brompton's stacking functionality.

Mark: From what I've seen on the Columbia website, I get the impression that you are modeling your instruction around the Disney pioneering model of the "brain bar" to simultaneously have iterative creation during the shoot. Do you try to emulate this method? On a small student budget, how do you limit the variables creatively available with the technology?

James: Yes, as much as possible. What this looks like in practice is that at least one student familiar with Unreal Engine takes on the role of operator; grip takes on monitoring tracking status at the camera; producer or AD may also work as VP supervisor.

There is a large amount of technical instruction for the operator, verifying node status, the multi-user session, version control, sync, and how Switchboard is running everything. Since ours is not an engineering program, this relies on students self-selecting, much like they do for other technical student worker positions elsewhere in the college.

The VAD students load the nDisplay configuration into the project prior to being on set, and I save some time by creating a Switchboard template. VAD is responsible for the environment being camera ready prior to filming, and between Discord, screenshots, and a final camera test with the volume, most of the iteration happens in pre-production, and only minimal changes need to be made by the operator on set.

When the operator and VP supervisor were communicating clearly with the director, expectations were realistic, and they were all very conscious of the limited amount of studio time available, so this set its own limitation.

Mark: I see that the IATSE is starting a program in coordination with the Los Angeles Community College District to introduce instruction for entry-level positions for the motion picture locals. The Animation Guild provides representation for virtual production. Do you offer any guidelines concerning union positions in the field?

James: Not specifically, as this is still emerging and inherently muti-disciplinary. That said, the overall body of knowledge aligns closely with a visual effects workforce, especially given the directions both fields are evolving in, so it would not surprise me to see this formalize there first.

Mark: As virtual production gains momentum, there will be many schools being challenged to offer this education. Do you have any advice to offer administrators starting from scratch?

James: There is a lot to be said for starting small. The initial test setup we used at Columbia was a VIVE Mars and real-time chroma-key compositing. It was a good way to gauge student interest since there was no flashy LED volume yet, but the classes filled quickly, and the interest was clearly there.

It is exciting and eye opening for students when they see the narrative potential within Unreal Engine and have an opportunity to "play" in a real-time environment. Because it's a tool they could take in numerous directions, it's a great place to start. Even after-school or high school programs introducing UEFN are laying the groundwork for a virtual production education.

Undoubtedly, there will be discussions about an LED volume. What I can say is that the cost may not be as intimidating as might be anticipated, and the resolution-to-cost ratio is always improving. It's worth looking into, particularly in a region with limited volumes. If an institution already has a model for leveraging facilities for commercial production, a volume can be a great resource for faculty and other local filmmakers.

It also doesn't need to be the massive scale of big studio volumes to be effective. Our volume is roughly 12 feet high by 22 feet wide with a three-degree curve. It's big enough to get most shots with enough camera movement for convincing parallax and throws enough light for reflections and IBL (image-based lighting).

Outside of filming, I think educational institutions are at an advantage, in that performance, presentation, and spaces for visualizing advanced research are all potential use cases for a volume as a shared resource.

On the curriculum side, it's a natural fit at institutions that have both filmmaking and game design programs already. Because it requires both skill sets, the goal is not so much an individual student who is a "virtual production master" but students in their respective areas who are fluent with virtual production.

Getting these groups to work together effectively is what it comes down to most often. Creating points of intersection and enough experience outside their core domains (without overwhelming them with highly technical details outside their areas of interest) is practical, given the number of shared fundamentals.

Mark: What do you find attracts your students the most about virtual production?

James: Creative opportunity. For some students, it is an opportunity to use knowledge they already have in completely new ways, and it opens up potential avenues for employment without requiring that they learn entirely new skills.

For other students it is the opportunity to bring creative visions to life that previously were not possible. Having access to the technology and the knowledge of what is required to effectively create high-level VFX shots is very empowering.

Working with a real-time process creates new opportunities for collaboration that are extremely appealing to students who are just discovering and refining their creative voices. It enables them to have meaningful creative input throughout the process in ways that were not previously possible, especially in the short amount of time available to complete productions.

I would say it's also because they "see it everywhere" except that like all good filmmaking techniques, when it's executed well, audiences don't know they are seeing it at all. Every semester, we look at recent productions that used virtual production and there are always some surprises.

Students want to be part of new and emerging areas because they are always looking to the future. Their minds are on where they could be after graduation, and virtual production is still evolving, so it is a field where they see a space for themselves to have meaningful impact and grow with, not just into.

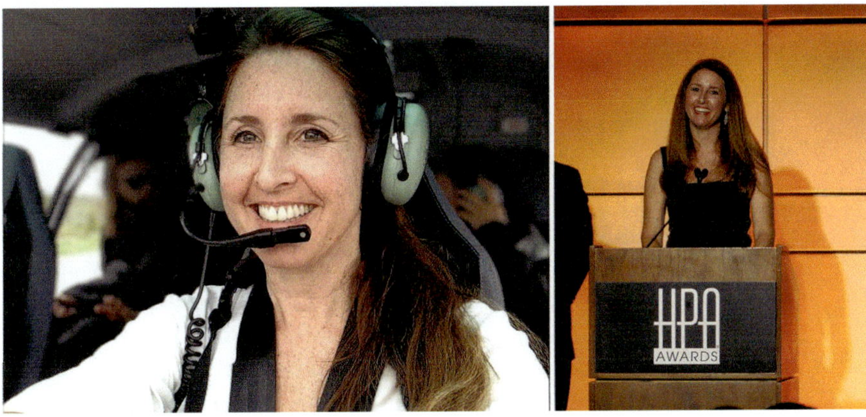

Figure 12.3 *Lindy DeQuattro.*

Lindy DeQuattro

Lindy DeQuattro is a visual effects supervisor known for Atlas (2024), Mission: Impossible – Ghost Protocol (2011) and Pacific Rim (2013).

Mark: You entered the industry right at the ignition point of the digital explosion. I place *Terminator 2* in 1991 as the defining moment. In those days, specialized teams of CG vendor companies were doing that specialized work, which would involve a small number of shots. When I look at the tremendous number of shots done for *Atlas*, I can't wrap my head around how a VFX supervisor handles all those challenges. Can you provide a snapshot of how a film of that magnitude is handled? How do you get hired? Do you have to make a pitch or a rough budget?

Lindy: As a production-side VFX supervisor, I get hired in one of two ways: either the client (studio, director, or producer) reaches out directly to me, or they reach out to MPC, who then acts as my agent and puts me forward for the job. In the case of *Atlas*, I knew the initial VFX exec on the project at Netflix, Kerry Shea, and she gave my name to the producer of the film, Jeff Fierson. I first had an interview with Jeff, and then once he had vetted me, he had me interview with the director, Brad Peyton. Basically, that initial director interview is an opportunity for me to pitch my ideas for the work and how best to approach it, but we weren't talking budgets at that point. It was more of a creative discussion to be sure we were all on the same page. Once I signed on to the project, that's when I started getting into breakdowns and budgeting. That said, every project is a bit different, and sometimes, if you get brought onto a project a bit later in the development, you might jump right into bidding. In the case of *Atlas*, I started on the project at the very beginning, so we hadn't gotten into that yet.

Budgeting a project the size of *Atlas* is not something you do once. It is a process that is constantly evolving as the script changes and as the director and various other film departments begin to home in on how they are going to approach the work. I begin by making a breakdown of the VFX work in the film. A VFX breakdown is basically a huge spreadsheet showing every single shot in the film, whether it has VFX in it, and what the scope of that VFX work is. Then I work with the VFX producer to assign costs to each line of the spreadsheet. These initial $ figures are only estimates of what we expect the work to cost. Eventually, we send out that breakdown to the various VFX vendors that we are interested in working with on the project and have them give us a bid for the portion of the work we want to award them. Those numbers are the actual costs for the VFX work that go into the final budget. We also need to account for all the other VFX costs on the film such as previz, post-viz, on-set personnel, LiDAR, scanning, etc. Once we have all these numbers, then we can go back to the producer and the studio with the actual VFX cost for the project. Usually, at this point, we are told to cut the budget by X dollars, and then I work with the director and the other department heads (or HODs) to reduce the scope of the VFX work either by eliminating shots or sequences or by altering some of the creative choices to reduce the need for VFX work while still preserving the shot. This bidding process can go on for many months or sometimes even years before the film is greenlit, and the work is awarded to the VFX vendors. In the case of *Atlas*, we ended up with 1610 VFX shots in the final cut of the film. We had three main vendors: MPC, Scanline, and ILM. We had two main vendors doing the graphics work: Territory and Cantina. Our previz and post-viz vendor was Halon. In addition, we had eight VFX artists working directly for me as our in-house compositing team.

The only way to handle a project of this size is basically to break it down into more manageable-size chunks of work and then distribute those smaller chunks of work across multiple trusted vendors. Then create a tiered management structure that allows you to monitor each of those chunks and report up the chain. So, first of all, we don't give any one vendor more than about 500 shots. Then, on the production side, we assign a VFX coordinator to each vendor. The coordinators are responsible for making sure that their vendor is hitting their targets and then flagging any issues to the VFX production manager or VFX associate producer, who is ultimately responsible for all the vendors. Then that person answers to the VFX producer, who is responsible for all of that and also for interfacing with the studio and with the film's producers. Each of the VFX vendors have similarly large production teams to track all the shots through all the departments within their facility.

On the creative side, the VFX vendor pipelines have become much more of an assembly line than back in the 1990s. In the early days of the industry, if you were assigned a VFX shot, you would probably do everything yourself: match move, animation, lighting, compositing, and sometimes even roto and FX sim. All artists were generalists to some extent. These days, artists are generally very specialized, and the pipelines are set up to hand the shot from artist to artist as it moves towards completion. Each department generally has a lead who reports on any pipeline issues to the supe above them. Each sequence generally has a sequence supervisor who is keeping an eye on the creative continuity of the sequence and then reports up to the CG supervisor. The CG supervisor is generally in charge of the pipeline for the entire show within their facility, and they report up to the digital production supervisor or associate VFX supervisor or VFX supervisor, depending on the size of the shot. Ultimately, the VFX supervisors at each of the vendors report to me as the production-side VFX supervisor, and it is my job to make sure there is creative continuity across the entire show, make sure that all the work is moving along at the expected pace, and to pass along any creative feedback from the client (director, editor, producers, studio).

As the production-side VFX supe, I need to trust that a lot of people are doing what they are supposed to be doing because I personally cannot keep an eye on all 1610 shots and every artist who is working on them. Communication is vitally important as are relationships that are built over time. If I've worked with a vendor before and they did a great job for me, then I'm much more comfortable bringing them work on my next show and trusting that they will deliver.

Mark: You mentioned that you transitioned from VFX supervision on the post side to moving over to production. What are the differences in the challenges of being on each side?

Lindy: The job of a production-side VFX supervisor is actually completely different from being an internal VFX supervisor at a VFX vendor. The internal VFX supe works for the vendor company, and the prod side VFX supe works for the director (and, to some extent, for the studio as well). I was surprised by how little overlap there is. As an internal supervisor, you are generally not involved in prep at all. You may or may not be involved in plate photography because you don't start until the VFX contract is awarded to your company, which often happens in post. Even if you are involved in plate, you are generally only covering second unit or just visiting set for certain sequences, but all the decision-making in terms of how to approach the shoot has already been done. You generally don't interface with any of the other film departments except possibly for editorial. In post, you are the creative liaison between the production-side VFX supervisor and your internal team of artists. You are responsible for managing the crew and the pipeline that will be used to execute the VFX work. Most of your time is spent managing the internal artists and giving feedback on their work, which you then present to the client at regular intervals. The creative impact you can have on the film is generally somewhat limited as a lot of the concept art and look development has already been done by the client-side art department before you come on the show. You may or may not interface directly with the director or anyone else on the client side other than the production-side VFX supervisor.

As a production-side VFX supervisor, you are brought onto the project much earlier. When I first started on *Atlas*, the only other person besides the director that had already been hired was the production designer. The three of us met and worked alone together for months before prep even began to hammer out script changes and concept art that would reduce the scope of the project to fit within the budget the studio had given us. Bidding the show and proposing cost-effective solutions to budgeting issues is a big part of the job. As a production-side VFX supervisor, you are also responsible for planning the shoot. Meaning that you need to plan and budget for anything that will be needed during plate photography. This planning work is done during prep. If you expect other departments to do certain aspects of the work, you need to discuss that and plan it with those HODs. For example, if you expect a certain explosion to be practically done by the SFX dept, then you need to make sure they have planned for that and have it covered in their budget. The VFX department often shares work and methodologies with SFX, stunts, camera, lighting, video assist, grips, script supervision, costume, art dept, and makeup (among others), so you need to develop good relationships with those HODs and be in constant communication. Another aspect of planning the shoot is determining where you need process screens and what color they should be (digi blue, chroma blue, digi green, chroma green, black, etc.). If you are shooting outside the US, you may need to hire a VFX rigging crew as, in many countries, that won't be covered by the main rigging crew. You will need to determine which sets, actors, and costumes need to be scanned. These are just a few examples of the types of decisions that need to be made during prep, but the list is truly endless. You also need to keep your VFX producer well informed of any changes to the scope of the VFX that come about during the planning process.

During plate photography, you need to obtain photographic reference on set – either shoot it yourself or have additional crew to assist with this work: HDRIs, texture ref, photogrammetry, LiDAR, actor scans, etc. Sometimes you need to have access to 3D puppets or stand-ins for CG characters that you need to plan for and obtain ahead of time. I find that a lot of my job on set during plate is to simply explain to everyone what the VFX department is doing. There is often a lot of confusion about what we can and cannot achieve and the data we need to do so. I carry previz around with me on an iPad and show it to all the other HODs so that they understand where the scene will end up. A lot of times, I need to problem solve on the fly. For example, if a piece of equipment malfunctions or if something that was supposed to be done by another department doesn't work, I'm there to let them know if VFX can absorb the work and to ballpark the additional costs. Some scenes are extremely VFX heavy like LED walls or motion base work. Some scenes may just have a peek of a view out the window. In either case, it is necessary for the VFX supe to be present and knowledgeable about everything that's happening on set as it will all affect the final plates that VFX will use to execute the work in post.

Once we're in post, I generally have an office in or near editorial where I work with the director and editor very closely to be sure the work is progressing as expected; to be sure they have any temps they might need for various deadlines like studio screenings, teasers, and trailers; and to be in the loop on any editorial or sound changes that necessitate changes in the VFX work. I meet regularly with the internal VFX supervisor at each of the vendors to give them feedback on the work they are sending over and to flag any issues I see in terms of schedule or quality. I meet regularly with the director and the studio as well to keep them updated on the progress of the work and any issues I'm seeing at any of the vendors. The exact structure of the VFX reviews is different on every show. Sometimes the directors like to meet directly with the VFX vendors, and in that case, I will prescreen the VFX work to pull anything that is particularly problematic but will otherwise let them present their own work. In many cases, the directors don't like to be put on the spot like that, so I will present the work to the director with a small number of other people in the room, like the producer and editor. Then I will present the feedback to the vendor afterward in a separate review. Sometimes it's not possible for the director to meet directly with the vendors because they are in different time zones or have other scheduling conflicts.

Mark: You have had a long stellar career at ILM working on many high-end projects but have admittedly encountered that glass ceiling for women to advance. You have most certainly put a hole in it. What more needs to be done to have more diversity in the VFX field?

Is there a difference between dealing with traditional studios like Warner Brothers as opposed to newcomers like Netflix and Amazon?

Lindy: There is definitely a different culture at the new streamers compared to the old Hollywood studios. Netflix is very serious about diversity and inclusion. This is clear if you watch *Atlas* and look at the racial and gender diversity of the lead actors and even the extras. That was very intentional, and Netflix was very vocal about pushing that agenda. This was true behind the scenes as well, where they pushed for diversity among the crew. Unfortunately, I don't think the old-fashioned studios are changing fast enough. The Academy tried adding some language to their qualification requirements, but unfortunately, it was just too easy to work around it. I'd like to see all the guilds require quotas in their next round of contracts and then see those quotas raised year over year until we reach parity so you can't work with the WGA, DGA, PGA, SAG, IATSE, etc. until you agree to the quotas. If 14% of the US population is black, then 14% of US film crews and HODs should be black. If 50% of the US population is female, then 50% of US film crews and HODs should be female. No, we can't just flip the switch and get there overnight, but if we had a slowly increasing quota structure, then we could at least get there in my lifetime. We also need more men who are allies to our cause. It's easier to make changes when you are already in power, and the people in power right now are white men, so if we can get more of those people to insist on fair hiring and fair compensation and make that a condition in their contracts, then that would certainly help as well. Finally, we need to raise up and publicize the minorities and women who are competing and succeeding so that everyone can see that it is possible and hopefully encourage others to get into the industry.

Mark: You mentioned that *Atlas* at one time considered doing some virtual production process. I see a credit for the virtual production executive at Netflix, but Netflix decided to go another route. Had you planned the use of VP and had to switch gears at the last moment, or was that decision made early on, and what were the concerns?

Lindy: The initial plan was definitely to use an LED volume for all the shots of Jennifer Lopez inside the cockpit. A cockpit like that is actually the ideal scenario for LED volume work, just like a driving shot, and Netflix was totally on board with the idea. They were planning to build several volumes, so we were working with them to see if our shoot would work in one of the volumes they were already planning. The first issue we ran into was that the ideal dimensions of the volume we needed didn't exactly work with the generic volumes they were already planning. Because we had a relatively small cockpit (about eight feet in diameter) but we needed it to be up on a motion base, we needed a relatively small but very tall volume. The next issue was that the timeline wasn't really working. The volume we were discussing wasn't ready yet, and it was outside the US, but Jennifer didn't want to leave Los Angeles, and we were going for the LA tax credit, so it didn't really make sense. We then started looking into building our own volume, but the cost of that was several million dollars, which still might have been cost effective, but it's a hard sell to pay that much up front. We also looked at some existing volumes around LA, but again, they weren't tall enough. Eventually, we got to a point where we were just out of time to make it happen since all the images for the LED volume would have to be completed before plate photography, and we just couldn't get it done in the time remaining before the shoot. It's a shame because I still think it would have been the right way to go, and it would have been very helpful for Jennifer to see the battles and events that were supposed to be taking place around her. That said, without the LED volume and the preprogrammed images, we were able to improvise a lot more while we were shooting, so there were certainly trade-offs.

Mark: Going over the credits of this film is jaw dropping. Most of the films I worked on had one producer; *Atlas* has 16. What is the process of evaluation of all this data? I don't know how all the opinions can be culled into a singular decision.

Lindy: The producer credit has gotten a bit out of control lately, and not just on *Atlas*. It's fairly common these days that every first AD on a film this size gets a producer credit. All major stars get a producer credit, as do their management teams. Often the studios have development deals with several producers, and sometimes, if they can't put a film together with those producers but they are still beholden by such a deal, they will add them as an additional producer on another film just to absorb those costs. So basically, only a small number of the people credited as "producer" are actually producing the film. And even out of those, there is generally one person who is the "creative producer" and actually has a lot of influence over the creative aspects of the film. For *Atlas*, that person was Jeff Fierson. He attended all VFX reviews, had an office in editorial, and was present every day of prep, plate, and post. The rest of the producers are more like consulting producers and may visit set occasionally, attend temp screenings, and funnel any feedback through the studio. Any feedback from the studio is generally collated and filtered through the top decision maker and then presented to the director to either address or push back on as they see fit. Unless something is going really wrong on the film, the director still has the final say on all creative decisions.

Mark: I see that *Atlas* has 64 stunt people credits, which is great. Many are concerned about the stunt performer being replaced by the disposable metahuman manipulated by mocap or animation. Any thoughts on this?

Lindy: I certainly understand the concern. At this point, I always prefer to have stunt performers where and when it is safe and possible. There is a certain chaos to human movements that is hard for an animator to duplicate. It also keeps directors from asking for digital performances that would never be believable, so it keeps the work grounded. That said, I do think it may be possible in the not-too-distant future for AI to be able to generate pretty believable stunt performances. After all, it would be learning from previous existing stunt performances. As with any aspect of filmmaking, stunt performances need to be directable. In other words, they need to be able to be modified based off feedback from the director or other creatives. Currently that's not something we have the ability to do well with AI-generated performances, but I could see it happening in the future. I don't see a world where no stunt performers would be needed, but we may need fewer or only at a supervisory level. I'm certainly not advocating for that, but I am afraid that is where we are headed. Stunts is just one of many film departments which I fear will lose jobs to AI because making films is incredibly expensive and therefore incredibly financially risky, and all studios are looking for ways to reduce those costs.

Mark: In past generations, it was much easier to break into the industry if you met people, demonstrated your passion, and a cinematographer or artist would take you under their wing as an apprentice. You mentioned that today the route would be through internships. Can you share your thoughts about making a career in VFX?

Lindy: It's so hard right now. The industry is in shambles after the WGA and SAG strikes along with the emergence of AI, the transition from old Hollywood studios to streamers, and the emergence of YouTube and the like taking viewership away from film and TV. Nobody is sure where the industry is headed, and so in response, very few projects are being greenlit. This is especially true of the big-budget projects that generally require a lot of VFX work. As a result, even senior artists are out of work right now and have been for a year or more. It's a terrible time to be trying to get into the industry. My daughter, who is 22 and just graduated from UCSD with a major in computing and the arts with a minor in comp sci, is looking to get into VFX. I told her to apply for every internship she could find for the summer after she graduated, and she didn't get any of them. I told her to apply to film school for the fall so she could network with other people in the industry, and they told her to reapply next year. Keep in mind that this is a girl who has industry experience because I hired her as a compositor on *Atlas*. Both her parents are in the VFX industry, and she is a great artist. I know most of the instructors at the film school where she applied, and still, she couldn't get her foot in the door. Now I have her taking online classes and working on small projects so she can continue to build up her reel and reapply to film school next year. You need experience to get hired. That's the headline. So you need to figure out how to get experience if nobody is paying you for it. Apply to every internship and junior position you can, and in the meantime, work on your own independent projects to keep learning and building up your reel. If you can afford to go back to school full time, this is a great time to do it, and the networking and job placement assistance at most VFX schools are really helpful. I know none of this is cheap, so you may have to move back in with your parents or work a side job to afford it, but if you're serious about breaking into VFX, then you need to keep creating and evolving. If there is a YouTube channel or an influencer you really enjoy, try reaching out to the creator and offer to do some VFX for them for cheap or free. Learn Unreal, play with AI, stay on the leading edge of technology, and hopefully, when the industry turns around you will be ready for the opportunities. The best advice I can give to somebody starting out right now is that you need to keep moving forward. Momentum is key.

Mark: In your CGPro interview, you said we are slowly coming out of a tough time in the film industry as a result of COVID-19. It also seems that there is a glut of studios and content out there, and the production of the larger tentpole pictures has become more challenging than ever. How do you see the industry evolving?

Lindy: Nobody really knows where the industry is headed right now. There is a lot of uncertainty. Episodics and lower-budget films have definitely been the first to bounce back after the strikes, and there is a lot activity in these areas right now. The larger-budget tentpole films, which are where most of the VFX work lies, have been much slower to recover. Personally, I do believe that they will return because I feel like there is still audience demand for them. Currently, I'm seeing more activity with these larger projects at

Amazon, Apple, and Netflix than I am at the legacy Hollywood studios. These types of films are obviously very high risk because of the budget size, and the tech companies are much more flush with cash than the old studios, so they are willing to take a larger financial risk right now. Given the younger generations' interest in streaming and unconventional entertainment platforms like YouTube, I think we're going to see a broadening in the client base of VFX work, but overall, I think the budgets will come down so it will be interesting to see how the big VFX companies adapt to this. In all likelihood, they will need to take on 100 smaller projects per year instead of the 10 large ones that they have done historically in order to bring in the same revenue. They will probably employ fewer artists overall, and some disciplines and positions are replaced with AI technology. I do think big changes are coming to the industry, but I don't see it going away entirely. We aren't going to have AI doing end-to-end VFX work on entire films any time soon. That said, I certainly wouldn't want to be in the theater business because I sadly foresee much lower demand for theatrical releases moving forward as the younger generations seem to consume most of their media on phones and computers.

Mark: It is very timely that *Atlas* has the theme of AI gone bad. The image creation tools are astounding and drastically narrow the script-to-screen timeline at the expense of all the disciplines of the motion picture industry. It seems to lack continuity and consistency but is an excellent previz tool. How do you see AI being utilized as a VFX supervisor? Instead of fixing it in post, will it become "fix in AI" or perhaps vice versa?

Lindy: Currently we have a bit of a logjam with using AI in VFX at the big VFX vendors because even though AI is capable of improving a lot of our current workflows, the studios have put a full stop on any generative AI imagery actually being used in their films until the legalities have been settled. There is a lot of conversation about whether generating an image using AI constitutes copyright infringement, and until that matter is settled in court, no studio is willing to risk being sued for their film profits. In the meantime, most VFX vendors are investigating the use of AI for aspects of VFX work that don't actually create new images used in the film. For example, using it for planning work like concept art, look development, and previz. In addition, it is probably okay to use it to generate technical data like roto or depth mattes or to modify existing imagery from the film like relighting, re-aging, and dialogue lip sync changes. We can also use it to refine work in progress, so if you have a shot that is not quite looking "real" for some reason, you could feed it through an AI model to take a photoreal pass at it or to show you what it would look like using a different lens, that kind of thing. The issue with this last AI usage that I've outlined is that it requires you to feed your existing image into the AI model in order to get the modified output, and as soon as you do that, then it becomes input to the AI model itself and is no longer secure, which goes against the security agreements that all VFX companies have with their clients. To summarize, I don't think there is a lot that the big VFX companies can do with AI currently until two things happen: 1. The legalities of the potential copyright issues with generative AI are settled, and 2. There is a way to four-wall an AI model so that the imagery fed into it remains secure and proprietary. There are some companies already that are working on building AI models using only traceable and licensed input artwork, and that would certainly solve the first issue, so we may be close to opening the floodgates on using AI in VFX. Certainly, it is an area that all the VFX companies are studying closely right now.

Mark: In our book, we are seeing a technological democratization of virtual production where iPhones and clever post-production can mimic the same shots that involve a huge capital outlay. I think the high-end systems will survive because you need them for real-time in-camera finished shots that promise to reduce the cost of post-production. As an Academy member, do you see this access to technology as a positive move forward for diverse production personnel?

Lindy: The Academy is all about celebrating great film and great filmmakers. Ideally, nobody's creativity would be constrained by the tools (or budget) available to them. In my opinion, the more options artists and filmmakers have available to them, the better. I agree that there will always be a demand for higher-end work just as there will always be a demand for quick and dirty work because each film has different requirements to tell the story that filmmaker is trying to tell. At the end of the day, VFX is a suite of tools, and it's all about choosing the right tool for the right project. I always laugh when people say they hate VFX, or films were so much better when everything was done practically. That's like saying you hate a hammer. A hammer is great if you need to put in a nail, but not so great for a screw or if you want to install an entire deck. You must choose the tool that makes the most sense for what you are trying to achieve creatively and which fits within your available resources.

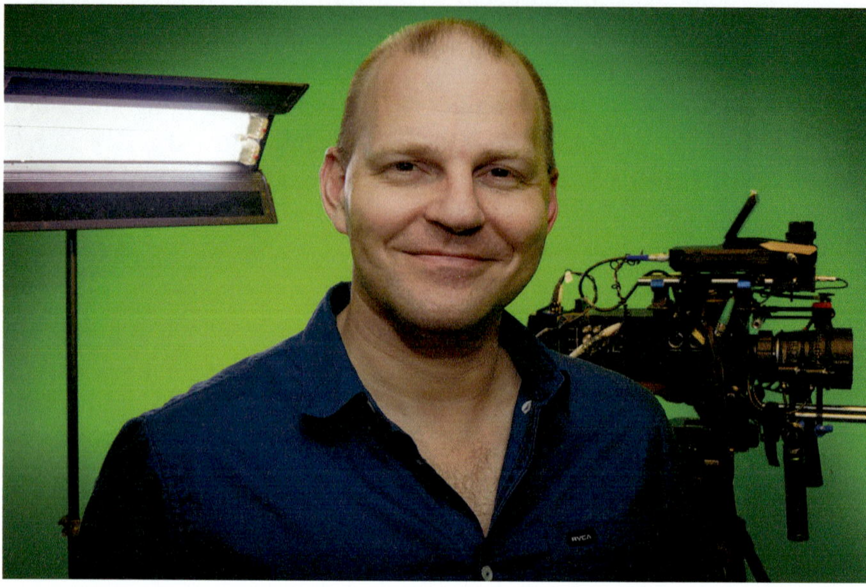

Figure 12.4 *Eliot Mack.*

Eliot Mack

Designed original iRobot Roomba. Founded Lightcraft Technology. Shipped Previzion, Halide, and Jetset virtual production systems. Eng. Emmy 2013.

Mark: In your original design, you had a camera looking up at targets that helped to match with the taking lens. The iPhone has three lenses, which I imagine provide a nesting arrangement so that when you zoom in on the image, the quality is maintained. Are there three sensors for each lens that are blended somehow? I assume you use the default setting and not zooming on the iPhone. How is the video information used for tracking other than the LiDAR.

Eliot: ARKit uses a technology called "visual odometry," which detects natural features in the scene and couples that with the LiDAR data to assign a 3D position to each feature. Once enough features are recognized, it's possible to calculate the real-time position of the phone optically. The optical-only solve has a lot of noise, however, so almost all systems like this use an integrated IMU (inertial measurement unit), which detects accelerations on the XYZ and rotational axes and mixes that data with the optical solve to make for a stable output position.

To my knowledge, the real tracking on the iPhone only uses the "middle" lens, and the "normal" iPhone digital zoom is disabled. In

Jetset or Jetset Pro, where we are recording iPhone video, we provide a set of simulated focal lengths (so that you can see what a shot would look like on a 24mm/28mm/32mm/etc. lens), but we achieve that by cropping in on the rendered image.

We always save the camera original at full resolution.

Mark: I remember visiting you on your stage a while back, and you mentioned during your research, you had burned out a laptop processing all the calculations. I've felt how hot the iPhone gets without the cooler solution. Was there an epiphany moment during your process that you said, "Of course, the iPhone!" Or perhaps it was "Eureka"?

Eliot: I bought an iPhone 11 Pro and was testing the tracking on our stage, and it was tracking better than I had seen previously. (I had tried ARKit on my older iPhone 6s.) It really surprised me how well it worked. It wasn't quite at the level of our custom-built hardware trackers, but it was close enough to rethink how we approach tracking.

Mark: You said that the tracking system in the iPhone only functions at 30 fps. I suspect that 30 was chosen as iPhones are more of a tech relative of video than film. When film [is] shot at 24 and transferred to video, it is run slightly slower at 23.97 to make the math of the 3:2 pulldown work with the video frame rate of 29.97. If the tracking only works with the phone running at 30 but only provides tracking data, I assume the slower speed isn't needed, and, in fact, the cine camera can shoot at either 24 or 23.97 or high speed or below 24. Is this correct, or will some frame-rate conversion need to be made in the compositing process?

Eliot: We convert the 30p tracking from the iPhone to 24p or 25p via interpolation when shooting with Jetset Cine. We use the flashing marker codes on the Jetset digital slate to provide a timing reference for both Jetset and the cine camera and automatically detect those timing markers in Autoshot so that the time alignment is automated.

We're also adding support to use embedded timecode from a Tentacle Sync E device to automate take sync, removing the need for the digital slate. (But it's still a good idea!)

Mark: Is it advantageous for the cine camera to shoot at a higher frame rate to improve tracking and ramp down to normal speed in post?

Eliot: The tracking in the iPhone is independent of the cine camera rate. We interpolate the tracking data in post to whatever the cine camera uses, which works well for shots that don't have extensive ground contact. If you have a visible CGI/live action seam, you'll want to use our post-production tracking refinement process with SynthEyes to rapidly nail down sub-pixel tracks in minutes.

Mark: In some live-tracking systems, the calibration is so sensitive that the mere removal of the same lens and putting it back again will cause a need to recalibrate if the seating of the lens is just slightly off. Is this a consideration with your system? Many cinematographers prefer using a set number of fixed focal length lenses for a show rather than a zoom. Is a zoom lens preferable for virtual production with your system?

Eliot: The system is designed to be pretty robust in production use. We recommend using a SmallRig-type phone cage that is rigidly mounted to the main camera. The key thing is maintaining the position of the iPhone with respect to the lens, but a rig holds the iPhone pretty rigidly. You'll need to calibrate your various lenses with the iPhone attached in its correct position, but once the lenses are calibrated, you can switch back and forth between them rapidly without recalibrating as long as the iPhone stays put.

We don't yet track zoom lenses in real time, so primes are the current method. You could calibrate a zoom lens at different points and then just recall the lens calibrations for different focal lengths.

Mark: The LiDAR scan of the set seems to provide good depth information that is used to inform tracking points for the 2D image when massaging the tracking in post. Will a simple scan of a stage floor be sufficient for this purpose, or does it help to have more three-dimensional set pieces to reference?

Eliot: It all depends where the tracking points are. If you have a green screen with tape crosses on it, you'll want to scan the green screen so that you know where those tape marks are in 3D. The LiDAR-based iPhone scanning in Jetset is incredibly convenient because it can give you survey data in a matter of seconds on a shoot. That makes all the difference in terms of the ease of post-production tracking work. Seconds versus hours.

Mark: Would your system be effective with LED volumes? You've demonstrated that the iPhone can do real-time tracking, but if the data has to go through a pipeline of a virtual camera output going to a wall, I imagine there would be a time delay involved. Would you say your system is more of a high-quality post-process system?

Eliot: We can send real-time data to Unreal, which could be used to drive a volume. The real-time view of the composite in the Jetset app is extremely low latency – so much so that you can shoot rapidly moving animated characters with it.

Mark: Do you anticipate that LiDAR and motion-sensing capabilities of iPhones will be incorporated into production cameras, much like lens distortion data is now stored in come lenses along with an output port? I suppose it could go this way or the next iteration of iPhone would be able to put out cine-quality images without the need to translate tracking targets between two imaging systems.

Eliot: It's possible the camera manufacturers will include this, but unlikely. Apple spent an incredible amount to get the real-time tracking to the level that it is, and the camera manufacturers would need to add the hardware equivalent of an iPhone to their camera.

Mark: How is AI being incorporated into your brilliant virtual production tracking method? The Autoshot software is quite robust but also has a large number of menu choices between it and Unreal. Do you foresee the future cine versions having a standard default pipeline that serves less technical creatives, much like your starter Jetset does with 2D or 360 imagery? I imagine it's tough to develop a product that is asked to be all things for all people without being complex.

Eliot: We're releasing a new in-phone re-rendering pipeline that uses the stored data in the iPhone along with a Gaussian splat model (also loaded into the iPhone) to render out high-quality tracked backgrounds that can be easily composited in a normal nonlinear editor timeline. This is a huge simplification of the virtual production process, and we think it will be very attractive for groups doing longer projects that don't [have] to deal with the complexity of traditional VFX.

Mark: Your system detects frame drops after the take. If that take becomes a hero take, is there a remedy to fix frame drops in tracking?

Eliot: Yes. The tracking data is automatically interpolated for both our traditional VFX workflow and our in-phone re-rendering workflow, so minor frame drops only really affect the recorded iPhone camera original video. (If a take has a ton of drops, the tracking data will be compromised.)

I'm finishing a tutorial of a take recorded with Jetset with a couple of frame drops, and it's easy to fix a couple of frames while editing in Resolve.

Index

Note: Page numbers in *italics* indicate a figure and page numbers in **bold** indicate a table on the corresponding page.